BEST
MUSIC
WRITING

2007

BEST
MUSIC
WRITING

2 0 0 7

Robert
Christgau
GUEST EDITOR

Daphne
Carr
SERIES EDITOR

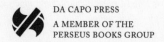

DA CAPO PRESS
A MEMBER OF THE
PERSEUS BOOKS GROUP

Designed by Timm Bryson
Set in 10.5 point Caslon by The Perseus Books Group

Cataloging-in-Publication data for this book is available from the Library of
Congress.

First Da Capo Press edition 2007
ISBN-13: 978-0-306-81561-4
ISBN-10: 0-306-81561-3

Published by Da Capo Press
A Member of the Perseus Books Group
http://www.dacapopress.com

Da Capo Press books are available at special discounts for bulk purchases in the
U.S. by corporations, institutions, and other organizations. For more
information, please contact the Special Markets Department at the Perseus
Books Group, 2300 Chestnut Street, Suite 200, Philadelphia, PA, 19103, or call
(800) 255-1514, or e-mail special.markets@perseusbooks.com.

10 9 8 7 6 5 4 3 2 1

CONTENTS

Introduction   *xi*
By Robert Christgau

CARL WILSON   1
If Music Is the Answer, What's the Question?
Said the Gramophone (saidthegramophone.com)

ANN POWERS   5
Latinos Give New Life to Neil
   Diamond Anthem
Los Angeles Times

MICHAELANGELO MATOS   10
A Double History of the Supremes'
   "Love Child"
Back and Forth (beatresearch2.blogspot.com)

JANE DARK   19
white bread black beer
jane dark's sugar high! (janedark.com)

SASHA FRERE-JONES   22
On Top: Mariah Carey's
   Record-Breaking Career
The New Yorker

DAPHNE A. BROOKS   27
Suga Mama, Politicized
The Nation

CHRIS RYAN
YEAH I'M THREATENING YA! I KEEP
    HEDGE FUNDS!   36
BUY KINGDOM COME AND GET A FREE
    FUCKING TOTE BAG!   37
I'MA FUCK AROUND AND BARF!   39
Gabe Said "We're Into Movements"
    (gabesaidwereintomovements.blogspot.com)

JONATHAN LETHEM   42
Being James Brown
Rolling Stone

DAVID KASTIN   79
Nica's Story: The Life and Legend of the
    Jazz Baroness
Popular Music and Society

ERIK DAVIS   109
Always Coming Home: Joanna Newsom
Arthur Magazine

ROB HARVILLA   141
Spankmaster and Servant: On the
    Psycho/Genius Double Helix and XXX
    Appeal of Kool Keith
Village Voice

JODY ROSEN   145
G-d's Reggae Star: How Matisyahu Became a
    Pop Phenomenon
Slate (slate.com)

ARYE DWORKEN   150
Straight Outta Israel
Flaunt Magazine

**JACK ERWIN, SEAN A. MALCOLM, ANDRÉA DUNCAN-MAO,
ADAM MATTHEWS, JUSTIN MONROE, ANSELM SAMUEL,
AND VANESSA SATTEN**   161
Told You So: The Making of *Reasonable Doubt*
XXL

kris ex   186
The History of Cocaine Rap: All White
XXL

ELISABETH VINCENTELLI   192
Bulgarian Idol
The Believer

DAVE SIMPSON   213
Excuse Me, Weren't You in the Fall?
The Guardian

WILL HERMES (AS ROBERT BARBARA)   221
#32—Just Because It's a Song Doesn't Mean
    It's True
Loose Strife (loosestrife.blogspot.com)

BRANDON PERKINS   226
   Industrial Psychology
   URB Magazine

SARAH GODFREY   232
   Multiple Personality Disorder
   Washington City Paper

DYLAN HICKS   238
   Man in Love: Barbra Streisand, Barry Gibb,
      and the Autobiographical Criticism of
      Doug Belknap
   The Rake

JESSICA SHAW   249
   People, People Who Love Barbra
   Entertainment Weekly

NITSUH ABEBE   256
   Making Plans for Daniel
   Pitchfork Media (pitchforkmedia.com)

JESSICA HOPPER   273
   SWF, 45
   Chicago Reader

JAY BORONSKI   278
   Gimme Back My Bone: Pondering the
      Ineffable Sound of "Classic Rock That
      Rocks"
   San Francisco Bay Guardian

DAVID BYRNE   282
   Heavy Theater
   David Byrne Journal (journal.davidbyrne.com)

NICK SOUTHALL   284
  Imperfect Sound Forever
  Stylus (stylusmagazine.com)

ROBERT FORSTER   302
  A True Hipster
  The Monthly

RICHARD HELL   310
  Rock 'n' Roll High School
  New York Times

JOHN SWENSON   313
  The Bands Played On
  Offbeat Magazine

KELEFA SANNEH   323
  New Orleans Hip-Hop Is the Home of
     Gangsta Gumbo
  New York Times

DOUGLAS WOLK   329
  The Syncher, Not the Song: The Irresistible
     Rise of the Numa Numa Dance
  The Believer

  Other Notable Essays of 2006   337
  List of Contributors   341
  Credits   348

INTRODUCTION

Mary Gaitskill began her introduction to the 2006 edition of this series by noting that, actually, she didn't regard her selections as 2005's "best music writing"—"not in the set-in-stone type way." They were more "a mix tape of sounds one might hear in life." Respect to her— I think Gaitskill's collection surpassed all six of its predecessors. But I came in with a different program. Set in stone, nah—even for a guy whose claim to fame is letter grades, stone would be pushing it. But as the only full-time rock critic, experienced music editor, or for that matter professional journalist ever to assemble one of these books, I had something to prove and only one way to prove it. So to be perfectly clear I'll yell a little: I wanted the best *writing*. ***THE BEST WRITING***.

These essays—a term I use loosely but advisedly—comprise no sampler, mix tape, cross-section, genre survey, affirmative action program, rich tapestry, or tasty gumbo. I chose them without considering how they'd fit together except in a worried, uh-oh kind of way. I omitted good work by friends of mine because I thought there was better work in the pile, sometimes by people I'd never heard of (though one disadvantage of giving a pro this job is that the pro in question has met a majority of those who made the cut, half a dozen of whom do qualify as his friends). As someone who designates himself a "rock critic" on the grounds that "music writer" is a weaselly anti-intellectualism, I ended up with fewer than ten examples of criticism in the narrow sense. Early plans to include a section of 100-to-300-word album reviews, the meal ticket of critics with no stomach for arbitrary trend pieces or low-access celebrity profiles, were abandoned when I tallied up the superb longer work at my disposal—including several profiles and trend pieces.

So what was my program? To demonstrate, within the limits of the available evidence, that even in this diminished time—with commercial journalism often cynical pap, alternative journalism redefined as leisure guidance, and the Web a trackless waste of hastily composed one-upsmanship—the music I imperialistically call rock and roll continues to inspire more acute, original, informative, engaging, funny, and idiosyncratic writing than can be stuffed into a 300-page book. Going in, I wasn't sure the evidence would be there. Coming out, I will have the luxury, before this introduction is through, of urging readers to seek further proof from the "Other Notable Essays of 2006" list in back, much of which can be located on the trackless waste to which I just referred.

In the interest of transparency and my argument, let me describe our process. The bulk of the work is done by series editor Daphne Carr, who finds candidates by logging her year's reading, soliciting nominations, networking, and nosing around. Between December and February, Daphne winnows more than 1000 possibilities down to 100 or so (this year it was around 115). Understandably, Daphne doesn't finish reading everything she starts, and I didn't expect to either—once I decided something fell short, I'd save time by moving on. But not counting a couple of late, long entries, that never happened. I downed 81 in a three-day weekend, some less than 1000 words, others more than 8000; even the few of Daphne's choices I thought rather bad were bad in a sufficiently fascinating way that I always got to the end. To these I added several dozen possibilities I rounded up on my own, although only two of my final choices weren't among those Daphne preselected. It was hard work, all this reading. But it was also tremendous fun—a lot more fun than editing Pazz & Jop Critics' Poll comments for the *Village Voice*, which is how I used to catch up every winter. We squeezed in thirty-two titles, every one surefire by me, with others I truly regret excluding. In short, I read three books' worth of music writing, most of it rock criticism by my broad standards, and enjoyed the bejesus out of at least two-thirds of it.

Granted, there's a professional reason for my enjoyment that most readers don't share. Knowledge of music is my stock in trade, and editing this book proved an exceptionally pleasant way to beef it up— beats scrolling through MP3 blogs, believe it. Many rejects—Lemmy Kilmister and Horace Tapscott, Frank Sinatra Jr. and Lady Sovereign, Paul Nelson and Michael Jackson, Joe Meek and a second exegesis on the Fall, to choose a few I can put proper names on—will now proceed to my permanent files. But when I said I was on the hunt for *writing* I wasn't kidding, and that mission sharpened my ever-evolving conception of what good writing is.

My first principle was to take it as a bad sign if I caught my attention flagging, although with Nick Southall's disquisition on compression (one of the most widely noticed pieces of the year, I later learned), I then found myself thinking about the damn thing for days, a very good sign that turned me around. Then again, note that my heart sank when I saw that a writer I know slightly and like a lot had submitted an immensely long profile of Joanna Newsom, whose much-praised second album I can't stand. OK Bob, I said to myself, grit your teeth and get through it first thing tomorrow morning, when you're fresh. Forty-five minutes after breakfast, I was so engrossed I hadn't budged from my chair. You will find Erik Davis's labor of love grouped with the one selection I was sure of going in, Jonathan Lethem's epic portrait of James Brown, accounted by me the greatest rock and roll musician of all time.

But boredom is a crude criterion. Active interest is subtler. One test is that I want to learn something I didn't know. Thus, the journalistic nitty-grit of good reporting can shore up the literary ideal of good writing. But often something new is a gift of style, voice, verve, and either ideas that make you think or, much harder for some writers although very closely related, jokes that make you laugh. Rock criticism has always been indulgent about style—from the underground-newspaper era until the Internet, a realm of rants, spoofs, slanguage, and barbarism, of corn and pretension and half-cooked academese. Reading through, the line editor in me did some cringing. Erik, what's with this "apotheosis"? Arye, couldn't you do better than "beliefs revolve around a distinction that is gaining popularity"? Daphne Brooks, no matter how much you owe Hazel Carby you don't need to name-check her. But big deal. In the end, most of what captivated me was lumpier than a lot of what didn't. Much of the best-edited and hence "best-written" work came from high-end periodicals that invest serious money in clarity and consistency, which in themselves are virtues (cf. Lethem on JB). But finally, this work did often feel "slick," a characterization beloved of oafs hoping to devalue levels of craft that are beyond them, because structurally and, sometimes, intellectually, I knew what was coming: the quick ID, the deft kicker, the supporting quote, the balanced conclusion.

So although I would have filled the book with *New Yorker* reprints if that was how the cookie crumbled, in fact, only three periodicals placed even twice: *XXL*, easily the most self-possessed of the mags jammed into hip-hop's stretch limo; the *New York Times*, with help from the op-ed page where Richard Hell placed his CBGB gem; and the essayist's new best friend, *The Believer*, with an asterisk. The asterisk is because Douglas Wolk debuted our finale, his "Numa Numa Dance" saga, not in print but as an AV-enhanced lecture at Seattle's EMP Pop Conference, which is also where I first encountered Dylan Hicks's tribute to legendary Streisand crit Doug Belknap, as well as Michaelangelo Matos's miraculous tale of how the most important rock and roll fan he's ever known misprised the Supremes' "Love Child." Like Wolk, Hicks eventually received a check for his effort (from the Twin Cities–based *The Rake*), but Matos published his jaw-dropper for nothing on the *Back and Forth* R&B blog. EMP doesn't pay either. Yet every year since 2002 it has brought together an amazing array of distinguished rock criticism and research—some by academics, whose job description includes attending conferences, but just as many by journalists and amateurs, who every year vie to collect their thoughts at this forum for the pleasure and pride of it. EMP is like the blogosphere with gatekeepers. The punch line being that this anthology is too.

Most of my little online reading is devoted to politics. I'm sure I'm missing stuff, but I'm also sure this is efficient time management. Even setting aside my firm beliefs that writing takes time and requires editorial oversight, up-to-the-minute imperatives like the Internet's have been cheapening what's-hot journalism for generations and would seem to guarantee the failure of Web posts to weather any reasonable look-back period—three months, much less our twelve. But complaining about the Web as if it's a single thing is like complaining about television—it's too big. And as it turns out, eight of our thirty-two selections were first published there, only one for money—Nitsuh Abebe's gratifyingly unromantic Daniel Johnston profile for, of all places, *Pitchfork*, a publication long responsible for more godawful prose than *Murder Dog*, *Variety*, and *PMLA* combined. Moreover, though most of these Web finds presumably took time, none except Abebe's was edited at all. Moreover moreover, they didn't just sneak under the wire: Chris Ryan's mad fake emails and Jane Dark's/Joshua Clover's sweet takeout on Scritti Politti are both in my top five. And Carl Wilson, a Toronto *Globe & Mail* editor I knew better from his *Zoilus* blog, opens the book because his non-*Zoilus* post summed things up.

"Forgive me; this won't be brief," Wilson begins. And it won't. This book is for readers; as I'm always explaining to my bosses, rock criticism isn't for rock fans, it's for, duh, rock criticism fans. On one of those MP3 blogs I have no use for, Wilson resurrects a lost song I recall fondly from Pere Ubu's *The Tenement Year*. But Wilson reads more into it than I did—in part, one infers, because he's living through the kind of marital trauma he believes inspired it. He parses David Thomas's meanings like Christopher Ricks unpacking Dylanesque vernacular, only to end by admitting that the song he remembers, and has just put into words, is more powerful than the one he reconnects with when he finally locates a copy to upload. Reading Wilson's piece a second time, I had to play "We Have the Technology" myself, just so I could find out what I thought was there. I went to my vinyl. *The Tenement Year* was gone. I Googled Wilson's post. The song link was dead. So I'm left with "If Music Is the Answer, What's the Question?" It's not enough—I still want the music. But it's something. It's a lot.

The pious thing to say about music writing is that it's for the *music*, man. And sometimes that's true. Read in *The Nation* (online-only, so make that nine Web pieces, two paid, and oh right, Jody Rosen in *Slate* makes it ten and three), Daphne Brooks's explication of Beyoncé's *B'Day* changed a record I'd played plenty without grokking—suddenly I could hear its moneyed sheen and cool heat as troubling, aestheticized, politically significant assertions of sass and substance. Jessica Hopper sent me to my unplayed shelves to grab a Mecca Normal album I'd kept even though I'd always thought they were a crock, and how about that, this one had something. *XXL*'s

takeout on Jay-Z's *Reasonable Doubt* convinced me to replace my
home-taped version with a CD. But Ann Powers, who's been talking
up Neil Diamond for years, won't turn me into a fan even with every
Latino-American in L.A. backing her up. Sasha Frere-Jones is always leading me to slick elixirs like Mariah Carey without making
me drink. I'd rather be subjected to a David Byrne solo album than
attend one of the Sunn0))) shows he describes so swiftly and astutely. Daniel Johnston remains a pet peeve. And for thirty-five years
I've had enough of Barbra Streisand, who hams up two pieces here.
Far from leading me to new music, these essays saved me from it.
With a good writer, reading about music you don't like often beats
listening to it. You gain cultural grasp with no loss of ear time.

And of course, not all music writing, or music criticism, practices
advocacy. In addition to pans—Matisyahu, meet Jody Rosen, his
erudition a blessing and a curse (for us and for you, respectively)—
there is simply writing that honors all the worlds that music crystal-
lizes and creates. The finest thing in Gaitskill's collection was John
Jeremiah Sullivan's mammoth *GQ* report on a Christian rock festival, which in thirty-three pages detailed barely any music at all.
While nothing quite so extreme surfaces this year, in its low-budget
way Will Hermes's yarn about an imaginary blogger's encounter with
a delusional friend of the Hold Steady comes close. Elisabeth Vincentelli's medium-budget report on the Eurovision Song Contest
and Dave Simpson's quixotic attempt to locate forty-three former
members of the Fall are tales of musical obsessions 180 degrees
apart, only where does that leave Jessica Shaw's Streisand fans?
(Over near Vincentelli, I guess.) Arye Dworken and kris ex look inside two hip-hop subcultures that are almost as diametrical, while
Sarah Godfrey, Rob Harvilla, and Brandon Perkins break down hip-
hop obsessions barely distinguishable from dementia—although in
Perkins's case the dementia is the fan's, and the only advice he can
extract from Lil' Wayne, Ph.MF.D., is "Get money. Fuck bitches."

Jay Boronski's analysis of how classic rock has been reconceived at his favorite radio station describes an obsession he's not embarrassed to depict as ridiculous. David Kastin's reconstruction of the life of bebop benefactor Pannonica de Koenigswarter describes an obsession he's not embarrassed to depict as noble. And then there's some really serious stuff.

I know/knew these guys a little bit, and wrote an obituary myself, so my emotions are suspect, but for me the most moving piece here is Robert Forster's tribute to his late friend and fellow Go-Between Grant McLennan—making Forster one of three musicians to end up among my best music writers, which like the Web presence surprises me. This is hardly to say I didn't think David Byrne or, God knows, distinguished novelist and critic Richard Hell could write prose. But as Forster climaxes by pointing out, McLennan (and by association his partner) represented a special case—although he probably wasn't the only rock and roller with a subscription to *The New York Review of Books* (wouldn't put it past Byrne, or Sting), he was one of the few. Advocacy moment: rock criticism fans who have never heard his music should get on the Go-Betweens now. Start with *Tallulah*. Maybe *The Friends of Rachel Worth*.

The other obituaries here aren't. Both concern New Orleans, and neither is giving up now. Nostalgia-averse though I happen to be, I was almost persuaded by several impassioned arguments for the stubborn vitality of New Orleans trad in the teeth of a disaster rapper B.G. summed up all too well: "New Orleans gone." The militantly unsentimental Kelefa Sanneh won't give up because he's certain that, one way or another, N.O. bounce and all its crunky cousins will continue to thrive, and he notes with his usual acerbity that the refusal of New Orleans music advocates to respect its hip-hop is a scandal that long preceded Katrina. What's more surprising, however, is how unsentimental the traditional advocates are. The piece I loved was just reporting, its facts more eloquent than any rhetoric: John Swenson's band-by-band account of where and when who started playing again. And high among the Other Notables is a Geoffrey Himes profile of singer John Boutte, who always says "when the levees failed" where others would say "after the storm," and some poli sci from Ned Sublette, who explains why Ray Nagin is Clinton's candidate—George Clinton's. Check it out—*The Nation*, online.

So, this is my 2006, on August 31 of which I was fired by the *Village Voice* after 32 years. I had long feared the moment, but it worked out great—a publicity coup that among other things got me this gig. I found myself transformed into a symbol of the perfidy of the Phoenix-based New Times Media, which had swallowed Village Voice Media's alt-weekly chain and assumed its hallowed name. Without going much further I will note that most of what I've seen of the rock criticism at New Times Media, to call it by its rightful moniker, is leisure guidance at its most reflexive—but that that doesn't include Rob Harvilla, who replaced me at the *Voice*. With his sly diffidence, high joke density, and nonexistent nasty streak, he makes something of New Times's Joe Clubrat shtick. It's just another way of doing things—the Jay Boronski essay here, written for a sworn enemy of the New Times empire in San Francisco, also does well by the approach, though Boronski doesn't seem as nice a guy. Anyway, my brief celebrity status got me interviewed a lot. And since I was expected to hold forth on the State of Rock Criticism, I decided I'd better develop a soundbite, which after some thought went like this.

The erosion of review length has been terrible for rock criticism—for criticism in most genres, although music's product glut exacerbates the squeeze more than the panoply of outlets mitigates it. But that doesn't mean there isn't plenty of epigrammatic work being done at 100 to 300 words. And please, enough with the giants-in-those-days blather about the golden era of Lester Bangs (dead before the shit hit the fan), Richard Meltzer (who believes rock expired in

1968), and Greil Marcus (monthly column in *Interview* to this day). Since 2002, four major jobs have gone to superb younger critics. Kelefa Sanneh on the hot-and-new beat at the *New York Times* and Ann Powers on the humanist-overview beat at the *Los Angeles Times* are old-school adepts of social context and mega-significance. Sasha Frere-Jones at *The New Yorker* and Jody Rosen at *Slate* are new jacks, adding to that stuff a musical sophistication that, crucially with hip-hop, the new century's most formally complex genre, is even sharper about rhythm than about harmony, with Rosen exploiting a subspecialty in prerock pop and Frere-Jones one in studio technique. Although Powers occasionally puts her heart into trying, none of these critics makes the kind of grand cultural claims that were the bedrock of early rock criticism for the excellent reason that they wouldn't be true. Pop music won't change the world, not enough, so let's all try to make sure something else does. But all four evince more love of music than any MP3 flibbertigibbets or golden-age nay-sayers I'm aware of. And the same goes for every single writer in this anthology. If they didn't love music, they probably wouldn't write so good, now would they?

Robert Christgau
New York City
March 2007

CARL WILSON

IF MUSIC IS THE ANSWER, WHAT'S THE QUESTION?

Pere Ubu—"We Have the Technology" (Original)
Forgive me; this won't be brief. Because, to put it plain, this is one of my favourite songs. Yet a frustrating quest a few months ago could not turn up the original version, from the album *The Tenement Year*, anywhere in the digital wilds, legal or no. Weeks later, too late for the mix I'd been hoping to make, I got ahold of a "hard" copy. And tonight I realized that thanks to Said the Gramophone, I had the means to alter that reality for some other searcher out there.

So here we are. You and I. The moment is delicate. Don't press play yet. Already I have built the song into myth, the myth of a favourite song, and if you hear it and shrug, "*huh, whatever,*" this conspiracy between us, this chance for contact and sympathy, may vanish. Words cannot prevent it. Not all the words that have been spent enhancing the legend of Pere Ubu, certainly, by the likes of Greil Marcus or Jon Savage or most recently Simon Reynolds—

most of them devoted to the way in the mid-1970s the band trans-
figured the sonic scrapheap of post-industrial Cleveland, forged it
into a futurist vision of the American transcendental tradition, an alternate history of rock'n'roll, fated to be one of the most influential
obscurities in modern music. This is not that Pere Ubu. You can look
that one up.

This is the Pere Ubu of 1988, when it had regrouped after David
Thomas's more-scorned-than-heard, "eccentric nature-boy" solo
years. Now David Thomas lived in what he considered an exile in
England, making albums such as *Monster Walks the Winter Lake*, a
metaphoric suite about the breakdown of communication in a marriage. In those songs, he portrayed a failing marriage as a third entity,
a Frankenstein pastiche of "parts that don't matter," a hulk that comes
lumbering between two people, silencing them, dominating the horizon. And in the first years of the reanimated Pere Ubu this theme
persisted: Where to turn when the dynamic between people is beyond
their control, when it wrenches the torch from their hands and blazes
through the village? It needn't be a marriage; it could be a band.

All right, let it play now.

As so often, in a group that always made its art from the parts that
weren't supposed to matter in culture, from B-movies and sci-fi novels and comics and Germanic freak rock and abandoned buildings
and obsolete synthesizers and dinosaur books, Pere Ubu digs for inspiration in the trash: Here it's the opening sequence of the bone-
headed 1970s TV show *The Six Million Dollar Man*, in which the
surgeons intone over the prone body of the astronaut, "We can re-
build him. We have the technology." And somehow, presumably
with bits of early microwaves, Soviet satellites and HAL–9000, they
call the fallen man to rise, to run fast in slow motion, to face su-
pervillains and (not incidentally) fembots—too good to be good,
much less true.

But David Thomas isn't a kid any more. He doesn't want to fight cartoon threats, or even, for awhile, his pet cultural apocalypse. He wants to talk to his wife. What is that monster made of? It's made up of moments, intervals at which no one rises to the occasion, or all parties are too stubborn to prevent the inevitable crash. Where is the device to stop the action—time travel that goes not forward or back but within, as in Nicholson Baker's *The Fermata*, or in the current glib Adam Sandler variation with the remote control that could put life on pause, to let us "hold it to the light, study all the angles, and find out How and Why it's gotta go the way that it goes"? That's the only restoration for this man fallen to earth, this no-longer-young genius laid low by human banality.

The fantasy swells to overwhelm him. With his meaty hand he swats away apparitions of "thinkers and poets of the past—oh no!" There must be more than blind intuition. There must be a machine. And with that the utopia passes to dystopia, to eyes that are "beaming," to coming "unstuck completely, Flap A from Slot B, slapping in the wind!" It's a bit like the Internet, this flux of liberated information, of knowledge unhinged from wisdom. (In a couple of years Pere Ubu would be an early adopter, putting out CD-Rs and press materials in pre-Web hypercard stacks.)

Yet isn't the song itself made up of moments? With its anti-canonical poetic folds, and the anarchic presence of Allen Ravenstine's EML synthesizer—never before as assertive as on this album—this music seems to be splicing possibility with its every twist. Yet the hunted man inside this storm hasn't the patience, hasn't the hold on his desperation, to let him inhale its gusts or let its lightning travel through him to ground. Surely the solution must be elsewhere, beyond this song. And it's this error, the song's self-disregard, that tells the tale. "This moment" in which the song began has been bypassed in yearning for a higher power. Rewind, begin again and again, but it still goes the way that it goes. It ascends from the real to the sublime, and in that very apotheosis, it goes hollow and is lost.

And reader, my words won't save our moment, either. If you've listened to the track, you've heard what I did when I finally found it again: The 1980s sound is shallow, brittle, the recording not much more than a blueprint for the song I remember, the song it is supposed to be, the one that contains its own undoing and thereby its own fulfillment. Even David Thomas's maelstrom of a voice is more like a flat surface.

Stop. Let's study one more angle.

There is another, still-in-print version of this song on *Apocalypse Now*, a live recording made at Schuba's in Chicago in 1991, on a break from touring with Ubu acolytes the Pixies. Allen Ravenstine is absent (by now he'd quit music altogether), but some of the roar and absolutism of the song I recall is restored, its spontaneity, that unstuckness that my memory must have transferred from live experiences to the original recording. But here, the details of the fable, its path from reasonable question to irrational answer—a *Dr. Who* episode taken to its logical mad end—are muddled in the generalities of a rock show.

Pere Ubu—"We Have the Technology" (Live)

No, it's not out there, the "We Have the Technology" that I intended to share with you. Nothing correlates to the song inside me, just a chain of translations, representations that undo me, that won't shut up, that breed monsters only to fight the monsters who preceded them. You'll never understand. I don't understand it myself anymore. All I have is this story about where it all went wrong. Does it help, this autopsy? If I guessed why you don't love me, darling, might you love me again?

Ann Powers

LATINOS GIVE NEW LIFE TO NEIL DIAMOND ANTHEM

Amid the mariachi music, socially conscious *corridos* and civil rights hymns at last week's immigration-rights rallies, a surprising voice arose—a strong Jewish baritone usually favored by middle-aged women and retro-hip college kids. It was Neil Diamond, singing his own exodus anthem: "America," from the pop elder statesman's 1980 remake of America's first talkie, *The Jazz Singer*.

The recording opened and closed the May 1 speakers' program at City Hall. It's made its way into reports of rallies in Dallas, Kansas City and Milwaukee. Although hardly the official anthem of La Raza, "America"'s portrait of travelers "traveling light . . . in the eye of a storm" is outdoing more standard fare such as "If I Had a Hammer," giving Diamond something like the role Bob Dylan played during the civil rights era of the 1960s.

The journey of Diamond's "America" toward its current place within the immigrant movement says much about the open-border policies of inspirational pop. Powerful songs move and change—and not always as some think they should. Party music like reggae or

African mbaqanga can stir revolution. A giddy romp can become a heartbreaking plea (balladeer Ray Lamontagne's take on the Gnarls Barkley hit "Crazy," for example). And a song with a complicated past, like "America," can resurrect in new listeners' hands.

"It's the immigrant anthem," said Angelica Salas, executive director of the Coalition for Humane Immigrant Rights of Los Angeles (CHIRLA). "Every time I've been at different activities over time, you'll have the Neil Diamond song. It speaks to the experience."

The song is built like a footpath up a monument, the melody swooping downward to rise up again, its key changes and call-and-response elements ("They're coming to America!" "Today!") forcing the tension. Rooted in the Yiddish music of Diamond's Brooklyn youth, the song moves on to Broadway and the Borscht Belt and lands on the edge of disco—a border-crossing trek unto itself. This intentional hugeness, this insistence on being an anthem, makes "America" easy to mock but also impossible to resist.

Salas, though, was quick to shift the conversation toward Latino artists Los Tigres del Norte, Ricardo Arjona and CHIRLA's house band, Jornaleros del Norte, who helped lead the Wilshire Boulevard march. Arjona's poignant "Mojado," she noted, is becoming the Spanish-language equivalent of "America." Like many of Los Tigres' *corridos*, "Mojado" traces a migration similar to those made by Diamond's unnamed dreamers. And its clear connection to the current debate makes it a favorite among activists.

Diamond's "America," on the other hand, raised hackles. One organizer quickly dismissed the "knuckleheads" who played the song at City Hall; another hung up when pushed on the subject. It's not surprising that those in charge prefer to focus on clear expressions of Latino pride, like the hundreds of mariachi players participating in last Monday's downtown march.

What about "America" makes certain people uncomfortable, yet also leads it to surface again and again? One factor, of course, is its

English-language origin; though far less ubiquitous, it's akin to the rallies' ever more present American flags. "If you grew up in the U.S., this is a song you know," Salas said, articulating the song's bridge-building usefulness and its limitations. "Immigrants today don't really know it." Yet the language barrier doesn't defeat "America"'s irresistible hokeyness.

A DESCRIPTION BY DIAMOND

For his part, the 65-year-old Vegas veteran is delighted at the new interest in his 26-year-old song. "That's what it's there for," he said by phone from an undisclosed vacation hideaway. "That song tells the immigrant story. It was written for my grandparents and the immigrants who came over in the late 1800s, the Irish, Jews and Italians. But it's the song for the modern-day Latino coming as well."

Diamond describes its sound as sadness "counterbalanced with joy," and its dynamic and melodic drive is, indeed, satisfyingly overwhelming. The song's unusual history only intensifies its effect. Its association with *The Jazz Singer*, a cinematic flop with a platinum-selling soundtrack, raises the specter of American entertainment's most controversial border crossing—blackface minstrelsy. Al Jolson famously appeared "corked up" in the 1927 original and Diamond, briefly but embarrassingly, did the same in 1980.

Diamond's version underplays blackface by making it a literal disguise, not an effect; in general Diamond was less guilty of the rock era's version of minstrelsy than several of his peers (a certain skinny, lip-licking Englishman, for example). Yet by taking on the role once inhabited by Jolson, Diamond highlighted all of pop's complex existence on the boundaries of race and taste.

"America" lifted itself out of the film's context to become its own phenomenon. It's appeared on many Diamond compilations and is so popular with his fans that Diamond often opens and closes his shows with it. Schoolteachers across the country use it in their curriculum on immigration. Michael Dukakis, the son of Greek immigrants, adopted it as a theme during his ill-fated 1988 campaign against George H.W. Bush. After the attacks of Sept. 11, 2001, the radio conglomerate Clear Channel added it to a list of "lyrically questionable" (and supposedly dangerous) songs, because it mentioned immigrants entering the U.S. on planes.

"CHEECH" AND SONG

It was Chicano comic Richard "Cheech" Marin's 1987 comedy *Born in East L.A.*, however, that linked Diamond's Eurocentric anthem to California's Latino populace.

This picaresque tale follows Marin as Rudy, a native Angeleno falsely deported and forced to maneuver his way home from Tijuana. In the film's climactic scene, Rudy stands at the U.S.-Mexico border, frustrated and mocked by nearby immigration officers. Suddenly, a multitude of fellow border-crossers appear and rush the line. The chorus accompanying their triumphant entry? "They're coming to America!"

"One of the film's editors put the song in as a temp track," said Marin, reflecting on his unexpected mining of the Diamond catalog. "My experience is try not to add any music you'll fall in love with as a placeholder. But we did, and it just stayed. We showed Neil the movie and he signed on right away."

Marin's work is full of slapstick and low humor, but its balance of silliness and acerbic satire represents a strong line in Chicano art. The cartoonist and radio host Lalo Alcaraz, the theater troupe Culture Clash and the "Mexican Elvis" El Vez all similarly infuse their jokes with cutting political observations.

"It goes with the Chicano and Mexican tradition of always having two jobs at the same time," Marin said. "Taking on the subject of immigration in a comedy is the classic way. You're able to do two things at once, and people get it better—it goes down easier."

Raul Ramos, a professor of history at the University of Houston, seconds Marin's view. "Irony and satire are powerful tools often used by disenfranchised and marginalized groups," Ramos said. "During the Chicano movement, Luis Valdez used a style of agitprop theater at farmworker rallies throughout the San Joaquin Valley. Mexicans understand the power of humor and satire. It's a survival strategy, you could say."

In this light, the Latino resurrection of Diamond's "America" makes delicious sense. It's a joke that's not a joke, an embrace of something seemingly "other" that ends up an invocation of ethnic pride.

"Not only the Latino community but many other immigrants have told me they love that scene particularly," Marin said of *Born in East L.A.* "That moment of crossing the border and coming to a place where you don't know anybody and you're reduced to the smallest emotional element is something everybody identifies with. I think a lot of them expected that when they crossed the border they'd hear that song."

Given such agile appropriations, the idea of putting borders around any music—"The Star-Spangled Banner," for example, an all-star Spanish-language recording of which recently sparked criticism from conservative pundits—becomes ridiculous.

As Diamond himself says, "A song belongs to the world. . . . It took me a while to get used to that."

MICHAELANGELO MATOS

A DOUBLE HISTORY OF THE SUPREMES' "LOVE CHILD"

Let's start with a few facts. According to a study by the National Center for Health Statistics (NCHS), in 1960, for every 1,000 women aged 15–19 in the United States, 89.1 had a child—nearly 594,000 total. By 1970, the U.S. population had increased, and so had the raw number of women under 20 with children, to 656,460. But the numbers were actually down 2.1 percent, to 68.3 women per 1,000. In Michigan state during 1970, the number of births per 1,000 women aged 15–19 was 66—slightly lower than the national average.

I cite these numbers because when I decided to do my presentation on the Supremes' "Love Child," I figured the song was rooted in an increase in teen pregnancy, both nationally and more specifically in Detroit, the Supremes', and Motown's, hometown. Motown are not known as documentarians; their greatest records, however visceral, are as constructed as any in pop. But they're still plenty real, and no '60s Motown record sounds more real, more based on fact or lived circumstance, than "Love Child." In this case, though, it might seem that what Motown's hit machine decided to address was less a new problem than an old perennial.

Or at least a perennial with a new twist, because what did change over the '60s was the number of teenage mothers who weren't married. In 1960, 15 percent of teenage women who gave birth did so out of wedlock. In 1970 that number had doubled, to 30 percent. Teenagers began marrying less, too: in 1960, 60 percent of 19-year-old women remained unmarried, and in 1970 that number increased to 69 percent. A 1985 version of the NCHS study noted the following: "Teen parents . . . tend to have larger numbers of children, to face a higher probability of being a single parent, to experience poverty more frequently, and to be disproportionately represented on welfare."

These are the facts that underscore the song's urgency. The song isn't about the rejection of childbirth—it's about the avoidance of having kids out of wedlock. It's about not wanting to raise your children single, to avoid poverty and welfare, about not getting locked into a cycle of having even more kids you can't take care of as well as possible.

It's a pop-critical truism that Motown underwent a revolution when Marvin Gaye won the freedom to make *What's Going On* his way. The album is understood to have opened the door for the label's artists to write about what they wanted, how they wanted—as long as, you know, there were hits involved. It's striking to me how often "Love Child" is left out of this argument altogether, something that seems down more to intentional fallacy than anything. The lone genius questing for capital-T Truth against the wishes of the money men, after all, is a lot more romantic an image than that of four seasoned pros who've been sequestered in a hotel suite by their extravagant boss for the specific purpose of turning a fading act's fortunes. That was where "Love Child" was conceived, sired by Motown staff writers Henry Cosby, Frank Wilson, Pam Sawyer, Deke Richards, and R. Dean Taylor, and paid for by Berry Gordy, Motown's president.

The situation was simple: The Supremes had been Motown's flagship act since 1964, becoming the label's—and black America's—glamour queens, particularly their lead singer, Diana Ross, who would have probably been thrust out front even if she hadn't been dallying with the boss. Ten Number Ones later, they were in a rut. Their singles were only going Top 20, if that. Soul had taken on new contours thanks to Sly & the Family Stone, had subdivided into funk thanks to James Brown, had grown grit thanks to Stax and Aretha Franklin. As a whole, Motown was keeping up, but not the Supremes, who hadn't had a Number One in—heaven forfend—an entire year, since "Reflections," whose phased guitar intro was the label's nod to the Summer of Love.

"Reflections" was also the last Supremes Number One written and produced by Lamont Dozier and Brian and Eddie Holland. Late in 1967, the trio left Motown over royalty disputes and began working on setting up their own shop, or shops—the Hot Wax and Invictus labels would straddle the '60s and '70s with Supremes-modeled groups like Honey Comb and the Temptations-esque Chairmen of the Board. (Ironically, HDH would benefit from the blunter lyrical territory that "Love Child" helped open up: See Freda Payne's 1970 hit "Band of Gold," the greatest R&B song ever written about wedding-night erectile dysfunction.)

Dozier and the Hollands' departure threw the Supremes into a tailspin, at a time when they didn't need the help. At the beginning of 1967, the group had been renamed Diana Ross and the Supremes, and founding member Florence Ballard was replaced by Cindy Birdsong. Gordy, putting his coach hat on, decided to take action.

As anyone who prefers "It's the Same Old Song" to "I Can't Help Myself" is aware, Motown was never averse to working a formula until it fell down exhausted. (Indeed, they'd do it with "Love Child"'s follow-up, 1969's "I'm Living in Shame.") The title of "Love Child" seemed to reach back to the second Supremes Number One, "Baby Love"—just reverse the titles: "Baby Love," "Love Baby," "Love Child," simple. But in this case the topic came first, and anyway "Love Child" was fairly new territory for Motown: a song about a socially relevant topic that wasn't a cover. It doesn't seem like an accident that "Love Child" preceded, by only a couple of weeks, the Temptations' "Cloud Nine," another Number One, written and produced by Norman Whitfield. Clearly, Motown was ready to answer charges that they weren't socially relevant enough.

"Love Child" is a protest song in the same way "Blue Suede Shoes" was—a warning, or a plea, for someone to back off, in this case Diana Ross's boyfriend. He's pressuring her to have sex, and she wants to wait. 1968 was the year that the birth control pill, then on the market for eight years, was compared to the discovery of fire in terms of importance, but the sexual revolution wasn't yet in full swing, and anyway the Supremes were essentially singing for kids (not a pejorative). More to the point, Diana Ross was singing as a kid—the narrative voice is clearly that of a teenager even if no ages are mentioned—a teenager telling her boyfriend why she won't have sex with him—she will not get pregnant and continue the cycle of unwed, teenage motherhood.

Diana is also singing about something that Motown had previously used to less cutting ends: class. It came up sometimes, usually as a hurdle to be joyously overcome, as with Stevie Wonder's "Uptight," about "a poor man's son" who wins the girl. The poverty in "Love Child" isn't cute, though: It's something you deal with because you have no choice, and something that, however successful you become, you never completely escape. "Te-e-e-e-nement slum!" chant the background singers (none of them actual members of the Supremes) all through the song—stagy, a little comic, difficult to know how to take the first time through, even with the string slash and uptown-blues guitar-drum breakdown that leads the record off.

"In those eyes I see reflected / A hurt, scorned, rejected love child": Those lines are equally stagy, but they're also terse, brutal, unforgiving. Diana Ross didn't write those lines, but she inhabits them, each word rising—"hurt! scorned! REJECTED!"—as she lifts the lid off her own vanity and exposes what's beneath. For someone who'd recently taken star billing in a group she hadn't even sung lead in to begin with, it's a rather brave thing to do, and the closest she ever came to matching it weren't pieces of music but a movie, 1972's *Lady Sings the Blues*, in which she played Billie Holiday on junk, and an album cover, for 1980's *Diana*, in which she posed wearing almost no makeup. Both the cover and "Love Child" were statements—"I am real"—that served to ground her diva moves, i.e., the rest of her career.

In a way, Diana's divadom and Berry Gordy's tight grip on his charges' output make "Love Child" even more remarkable in its daring, even if social consciousness was selling. It helped open the doors for black pop to embrace lyrical realism on a widespread scale as much as any record ever made, even if, unlike "Love Child," a lot of what came through that door was pretty macho—the strong-male-leader-of-the-family bromides of early-'70s Gamble and Huff, for example.

It also opened the subject up for other songwriters to tackle, often men. First Choice's 1973 proto-disco cut "Smarty Pants" was written by Edward White and Mack Wolfson and was the straightforward cautionary tale that Gordy's crew and Diana's steely delivery never quite let "Love Child" become: A party girl goes after the best-looking guy around and ends up with his child and no him, thanks to her loose ways. (As in "Love Child," the narrator of "Smarty Pants" is never ID'ed as a teenager, but her name gives us a clue. Her name is also "Smarty Pants.") Madonna's "Papa Don't Preach," from 1986, is a plea for reconciliation between daughter and father after the daughter gets herself into, and I quote, "an awful mess"—not quite a cautionary tale, but one where, unlike either

"Love Child" or "Smarty Pants," adults are actively involved, which by default gives it a cautionary cast.

Two other songs take "Love Child" even further—one as a parlor tragedy, the other as a modern horror story. The title character of 2Pac's "Brenda's Got a Baby," from his 1991 debut *2Pacalypse Now*, is 12 years old. Her boyfriend is a cousin; her family cares less about her pregnancy than about the welfare check that accompanies it. Her boyfriend-slash-cousin leaves her and Brenda "ha[s] the baby solo . . . on the bathroom floor." She tries throwing the baby in the Dumpster, but thinks better of it. Then her mother throws her out: "You makin' me lose pay / The social worker's here every day." 2Pac grinds the details home, blunter and more horrific by the line: "She tried to sell crack, but end up getting robbed / So now what's next, there ain't nothing left to sell / So she sees sex as a way of leaving hell." Only she doesn't get to leave; 2Pac twists the knife the final time by having her murdered by a john.

Nothing that drastic occurs in Joni Mitchell's "Little Green," from 1971's *Blue*, thank god. But the performance is nearly as harrowing. "Little Green" is "Love Child" after Diana loses the argument, has the baby, and tries to care for it until she realizes she's in over her head and gives it up for adoption. This never feels (and it shouldn't) like a neat little narrative arc; on an album famous for its emotional rawness, "Little Green" is the song carrying the least amount of protective cover. 2Pac crafted a worst-of-all-possible-cases scenario; Mitchell's single, teenaged mother is simply left completely on her own.

Let me tell you now about a Supremes fan. The third-oldest of seven kids born to a snappish Irish Catholic mother and a Puerto Rican dad who was never around, Lorie Matos grew up on welfare in south Minneapolis, where she hung around with drug addicts, thieves, and hoodlums—her siblings, in other words. The Supremes were Lorie's favorite group; as with a lot of girls her age, they represented an apotheosis, a potentially reachable mixture of hood and glam.

Not long after puberty, Lorie began dating an older teenager named Nick Rahoutis; shortly thereafter, she became pregnant and went to stay at a Catholic school for girls. When she went to the Hennepin County courthouse to sign the papers putting her unborn child up for adoption, she changed her mind at the last minute, got on the welfare rolls, and moved into a Section 8 apartment. Nick Rahoutis joined the Marines. On February 18, 1975, Lorie took a city bus to Deaconess Hospital near downtown Minneapolis and after 11 hours of contractions gave birth to her first son. A week later, she turned 15. Mom's most cherished memory of my early years, she later told me, occurred during a snowstorm, during which she fished through couch cushions and various pants pockets in the hamper, cobbled together about two-and-a-half dollars, took me to a nearby drugstore, and spent three hours in the aisles, figuring out how to spend what at that point seemed like all the money in the world.

In Christmas 1979, Santa Claus got me a Fisher-Price record player and a copy of the *Grease* soundtrack. Not long thereafter, Mom picked up a double-LP Supremes best-of that had been compiled two years before "Love Child." She played it on my Fisher-Price, but the record, unlike the others she picked up for me at Target on the first of every month, belonged primarily to her.

In 1988, I was 13. Mom was 28, my sister Alex three, and my sister Brittany two. Mom bought a CD player and a copy of George Michael's *Faith*. Soon after came an early Supremes CD. She was especially excited about "Love Child," a song that I had never heard of. "Oh," she told me, "That's such a great song. I used to sing it to you when you were a baby." Mom put it on and began singing along in her fragile, tone-deaf voice. There was a line in the third verse that Mom pointed out right after it had passed to the chorus. "See?" she said. "She changes her mind: She was going to put her baby up for adoption but decides she loves it too much."

In 2000, when I was 25, I was working at an office and prone to going in on weekends to use the computer, since I didn't have one at home. One Saturday before heading over, I picked up a used copy of the Supremes' *Ultimate Collection*; I especially wanted to hear "Love Child," which I hadn't listened to in years. I played it loud on headphones; it sounded as tough and frightening and vulnerable as I remembered it. Everything was in place—until the third verse, when Diana Ross sang these lines:

> *Don't think that I don't need ya*
> *Don't think I don't wanna please ya*
> *But no child of mine'll be bearing*
> *The name of shame I've been wearing*
> *Love child*

The first two lines, if you missed them, are: "Don't think that I don't need ya / Don't think I don't wanna please ya." What Mom had told me when I was 13—and what I had been hearing as a result for a dozen years—was "Don't think I don't wanna FEED ya." What my mother heard—and, through her, what I heard for a dozen years—was a shift: Diana moving from addressing her guy to addressing a baby, the one Mom thought the song was about. But there is no baby. The song is about the fact that there won't be one. Mom had heard one word wrong and changed the song's entire meaning to fit the mishearing.

Or maybe she changed it to fit something else. I know exactly how stubborn, willful, and frankly delusional my mother can be, and she is notorious for mishearing pop-song lyrics. I once got into an argument with her about whether Prince, at the end of "Let's Pretend We're

Married," was saying "I'm in love with God" or, as she heard it, "I'm in love with guys." (It's "God," by the way.)

But I wonder whether she really did hear it wrong, because I wonder how possible it is to hear any song wrong, or interpret any work of art wrong short of it leading to murder. All art takes on a life of its own outside of its creators' intentions, especially pop songs. Undoubtedly, Mom heard "Love Child" as a justification, a *Yes* from figures she admired. Oftentimes pop tells us what we want to hear. I think "Love Child" told Mom what she needed to hear, at a time when it seemed that no one else would. And that's difficult to accept, because by all rights no one else should have told her that. I don't think 14-year-olds should be having children; I don't think 17-year-olds should, either. But they do, and I am both alive and an uncle as a result. My niece Veronica will turn a year old in a couple of months. My sister Brittany recently turned 19. And I wouldn't give up my life or trade my niece for anything. So my only real conclusion is that for all my ambivalence, I have little choice but to feel indebted to "Love Child." If a pop song can change your life or save it, this one feels like it helped to enable mine.

WHITE BREAD BLACK BEER

Once upon a time there was a boy named Scritti, and though this was a strange name, nobody teased him, for he had a beautiful voice, and a falsetto that was like honey injected into the veins. And he grew up with the desire to make jangly pop music woven from strands of romance, left politics, reggae, post-structuralist theory, black soul, and everything resting in the sentence, "the music of the Beatles and Bowie prepared me for every subsequent adventure, intellectually, politically, aesthetically, structurally."

One day a funny thing happened to Scritti, because funny things happen to everyone in history. As he was figuring out his jangly pop music and bringing discreet pleasure to several people, pop music itself became less jangly, in part because digital technology favored a sharper snap in general, and in part because it was part of a constellation that would eventually be called hip-hop. And Scritti liked this sound very much. He heard Michael Jackson and Run-DMC and it was good. So it came to pass that instead of giving this historical development the Heisman and insistently making a now-nostalgic jangle, Scritti made some romantic black-soul-loving pop music with digital snap, and brought indiscreet pleasure to many many people.

But this didn't make Scritti especially happy, and what's more, his headlong romantic leap into history's fastest pace meant that autumn would come as swiftly as summer, and before too long he found himself in a cool season with winter coming on. And so he retreated to the gloomy Usk Valley to spend a season drinking ale and thinking about what to do next.

A season turned into a few and then into many, as they tend to do when one is brooding in the gloomy Usk Valley, ancient kingdom of Gwent, where the coal miners mine coal and the years pass. And still Scritti puzzled over what to do next, or not. After a long while he came to an idea, and it grew and grew. His idea was that, though he had taken up the sonic snap that had so entranced him in the early Eighties, he had not truly taken up the hip-hop that he greatly loved.

And so it came to pass that Scritti walked out of the Usk Valley sometime near the end of the second millennium according to the Christian calendar, and released an album that featured his beautiful soul falsetto equally with several extremely minor pseudo-hip-hop characters, who had perhaps been chosen because they were open to nearly-forgotten intellectual Welsh pop singers with leftist leanings, and affordable by production budget of same, rather than because of their excellence. Though this strange brew had its moments, it was somewhat confusing to have pseudo-hip-hop songs which were also lovely falsetto parables involving Heloise and Abelard, and everyone was confused, Scritti not the least.

Perhaps the greatest confusion was the last song on the record, "Brushed With Oil, Dusted With Powder," which was the prettiest song but at the same time a ballad, and a remarkably gentle, soothing ballad at that, with no pseudo-hip-hop elements in the music, though the sweetly breathy lyrics did concern rides in police cars and, in some haunting manner, the song seemed to be taking place in the beauty of the Usk Valley and the scenario of American hip-hop at the same time. This was a true oddity and there was no way to make sense of it, but that seemed okay because it was the last song on the album and they are understood to be outside-the-work, and forgiven their incoherence, as a general rule.

After the last inconsequential song ended, some more years passed.

In those years a strange idea took hold in Scritti's mind. The idea was this: that the inconsequential, beautiful song was in fact the key to everything, or at least the key to his next album. He would make an entire record with no minor or even major hip-hop characters, but one charged with his love of early Eighties hip-hop, and his melancholy distance from it. But it would be an album of rock so soft that "soft rock" couldn't do it justice, an album that would make Quiet Storm radio formats feel like they might need to calm down a little and maybe attend a yoga class. It began with Scritti sighing "the boom boom bap. . . . " But he did not sound like KRS-One, he sounded like Scritti but older, honey dipped in morphine on a slow drip.

It was like the dream of Brian Wilson that Brian himself could never really approach, of an easy listening album that was at the same time a work of genius. And if Scritti was occasionally compelled to murmur the titles from an entire Run-DMC album in a distantly pretty bridge, or coo angelically to the effect that punks jump up to get beat down, sounding exactly as if he was blessing the beasts or inventing a lullaby for a child who had been dead for two decades, well, this was the sense of the album, though sense was not very much at stake. Something else was, though it was hard to be sure what, exactly, and this mystery was the album's greatness, or perhaps it was the invention of a previously unknown category of pop music, or the way a voice can trace its own history, and the relation of the individual to history, or how it felt to live in a beautiful and perfectly numb present, at the edge of a hole into which years and things one loved kept falling.

ON TOP

MARIAH CAREY'S RECORD-BREAKING CAREER

Mariah Carey is thirty-six years old, and, barring a debilitating ill-ness, or another movie as bad as *Glitter*, her 2001 vanity project, she will likely break the world record for the most No. 1 songs before she turns forty. The Beatles had twenty, and Carey is currently tied with Elvis Presley for second place, at seventeen.

She could almost break the record this year: her latest studio al-bum—her tenth—*The Emancipation of Mimi*, has what music pro-fessionals call "legs." It was the biggest-selling album of 2005—it has sold 5.5 million copies in the United States—and it has yielded two No. 1 songs: the gentle ballad "Don't Forget About Us" and "We Be-long Together," an equally gentle but catchier number that held the No. 1 spot for fourteen weeks, longer than any other song so far this decade. There are two singles from *Mimi* on the radio right now, the hip-hop dance number "Say Somethin'" and the churchy vocal work-out "Fly Like a Bird." If these songs don't take Carey to nineteen, she could still go on vacation for the next six months and finish the year with her résumé intact. She was the biggest-selling female artist of the nineties and is the first woman to have three studio albums sell more than eight million copies each in this country. She has written or co-written sixteen of her seventeen No. 1 hits, more than any other female composer, and has produced twelve No. 1 songs, more than any other woman.

Not all Carey's achievements are commercial, though: she co-wrote one of the few worthy modern additions to the holiday canon, the charming "All I Want for Christmas Is You" (from *Merry Christmas*, of 1994, which also happens to be the best-selling Christmas album of all time, but never mind that). And when she sang her perky dance hit "Emotions" at the 1991 MTV Video Music Awards, she reportedly sounded a G-sharp three and a half octaves above middle C, one of the highest notes produced by a human voice in the history of recorded music. (Party poopers say that the note was actually an F-sharp.)

Carey's freakish vocal ability explains part of her appeal. In the same way that people went to a San Francisco Giants game in order to see Barry Bonds hit a home run, people buy Carey's records in order to hear her do things with her voice that no one else can do. Her first No. 1 song, "Vision of Love" (1990), made it clear that her instrument was the story—and it has remained so, through a celebrity marriage (to Tommy Mottola, then the chief of Sony Music), rumored breakdowns, and the public's obligatory obsession with her weight. Carey can sing lower notes, like an alto, and extremely high notes, like a coloratura soprano, which says something about her range but little about her style. The brutish purity of her voice places her in pop's theatrical lineage, in the company of singers like Barbra Streisand, but Carey's aesthetic is not Broadway, or even particularly white. She is essentially an R&B singer, steeped in gospel, soul, and, especially, hip-hop, and she is a master practitioner of melisma, a vocal technique that dates back to Gregorian chant and is common in African-American church singing.

Melisma describes the act of taking one syllable of a lyric and stretching it over several notes—or, in Carey's case, sometimes ten or twenty. "Vision of Love" is the Magna Carta of melisma. Whitney Houston popularized it, but Carey made melisma a required move for both R&B singers and contestants on *American Idol*. (Five years ago, before a concert in Peoria, Illinois, Beyoncé Knowles told me that she started doing vocal "runs" after hearing "Vision of Love.") The song is a florid composition that expresses the philosophy that Carey has disseminated profitably for sixteen years: love will triumph and everything will be all right. (As she puts it in the song: "I had a vision of love, and it was all that you turned out to be.") It begins with several bars of lovely, wordless melisma, as if Carey were warming up, and it ends with two very loud passages of melisma, one of them an a-cappella expansion on the word "all" that can be roughly transcribed as: "ah-ha-uh-uh-oh-oo-oh-ooah-ha-uh-uh-oh-oo-oh-oo-ah-oh."

Calisthenics are only one aspect of "Vision of Love," however. The chord changes, which are played on electric piano, are reminiscent of early Billy Joel—obvious, consonant, and rich. Carey's sound changes with nearly every line, mutating from a steely tone to a vibrating growl and then to a humid, breathy coo. The melisma is what people remember about the song, like a ninth-inning grand slam, but that's not what made it a hit. Carey, who co-wrote it, knew that the singing should bob and weave while the verses move toward a climax—the words are secondary.

Carey couldn't have succeeded simply by persuading people that she was a craftsman. Her big ballads—"Vision of Love," along with No. 1 bromides like "Thank God I Found You" and "My All"—appeal to people who otherwise don't listen to pop. These are people who probably also like Andrea Bocelli and Céline Dion, singers who avoid the sexual tug of the blues and the glorious noises of rock and hip-hop in favor of tremulous expressions of chaste emotion. Yet Carey, more than any other musician, established R&B and hip-hop as the sound of pop. One of her frothiest and most delightful No. 1 hits was "Dreamlover" (1993), which features a loop of The Emotions' 1971 soul tune "Blind Alley," a song made famous by the rapper Big Daddy Kane, who sampled it in his 1988 track "Ain't No Half-Steppin'." Beginning in 1995, rappers started performing guest verses on Carey's songs. Suddenly, people who would cross the street to avoid listening to hip-hop were bringing rappers into their house, under the cover of Carey. It became standard for R&B stars, like Missy Elliott and Beyoncé, to combine melodies with rapped verses. And young white pop stars—including Britney Spears, 'N Sync, and Christina Aguilera—have spent much of the past ten years making pop music that is unmistakably R&B.

Among Carey's best and strangest collaborations with a rapper was a remix of her song "Fantasy," in 1995. After it was already No. 1, she invited Ol' Dirty Bastard, from the Wu-Tang Clan, to rhyme over the song, which is built around a sample of the chirping 1981 track "Genius of Love" by the Tom Tom Club. (Carey has often described herself as an "eternal twelve-year-old," an assertion borne out by her enthusiasm not just for rainbows, butterflies, and glitter—all of which appear on her album covers—but for the songs that were actually on the radio when she was a teenager.) Carey's sunny world view is a perfect match for the Tom Tom Club's twinkling keyboards; Ol' Dirty Bastard, on the other hand, who died of a drug overdose in 2004, was the last person you would imagine hiring for such a sanguine track, and the dissonance is entertaining. "Me and Mariah go back like babies with pacifiers," he begins his verse. At the end of the song, Carey coos about her "lucky boyfriend" while Ol' Dirty growls "sweet baby" behind her; he sounds drunk, as though he might fall over. (Ol' Dirty is apparently not the lucky boyfriend, but Mariah seems to like him anyway.)

The Emancipation of Mimi includes no songs as effortlessly cheery or as durable as "Dreamlover" and "Fantasy," partly because Carey's melodies now meander, in keeping with current trends in R&B, and have lost the clarity that pop demands. *Mimi* is Carey's most thoroughly R&B record; even the big ballads are in the "slow jam" vein and have little to do with Las Vegas, opera, or doo-wop. There are only a couple of Hallmark duds to skip over; you can enjoy Carey's expansive vocalisms without begrudging her moments of brassy self-affirmation.

In some ways, Carey resembles U2, another veteran act currently having extraordinary success late in a long career. (*How to Dismantle an Atomic Bomb*, the group's most recent release, won the Grammy for best album of 2005 and has sold three million copies in the United States.) Both acts have left experimentation to their juniors and are sticking to what they do best. In the case of U2, this means using the heavy rhythms and glassy guitar sound that first gained the band notice in the early eighties. In Carey's case, this means singing R&B but without the scenery-inhaling ballads that helped her sell millions of copies. Her decision largely to omit those ballads from *Mimi* is commercially gutsy—if multimillionaires can be gutsy—and it makes sense. The album's songs were produced by a host of people, including Jermaine Dupri, Kanye West, and the Neptunes, who have been guiding R&B and hip-hop during the past few years. Carey, having proved that she has the lungs of an opera singer, is now making the music that she has always listened to. Her idea of pairing a female songbird with the leading male MCs of hip-hop changed R&B and, eventually, all of pop. Although now anyone is free to use this idea, the success of *Mimi* suggests that it still belongs to Carey.

DAPHNE A. BROOKS

SUGA MAMA, POLITICIZED

The video for Beyoncé Knowles's latest single, "Ring the Alarm," shows the stunning 25-year-old singer, dressed in a caramel-colored trench coat that matches her glistening skin, being dragged away by policemen in riot gear and locked in a padded cell. An "alarmed" Beyoncé struggles and writhes, is brought to her knees and pulled by her arms and legs, in a scene that should ring familiar not only to fans of early Sharon Stone spectacles (the clip pays clear homage to *Basic Instinct*) but to those who still remember Diana Ross and her image-shattering star turn as a drug-busted and jailed Billie Holiday in 1972's *Lady Sings the Blues*. (Comparisons between Ross and Beyoncé are in abundance now as the latter jettisons her Supremes-inspired vehicle Destiny's Child for a full-fledged solo career and takes on the Ross-inspired lead of Deena Jones in the upcoming film adaptation of *Dreamgirls*.) The gloss and glitz of this shock-value video may cause casual viewers to write off Beyoncé's newest album, *B'Day*, as just another collection of sexed-up club jams. But they'd miss out on listening to one of the oddest, most urgent, dissonant and disruptive R&B releases in recent memory.

Much has been made of how Beyoncé's music of recent years has been a far cry from what pop culture critic David Swerdlick calls the "sistah grrl power" of early Destiny's Child recordings. On those records, and particularly on the multiplatinum *The Writing's on the Wall*, Knowles and her fellow "children" belted out densely arranged anthems with *Waiting to Exhale* themes of romantic distrust, material disillusionment and "ne'er do well" scrub boyfriends who were roundly criticized and kicked to the curb. The group's early hits— "Bills, Bills, Bills," "Bug a Boo" and "Independent Women, Part 1" among them—chart the young Texan's rise as a popular black female songwriter. The Beyoncé of old joyously rejected the stalker tendencies of needy men who persisted in "stressin'" her on her "beeper" and feckless freeloaders who "maxed out" her credit cards.

The Beyoncé on *B'Day* is anything but the "daddy's girl," "naughty but nice" icon who came bounding onto the scene with her first solo effort, 2003's remarkably successful *Dangerously in Love*. On *B'Day*, Knowles is unafraid of complicating and disturbing the image that won her fame. On these newer songs, the über-glam urban diva experiments with a startlingly abrasive persona that feels different from most contemporary pop divas (see, for instance, Christina Aguilera's "virgin-whore-virgin" dance, Britney's "virgin-whore-whore" dissolution or even Madonna's "whore"-to-mother moves). Instead of mistaking "edge" (the much-overused term) for raunch as her peers often do, Beyoncé finds different emotional notes to sound: spiritual discontent, romantic pessimism and self-control. Knowles especially stresses the pleasures of hard work as a means to overcoming despair. What's more, she packages her messages in a hard and frantic sonic register that sets this record apart from other MTV divas' pet projects. Quirky and unpredictable from beginning to end, this record hits a range of intriguingly sour notes that defy expectation. This alone seems reason for pop fans to take a second listen to *B'Day*—and to take note of the way the album shrewdly remixes R&B tales of "Resentment" (the title of the closing track), desperation and aspiration in contemporary black women's popular culture. It comes at a time when public and political voices of black female discontent remain muted and mediated in the public eye, from the scuffle between police and former Congresswoman Cynthia McKinney to the ubiquitous images of Katrina survivors—overwhelmingly black and female, who are spoken for by the media, politicians and corporate interests far more often than they are heard speaking for themselves.

In a genre known for its legion of Svengalis hovering over the talent, Beyoncé repeatedly boasts about doing it all: She is *B'Day*'s singer-songwriter, performer and one of the record's many co-producers. (All the tracks were co-written and co-produced by Beyoncé.) Her publicity team has stressed that she herself conducted and oversaw a compressed recording period and a studio dynamic that heightened its frantic sound. Recorded in two weeks in the wake of the *Dreamgirls* shoot—allegedly in secrecy from both her manager/father Matthew Knowles and from Columbia Records—*B'Day* has been repeatedly characterized by the artist herself as a Beyoncé-orchestrated endeavor: "Well, I made the movie and then I went to Miami to start that plan," Knowles told *Essence* magazine in September. "But when I got there, I had all these songs in my head. So I thought, Let me get into the studio. But it was all a big secret."

Whether you believe it or not, this is a rather unique and remarkable spin story for a female R&B artist's album: Everyone from Mariah Carey to Mary J. Blige to Christina Aguilera has aggressively centered the making of their recordings (and their success) around a producer. Knowles makes use of her own impressive array of production wizards (ranging from old stand-bys the Neptunes to Norwegian hitmakers StarGate), but she has also insisted on her own involvement in directing the multiple roles of her producers—arranging them to work in multiple studios simultaneously so as to reportedly capture the feel of "battling" MCs so prominent in the making of Jay-Z's Roc-A-Fella records. In many ways, the "independent woman" of Destiny's past has morphed on this record into a production Svengali in her own right—and into a woman who, in this behind-the-control-panels role, defies being pigeonholed as mere arm candy.

The power grab begins early, on the first track, "Déjà Vu," in which Beyoncé, as conductor, calls for bass, hi hat and 808 drum machine, and, finally, for Jay. (Online message boards and pop music critics alike expressed shock and disappointment with this lead single—called "flat" by some—but the track wisely uses the pair's notoriety to drum up interest in the album.) But Knowles quickly shifts gears, speeding up the tempo of the record on "Get Me Bodied," a Swizz Beatz-produced dancehall track. Combining Rasta beats with double-dutch syncopations and gorgeous vocal harmonies (by Knowles herself, natch), "Get Me Bodied" celebrates the joys of girls' night out. It's both more percussive than "Déjà Vu" and more resonant with the sounds of black girls' play—ropes twirling, handclapping and improvised cheers—games that, as ethnomusicologist Kyra Gaunt writes, are the backbone of black popular music culture.

The rat-a-tat doesn't let up. *B'Day* is an album that sounds like a battlefield—or at the very least a race of sorts, in which Beyoncé emerges victorious as a co-producer and entrepreneur engaged in multiple forms of self-reinvention and personal reparations. It might seem strange to credit an artist whose contributions to the culture have so far included readying us for her "jelly" with making a statement on one of the worst American tragedies in recent memory, but *B'Day* defies the odds by delivering a collection of songs that refract the emotional and material stress of post-Katrina Southern life. The tour of Gulf Coast culture begins with the images in the CD booklet: photos of a hard yet luscious *Jet* magazine centerfold Knowles—whose family hails from Houston and New Orleans—lifting a leg in a thigh-high juke joint mini on the dock of the bay, navigating twin crocodiles by the leash through verdant wetlands in high heels and a cut-out swimsuit, and walking the path of dusty railroad tracks in a leather and frills bodice. It's not exactly clear what showcasing the singer as sexually titillating against a landscape that resonates with (Eve's?) bayou imagery means (one should be "bootylicious" even when the levee breaks?), but it's clear that the rural American South that the world confronted in new and unsettling ways over the past year is front and center here. That uncanny South, the gothic and chaotic one of our nation's nightmare, provides a fitting backdrop to the controversial video "Déjà Vu," which recycles a historical déjà vu of the creepiest sort—a tricked out plantation setting with Knowles alternately draped across ornate Victorian furniture and dashing haltingly through everglades and (cotton?) fields looking like a deer in headlights or, perhaps more accurately, like a fugitive house slave on the run.

How to get free of this oppressive universe? On the record, Knowles runs headlong into the material world as a site of refuge. And no track sums up the theme of materiality more startlingly than "Suga Mama," a song that returns Beyoncé to her relationship with the (dollar) "bill" and her search for a partner who fits the bill. Promising her baby that she "won't let no bills get behind," Beyoncé effectively assumes the role that her Destiny's Child-era lover of her "Bills, Bills, Bills" days cannot fulfill. If her man of that song from the past can't "pay the automo'bills," then "Suga Mama" suggests she's more than ready to take the reins. Producer Rich (*Crazy in Love*) Harrison folds a gut-bucket blues guitar lick from J Wade & the Soul Searchers into a back-road beat as Knowles celebrates a nu-bile lover whose services are worthy of the gift of a "short set." Her (postcoital?) praise celebrates the purchasing power of the singer herself, whose love is seemingly not for sale but who is capable of providing the bling, the "new whip," the "new heavy on the wrist" to satisfy her lover's needs.

Even a seemingly innocuous R&B song like "Suga Mama" has the power to force post-disaster questions related to protection and survival. What, for instance, does it mean to be a "Suga Mama" with an "accountant waiting on the phone"? What does it mean to be a woman who proudly claims to be the "type to take care of mine" in an age of gross federal (read: patriarchal) failure to serve and to protect? In many ways, particularly given the example of Knowles's own mother, clothing designer and salon owner Tina, who has been responsible for most of Destiny's Child as well as Beyoncé's onstage costumes, there is something remarkable, almost parodic, about a track with a sinuous chorus ("Sit on mama lap / Hey, hey / Come sit on mama lap") that insists on the power and the allure of maternal entrepreneurialism.

On the surface, "Upgrade U," a battling MCs track of sorts that again features Jay-Z, is an astoundingly retrograde song, one in which the Beyoncé of Destiny's Child's controversial track "Cater 2 U" re-emerges and offers to "take care" of the home and her man. There is, though, perhaps a bit more to it than its cowboys-on-the-range horns and synthesizer arrangements. Even in a line as ludicrously overblown as "I can do for you what Martin did for the people," Knowles's fixation on material forms of uplift ("Audemars Piguet you / Switch your necktie to purple labels!") steers the track toward the theme of literal and figurative redress that hangs over *B'Day*. Rather than assuming the role of the helpless dream-girl, Knowles boasts about turning Jay-Z into a good product: "Unless you're flawless / Then ya dynasty ain't complete without a chief like me."

It would be easy to interpret the hit single "Ring the Alarm" as a familiar story of the "woman scorned." There is, after all, the chorus, an abrasive, in-your-face mantra in which Beyoncé yells a how-dare-you-step-out-on-me refrain that's punctuated by red alarm sirens. And its cathartic outrage recalls the kind of carefully marketed breakup ire voiced by the likes of pop songstresses like Alanis Morissette and Kelly Clarkson. But Knowles uses it to more complicated, tough-minded ends. "Ring the Alarm" gives loud, burning-down-the-house voice to a woman who's more concerned with losing her stuff, her "chinchilla coats," the "house off coast," "everything I own," than she is with losing love itself. Relationships and desire, in Beyoncé's cold, class-act world, are, in fact, all about business transactions: "I don't want you but I want it / And I can't let it go / To know you give it to her like you gave it to me, come on . . . " The "it" that Beyoncé laments losing—sex, money, power—is cause for starting a fire.

Fittingly, *B'Day* closes on a dissonant note with the song "Resentment," which loops a sample of Curtis Mayfield's melancholic "Think" with gospel and doowop-tinged harmonies to convey the pure depths of romantic bile. With shrill vocals stretched to the very extreme, "Resentment" is a difficult, visceral way to end an album. In its dulcet melody and intricate harmonies, the song recalls the early '70s soul arrangements of En Vogue's 1992 smash cover "Giving Him Something He Can Feel," but Knowles's version of retro-soul re-outfits electric sexual healing and "feeling" as shards of pain. This resentment is rushed, pulsing with emotion that comes from the crossroads of a choir solo and juke joint nightclub abandon. It's an extraordinarily uncomfortable crescendo, a jagged little pill for fans to swallow and one that reminds us, as Jody Rosen recently pointed out, that this is indeed a "tough record" produced by "a storm system disguised as a singer."

What may be "toughest" about it is the way that it gamely challenges century-old American myths about race, class and gender—ones that still portray black women as lazy, feckless, "degenerate" and unwilling to work, thus encouraging what scholar and critic Hazel

Carby has described as the "policing" of black women's bodies. Knowles's album stands as a musical response to black women's social dislocation in the wake of yet another massive migration, and it envisions a language of ownership that is at once perhaps almost liberating and disturbingly materialistic: So many poor and working-class African-American households, especially those headed by women, lost everything in the storm. *B'Day* expresses the wants and needs of a heroine actively contemplating what it means to lose, and to have, and to possess. While there is no way to get around Knowles's ultra-privilege (her extreme wealth dates back to her childhood, and she has roots that run deep in New Orleans), there is nonetheless something profoundly interesting and unusual about the drama that she sells on *B'Day*. She is neither the "hard-knock" heroine that Mary J. Blige has steadily cultivated as a persona over the past decade, nor the reigning tragic diva whose crown has been passed between Whitney Houston and Mariah Carey for some years now. On her second solo album, Knowles appears to be fashioning a coarse, hard-nosed character who stands apart from the R&B pack in expressing clear-sighted anger and efficient, pick-up-the-pieces resolve.

An even tougher challenge for fans and critics alike may be to take seriously the political dimensions of a pop music album by a glamorous black female artist when the semi-plagiarized "modern times" of other musicians still entertain the most studied attention of rock scribes. *B'Day* may not match the poetic commentary of Tracy Chapman or Joan Armatrading, nor does it offer the hard spiritual and sexual candor of Meshell Ndegeocello's finest work or the sheer experimental exuberance of brash newcomer Alice Smith. But it delivers a unique version of black female dissent in pop and R&B music culture. Beyoncé is part of a tradition of black women's musical expressions of personal and political discontent ranging from singers like Nina Simone and Odetta to MCs Lauryn Hill and Jean Grae to the brilliant new artist Keyshia Cole, who has released one of the most brutally visceral, emotionally assertive and convincingly combative R&B records of the decade, *The Way It Is*. Knowles's album of hard, militarized beats marches in defiance of a long history of public black women, from Sojourner to Superbowl Janet, who have been stripped and stressed and displaced and denied.

Many thanks to Christine Smallwood, Eric Weisband, and Reginald Jackson for their insightful suggestions and feedback regarding this piece.

Chris Ryan

YEAH I'M THREATENING YA! I KEEP HEDGE FUNDS!

BUY KINGDOM COME AND GET A FREE FUCKING TOTE BAG!

I'MA FUCK AROUND AND BARF!

TO: RAP'S GRATEFUL DEAD
FROM: THE DUDE NO PRISSY CHICKS WANNA FUCK WITH
RE: I'VE BECOME SO NUMB

THIS BEING SOME WEB 2.0 SHIT, BUT YOU PROBABLY BEING BUSY FAST FORWARDING THROUGH JOE BUDDEN'S LATEST DEMO, I THOUGHT I WOULD TAKE THE LIBERTY OF RESPONDING FOR YOU. THIS IS OF COURSE ASSUMING THAT YOUR RESPONSE ISN'T TO SEND MEMPH OVER TO THE CRIB TO OPEN BEER BOTTLES ON MY CHIPPED TOOTH. AHEM:

"WHY CAN'T I ENJOY, AND RAP ABOUT, THE MINUTAE OF MIDDLE AGE AND THE GLORIES OF THE FREE MARKET!? I DON'T MAKE THREATS ANYMORE! I BUILD BRANDS, BITCH!"

WORD. I AM A FIRM BELIEVER IN THE "YOU DO YOU" WAY OF LIVING. IF YOU WANNA MAKE AIMLESS, ARTLESS, EDGE-FREE RAP SHIT THEN BY ALL MEANS, GO FOR YOURS. JUST ONE THING, THOUGH:

I WANT TO LISTEN TO SHIT LIKE THAT ABOUT AS OFTEN AS I WANT TO READ ONE OF JOHN "BALLS-AND-MY-WORD" UPDIKE'S ELEGIAC ACCOUNTS OF SOME BASHFUL 60-YR-OLD ENGLISH PROFESSOR J-O'ING TO THOUGHTS OF WOMEN'S TENNIS. OR AS OFTEN AS I PLAN WEEKENDS AROUND FOLIAGE. OR AS OFTEN AS I LISTEN TO BLACKAFUCKINGLICIOUS!

CHECK IT: NPR RAP? WHATEVER GETS YOU THROUGH THE NIGHT, HOMIE. IT AIN'T MY THING, BUT IT STILL HAS THE CAPACITY TO BE GOOD SHIT. MAYBE. BUT THIS:

"I DIG A HOLE IN THE DESERT, THEY BUILD THE SANDS ON YOU, LAY OUT BLUEPRINT PLANS ON YOU. WE RAT PACK NIGGAZ, LET SAM TAP DANCE ON YOU."

YEAH IT'S ABOUT BODYING DUDES AND BUILDING CASINOS OVER THEIR MAKESHIFT GRAVES. BUT IT ALSO MAKES OTHER RAPPERS GRAB THE MAC FROM THE BACK OF THE AC AND FUCKING KILL THEMSELVES BECAUSE THEY WILL NEVER SAY IT BETTER. 40/40 CLUB'S APPETIZERS? SOME CONVO YOU HAD WITH THE IDIOT FROM MAD MONEY? WHO GIVES A SHIT. BUT RESPECT YOUR PAST FUCKING DARTS. YOU'RE MAKING ME FEEL LIKE I GOT ALZHEIMER'S UP IN THIS PIECE.

posted by Hawaiian Sophie's Ex at 2:19 PM
Thursday, November 16, 2006

****

TO: JAY
FROM: THE GUY WHO ACTUALLY SAID TO HIMSELF, "534 IS KINDA GOOD!" AND THEN ALMOST THREW UP IN HIS OWN MOUTH
RE: GOOD CREDIT AND SUCH

SO LET ME SET THE SCENE, BROSEPH. CUZ I THINK I FIGURED OUT WHY YOUR ALBUM IS SO DISTINGUISHED FUCKING GREY WITH A SODA ON THE SIDE.

SO YOU'RE IN BED WITH B. SHE'S IN AN AMBIEN COMA HUMMING SONGS FROM YENTL AS SHE DREAMS ABOUT UNICORNS AND SHIT.

WHICH IS GOOD, BECAUSE SHE DOESN'T BUDGE WHEN YOU WAKE UP IN A STATE OF UNHINGED TERROR, SHAKING AND SWEATING.

YOU THROW ON THE SLIPPERS AND GO TO THE KITCHEN, SCROLL THROUGH THE CRACKBERRY. RICHARD JEFFERSON WANTS TO KNOW IF YOU STILL MIGHT BE ABLE TO PUT A 16 ON HIS DEMO. GOTTA REMEMBER TO IGNORE HIM NEXT TIME YOU GO TO THE MEADOWLANDS. AND THEN THERE'S ONE FROM REDMAN. HE SAYS HE'S GOING TO KILL YOU.

YOU GRAB A YOPLAIT AND GET COMFY ON THE OTTOMAN. YOU'RE TRYING TO PARSE THE NIGHTMARE YOU JUST HAD. IT'S THE ONE THAT HAS BEEN HAUNTING YOU SINCE YOU RETIRED. FOR A SECOND YOU GET DISTRACTED, WONDERING IF YOU SHOULD GO TO THERAPY. IF THERAPY IS GROWN AND SEXY. BUT YOU DON'T NEED LORRAINE BRACCO. THE DREAM IS SIMPLE. IT BETRAYS YOUR GREATEST, DEEPEST FEAR.

IN YOUR DREAM, YOU ARE NAS.

YOU PUT OUT ALBUMS AND NOBODY CARES. YOU START BEEF AND NOBODY GIVES A SHIT. SIRIUS DOESN'T GET BACK TO YOU ABOUT HAVING YOUR OWN SHOW. YOU CALL NEW ALBUMS SHIT LIKE, STILL PLENTY OF REASON TO DOUBT. DJ DRAMA TELLS YOU HE'S "CRAZY BUSY." YOU DON'T OWN SUMMER.

BECAUSE THAT'S WHY YOU ARE PUTTING THIS SHIT OUT, RIGHT? IT'S NOT REALLY SOME FUCKING TAX BREAK FOR ISLAND. IOVINE ISN'T PAYING YOU TO COCK-BLOCK JEEZY. AND IT SURE AIN'T BECAUSE YOU HAVE A LOT ON YOUR MIND.

THE REAL REASON YOU COPPED HALF-A-DOZEN DRE BEATS THAT COULDN'T MAKE IT ON TO AN EVE ALBUM IS THAT YOU COULD NEVER ACCEPT THE IDEA OF NORMAL.

THAT YOU WOULD PUT OUT AN ALBUM AND CATS WOULD BE LIKE, "COOL, BUT I HAVEN'T LIKED HIS LAST 4 ALBUMS THAT MUCH. I'LL RAPIDSHARE THAT MOTHERFUCKER."

YOU HAD TO DO A DOUBLE CD, FOLLOWED BY YOUR LAST ALBUM, FOLLOWED BY YOUR COMEBACK. JUST LIKE YOU HAD TO DO A FINAL SHOW, FOLLOWED BY A REASONABLE DOUBT SHOW, FOLLOWED BY THE I-DECLARE-PEACE SHIT.

SO WHAT'S NEXT? DEATH? IT'S COOL. IT WAS ALL A DREAM.
posted by Hawaiian Sophie's Ex at 9:29 AM
Thursday, November 16, 2006

****

TO: WHEN I COME BACK LIKE JORDAN, WEARING THE 4–5, FUCKING UP KWAME BROWN FOR THE FORESEEABLE FUTURE AND BUILDING HOMELESS SHELTERS WITH ALL THE FUCK-ING BRICKS I'M PUTTING UP.
FROM: MY HAIR HURTS
RE: EVERYTHING IN ITS RIGHT PLACE

SO LET ME ASK YOU. DID I MISS THE FUCKING MASONIC RAP ILLUMINATI MEETING WHERE WE DECIDED THAT THERE WERE REQUIREMENTS FOR THROWING SHOTS AT SOMEONE? WAS THERE A FUCKING QUORUM?

WHY THE FUCK IS KAY SLAY TELLING LIL' WAYNE HE CAN'T GET A LITTLE ORNERY WITH YOU?! YEAH, I KNOW YOU WERE IN ST. TROPEZ PLAYING PUT-PUT WITH KENNY CHESNEY OR SOME SHIT. BUT THE WORLD KEEPS TURNING EVEN WHEN YOU'RE SNORKELING.

TO SUMMARIZE: BIRDKISSER BASICALLY SAID, HIP-HOP DOESN'T NEED SAVING. YOU'RE THE GOD. BUT STAY IN THE CLOUDS. THEN HE SAID HE WAS BETTER THAN YOU.

MEANWHILE, IN MANIC RADIO PERSONALITY LAND, KAY SLAY GOES OFF SAYING OF WAYNE, "YOU DON'T HAVE THE

AUTHORITY TO GO AT JAY-Z . . . " TO WHICH HE ADDED, "AND I'M NOT EVEN A BIG JAY-Z FAN."

PUTTING OUT THE MOTHERFUCKING STREETSWEEPER VOL. 2 . . . THAT'S OFFICIAL LICENSE TO BRACE MOTHERFUCK-ERS ON INTERNET RADIO AS PART OF YOUR DAILY BREAKFAST. BUT LIL' WAYNE NEEDS TO SHUT THE FUCK UP?! OK! COOL. JUST WANTED TO IRON OUT THE ORNATE REASONING! NO DOUBT, AT THAT VERY SAME MOMENT, SOMEWHERE IN BROOKLYN, PAPOOSE SCRAPPED HIS JAY-Z DISS RECORD THAT WAS COMPOSED ENTIRELY OF FUCKING PALINDROMES.

WAYNE IS BETTER THAN YOU BECAUSE YOU'RE NOT THAT FUCKING GOOD RIGHT NOW! YOU MUST KNOW THIS. OTHER-WISE WHY WOULD YOU SPEND THE THIRD VERSE OF THE "LOST ONES" VIDEO LOOKING LIKE YOU WERE A TEN-YEAR-OLD GIRL AT A SPELLING BEE!?

BUT BACK TO THE POINT: WHAT THE SHIT IS UP WITH, "YOU HAVEN'T EARNED IT"? HIP-HOP IS ALL ABOUT SLAYING THE FUCKING FATHER! RAKIM BODIED A WHOLE FUCKING DE-CADE OF RAPPERS WITHOUT SAYING A SINGLE NAME!

WEEZY, WHETHER YOU THINK HE'S THE BEST RAPPER ALIVE OR NOT, HE'S MADE THE GREAT AMERICAN RAP LEAP. YOU MADE IT (DEBATABLE AS TO WHEN . . . VOL. 2 TO VOL.3? DYNASTY TO BLUEPRINT? WE CAN TALK ABOUT IT AT THE SPOTTED PIG LATER). GHOST MADE IT. IT'S NOT JUST ABOUT A LEAP IN TALENT OR SKILL ON SOME, YO, HOW THE FUCK IS CRAIG BIGGIO HITTING 40 HOMERS WHEN HE LOOKS LIKE LIL MAN FROM WILLOW SHIT. I AIN'T TALKING ABOUT PUTTING SOME OF THAT CREAM AND A BIT OF THAT CLEAR ON YOUR RHYMEBOOK, G. OH RIGHT, YOU DON'T WRITE. YOU RECITE. FORGOT THAT 60 MINUTES SHIT.

NAH, I'M TALKING ABOUT THE MOMENT WHEN A RAPPER BECOMES THE MOMENT (MARINATE ON THAT SHIT!). IT'S THE

POINT WHERE HE UNDERSTANDS HOW GOOD HE IS, WHAT HE MEANS TO PEOPLE, BUT AT THE SAME TIME SEEMS COMPLETELY UNSHACKLED FROM ALL THAT SHIT. ID! EGO! IT'S LIKE A FUCKING CANIBUS SONG!

ALL I'M SAYING IS DON'T BE SO SENSITIVE, DEATH CAB FOR CUTIE! WHEN JAYO FELONY TOOK A SHOT AT YOU WHAT DID YOU DO? SHOVED BLEEK OUT THE BOOTH (AN UNREMARKABLE OCCURRENCE, I BET) AND THREW SOME SUB ZERO SHIT HIS WAY ON "1, 2, Y'ALL." IF WAYNE WANTS TO FUCK WITH YOU, DON'T ACT LIKE HE NEEDS TO FILL OUT SOME FORM IN TRIPLICATE. HIT HIM BACK! OR DON'T PAY ATTENTION TO THE SHIT AND GO BACK TO CHECKING THE AMAZON COMMENTS FOR KINGDOM COME! BUT IF YOU PIC UP A MIC, YOU GET TO SAY YOUR PIECE. GOT TO. IT'S AMERICA, MAN.

posted by Hawaiian Sophie's Ex at 1:43 PM
Saturday, December 09, 2006

BEING JAMES BROWN

In Augusta, Georgia, in May 2005, they put up a bronze statue of James Brown, the Godfather of Soul, in the middle of Broad Street. During a visit to meet James Brown and observe him recording parts of his new album in an Augusta studio, I went and had a look at it. The James Brown statue is an odd one in several ways. For one, it is odd to see a statue standing not on a pedestal, flat on its feet on the ground. This was done at James Brown's request, reportedly. The premise being: man of the people. The result, however: somewhat fake-looking statue. Another difficulty is that the statue is grinning. Members of James Brown's band, present while he was photographed for reference by the statue's sculptor, told me of their attempts to get James Brown to quit smiling for the photographs. A statue shouldn't grin, they told him. Yet James Brown refused to do other than grin. It is the grin of a man who has succeeded, and as the proposed statue struck him as a measure of his success, he determined that it would measure him grinning. Otherwise, the statue is admirable: flowing bronze cape, helmetlike bronze hair perhaps not so much harder than the actual hair it depicts, and vintage bronze microphone with its base tipped, as if to make a kind of dance partner with James Brown, who is not shown in a dancing pose but nonetheless appears lithe, pert, ready. Still, as with postage stamps, statues of the living seem somehow disconcerting. And very few statues are located at quite such weighty symbolic crossroads as this one. The statue's back is to what was in 1993 renamed James Brown Boulevard, which cuts from Broad Street for a mile, deep into the neighborhood where James Brown was raised from age six, by his aunts, in a Twiggs Street house that was a den of what James Brown himself calls "gambling, moonshine liquor and prostitution." The neighborhood around Twiggs is still devastatingly sunk in poverty's ruin. The shocking depths of deprivation from which James Brown excavated himself are still intact, frozen in time, almost like a statue. A photographer would be hard-pressed to snap a view in this neighborhood that couldn't, apart from the make of the cars, slip neatly into Walker Evans' portfolio of Appalachian scenes from *Let Us Now Praise Famous Men*. Except, of course, that everyone in Augusta's Appalachia is black. So, the James Brown statue may seem to have walked on its flat bronze feet the mile from Twiggs to Broad, to which it keeps its back, reserving its grin for the gentlefolk on and across Broad Street, the side that gives way to the river—the white neighborhoods to which James Brown, as a shoeshine boy, hustler, juvenile delinquent, possibly even as a teenage pimp, directed his ambition and guile. Policemen regularly chased James Brown the length of that mile, back toward Twiggs—he tells stories of diving into a watery gutter, barely more than a trench, and hiding underwater with an upraised reed for breathing while the policemen rumbled past—and, once the chase was over, he'd creep again toward Broad, where the lights and music were, where the action was, where Augusta's stationed soldiers with their monthly paycheck binges were to be found. Eventually, the city of Augusta jailed the teenager, sentenced him to eight-to-sixteen for four counts of breaking and entering. When he attained an early release, with the support of the family of his friend and future bandmate Bobby Byrd, it was on the condition that he never return to Augusta. Deep into the Sixties, years past "Papa's Got a Brand New Bag," James Brown had to apply for special permits to bring his band to perform in Augusta; he essentially had been exiled from the city for having the audacity to transverse that mile from Twiggs to Broad. Now his statue stands at the end of the mile, facing away. Grinning. Resolving nothing. James Brown, you see, may in fact be less a statue than any human being who ever lived. James Brown is kinetic; an idea, a problem, a genre, a concept, a method—anything, really, but a statue.

This we know: The James Brown show begins without James Brown. James Brown, a man who is also an idea, a problem, a method, etc., will have to be invoked, summoned from some other place. The rendezvous between James Brown and his audience—you—is not a simple thing. When the opening acts are done and the waiting is over, you will first be in the hands of James Brown's band. It is the band that begins the Show. The band is there to help, to negotiate a space for you to encounter James Brown; it is there, if you will, to take you to the bridge. The band is itself the medium within which James Brown will be summoned, the terms under which he might be enticed into view.

The James Brown Band takes the form, onstage, of an animated frieze or hieroglyphic, timeless in a very slightly seedy, showbiz way but happily so, rows of men in red tuxedos, jitterbugging in lock step even as they miraculously conjure from instruments a perfect hurricane of music: a rumbling, undulating-insinuating (underneath), shimmery-peppery (up on top) braided waveform of groove. The players seem jolly and amazed witnesses to their own virtuosity. They resemble humble, gracious ushers or porters, welcoming you to the enthrallingly physical, jubilant, encompassing groove that pours out of their instruments. It's as if they were merely widening for you a portal offering entry into some new world, a world as much visual and emotional as aural—for, in truth, a first encounter with the James Brown Show can feel like a bodily passage, a deal your mind wasn't sure it was ready for your body to strike with these men and their instruments and the ludicrous, almost cruelly anticipatory drama of their attempt to beckon the star of the show into view. Yes, it's made unmistakable, in case you forgot, that this is merely a prelude, a throat-clearing, though the band has already rollicked through three or four recognizable numbers in succession; we're waiting for something. The name of the something is James Brown. You indeed fear, despite all sense, that something is somehow wrong: Perhaps he's sick or reluctant, or perhaps there's been a mistake. There is no James Brown, it was merely a rumor. Thankfully, someone has told you what to do—you chant, gladly: "James Brown! James Brown!" A natty little man with a pompadour comes onstage and with a booming, familiar voice asks you if you Are Ready for Star Time, and you find yourself confessing that you Are.

To be in the audience when James Brown commences the James Brown Show is to have felt oneself engulfed in a kind of feast of adoration and astonishment, a ritual invocation, one comparable, I'd imagine, to certain ceremonies known to the Mayan peoples, wherein a human person is radiantly costumed and then beheld in lieu of the appearance of a Sun God upon the Earth. For to see James Brown dance and sing, to see him lead his mighty band with the merest glances and tiny flickers of signal from his hands; to see him offer himself to his audience to be adored and enraptured and ravished; to watch him tremble and suffer as he tears his screams and moans of lust, glory and regret from his sweat-drenched body—and is, thereupon, in an act of seeming mercy, draped in the cape of his infirmity; to then see him recover and thrive—shrugging free of the cape—as he basks in the healing regard of an audience now melded into a single passionate body by the stroking and thrumming of his ceaseless cavalcade of impossibly danceable smash Number One hits, is not to see: It is to behold.

The James Brown Show is both an enactment—an unlikely con-juration in the present moment of an alternate reality, one that dis-sipates into the air and can never be recovered—and at the same time a re-enactment: the ritual celebration of an enshrined histori-cal victory, a battle won long ago, against forces difficult to name—funklessness?—yet whose vanquishing seems to have been so utterly crucial that it requires incessant restaging in a triumphalist cere-mony. The show exists on a continuum, the link between ebullient big-band "clown" jazz showmen like Cab Calloway and Louis Jordan and the pornographic parade of a full-bore Prince concert. It is a glimpse of another world, even if only one being routinely dwells there, and his name is James Brown. To have glimpsed him there, dwelling in his world, is a privilege. James Brown is not a statue, no. But the James Brown Show is a monument, one unveiled at select intervals.

James Brown lives just outside of Augusta, so while he is recording an album, he sleeps at home. He frequently exhorts the members of his band to buy homes in Augusta, which they mostly refuse to do. Instead, they stay at the Ramada Inn. James Brown, when he is at home, routinely stays up all night watching the news, and watching old western movies—nothing but westerns. He gets up late. For this reason, a day in the recording studio with James Brown, like the James Brown Show, begins without James Brown.

Instead, I find myself in the company of James Brown's band and his longtime personal manager, Charles Bobbit, approximately four-teen people whom I will soon in varying degrees get to know quite well but who for now treat me genially, skeptically, shyly but mostly obliviously. They've got work to do. They're working on the new James Brown record. At the moment they're laying down a track without him, because James Brown asked them to, and because since they're waiting around, they might as well do something—though they do this with a degree of helpless certainty that they are wasting their time. It is nearly always a useless occupation, if you are James Brown's band, to lay down a track while he is not present. Yet the band members do it a lot, wasting time in this way, because their time is not their own. So they record. Today's effort is a version of "Hold On, I'm A-Comin'," the classic Sam and Dave song.

The setting is a pleasant modern recording studio in a bland corner of Augusta's suburbs, far from where the statue resides. The band occupies a large room, high-ceilinged, padded in black, with a soundproof-windowed booth for the drummer's kit and folding chairs in a loose circle for the band, plus innumerable microphones and cables and amplifiers and pickups running across the floor. On the other side of a large window from this large chamber is a room full of control panels, operated by an incredibly patient man named Howard. It is into this room that James Brown and the band will intermittently retreat in order to listen to playback, to consider what they've recorded. Down the hall from these two rooms is a tiny suite with a kitchen (unused) and a dining room with a table that seats seven or eight at a time (used constantly, for eating takeout).

The band is three guitarists and one bassist and three horn players and two percussionists—a drummer in the soundproof booth and a conga player in the central room. They're led by Hollie Farris, a trim, fiftyish, white trumpeter with a blond mustache and the gentle, acutely Midwestern demeanor of an accountant or middle manager, yet with the enduring humor of a lifelong sideman; a hipster's tolerance. Hollie now pushes the younger guitarists as they hone the changes in "Hold On, I'm A-Comin'." Howard is recording the whole band simultaneously; this method of recording "live in the studio" is no longer how things are generally done. Hollie also sings to mark the vocal line, in a faint but endearing voice.

One of the young guitarists, cheating slightly on the "live in the studio" ethos, asks to be allowed to punch in his guitar solo. This is Damon Wood: thirtysomething, also blond, with long hair and a neat goatee. Damon, explaining why he screwed up the solo, teases Hollie for his singing: "I can't hear myself with Engelbert Humperdinck over there." Howard rewinds the tape and Damon reworks the solo, then endears himself to me with a fannish quiz for the other guitarists—Keith Jenkins, another white guy, but clean-cut, and Daryl Brown, a light-skinned, roly-poly black man who turns out to be James Brown's son. "What classic funk song am I quoting in this solo?" Damon asks. Nobody can name it, not that they seem to be trying too hard. "'Lady Marmalade,'" Damon says.

"Well," says Hollie, speaking of the track, "we got one for him to come in and say, 'That's terrible.'"

Keith, a young man with a trace of disobedience in his eyes, asks if they're going to put the horns on the track. Hollie shakes his head. "He might be less inclined to throw it out," Keith suggests. "Give it that big sound. If all he hears are those guitars, he'll start picking it apart."

Hollie offers a wry smile. He doesn't want to add the horns. Hollie, I'll learn, has been James Brown's bandleader and arranger on and off since the early eighties.

It is at that moment that everything changes. Mr. Bobbit explains: "Mr. Brown is here."

When James Brown enters the recording studio, the recording studio becomes a stage. It is not merely that attention quickens in any room this human being inhabits. The phenomenon is more akin to a kind of grade-school physics experiment: Lines of force are suddenly visible in the air, rearranged, oriented. The band, the hangers-on, the very oxygen, every trace particle is charged in its relation to the gravitational field of James Brown. We're all waiting for something to happen, and that waiting is itself a kind of story, an emotional dynamic: We need something from this man, and he is likely to demand something of us, something we're uncertain we can fully deliver. The drama here is not, as in the James Brown Show, enacted in musical terms. Now it is a psychodrama, a theater of human behavior, one full of Beckett or Pinter pauses.

James Brown is dressed as if for a show, in a purple three-piece suit and red shirt, highly polished shoes, cuff links and his impeccably coiffed helmet of hair. When we're introduced, I spend a long moment trying to conjugate the reality of James Brown's face, one I've contemplated as an album-cover totem since I was thirteen or fourteen: that impossible slant of jaw and cheekbone, that Pop Art slash of teeth, the unmistakable rage of impatience lurking in the eyes. It's a face drawn by Jack Kirby or Milton Caniff, that's for sure, a visage engineered for maximum impact at great distances, from back rows of auditoriums; I find it, truthfully, terrifying to have that face examining mine in return, though fear is alleviated by the rapidity of the process: James Brown seems to have finished devouring the whole prospect of me by the time our brief handshake is concluded.

I'm also struck by the almost extraterrestrial quality of otherness incarnated in this human being. James Brown is, by his own count, seventy-two years old. Biographers have suggested that three or four years ought to be added to that total. It's also possible that given the circumstances of his birth, in a shack in the woods outside Barnwell, South Carolina, in an environment of poverty and exile so profound as to be almost unimaginable, James Brown has no idea how old he is. No matter: He's in his mid-seventies, yet, encountering him now in person, it occurs to me that James Brown is kept under wraps for so long at the outset of his own show, and is viewed primarily at a distance, or mediated through recordings or films, in order to buffer the unprepared spectator from the awesome strangeness and intensity of his person. He simply has more energy, is vibrating at a different rate, than anyone I've ever met, young or old. With every preparation I've made, he's still terrifying.

James Brown sits, gesturing with his hand: It's time for playback. Mr. Brown and Mr. Bobbit sit in the two comfortable leather chairs, while the band members are bunched around the room, either seated in folding metal chairs or on their feet.

We listen, twice, to the take of "Hold On, I'm A-Comin'." James Brown lowers his head and closes his eyes. We're all completely silent. At last he mumbles faint praise: "Pretty good. Pretty good." Then, into the recording room. James Brown takes his place behind the mike, facing the band. We dwell now in an atmosphere of immanence, of ceremony, so tangible it's almost oppressive. James Brown is still contained within himself, muttering inaudibly, scratching his chin, barely coming out of himself. Abruptly, he turns to me.

"You're very lucky, Mr. ROLLING STONE. I don't ordinarily let anyone sit in on a session."

"I feel lucky," I say.

Fussing his way into place, James Brown decides he doesn't like the microphone. "I want one with no felt on it. Get me a cheap mike. I made all those hits on a cheap mike." The mike is swapped. He's still irked, turgid, turned inward. "Are we recording this?" he asks. The answer comes back: Yes. "The one we throw out will be the best one," he admonishes, vaguely.

Now he explains to the band that it's not going to bother with the track it recorded before he arrived. Go figure: Hollie was right. "Sounds good," James Brown says, "but it sounds canned. We got to get some James Brown in there." Here it is, the crux of the matter: He wasn't in the room; ipso facto, it isn't James Brown music. The problem is fundamentally one of ontology: In order for James Brown to occur, you need to be James Brown.

He begins reminiscing about a rehearsal they enjoyed the day before, in the practice space at the Ramada. The Ramada's room provided a sound James Brown liked, and he encourages his band to believe they'll recapture it today: "Gonna bring that room in here."

Now that the gears are oiled, a constant stream of remarks and asides flows from James Brown's mouth. Many of these consist of basic statements of policy in regard to the matter of being James Brown, particularly in relationship to his band: "Be mean, but be the best." These statements mingle exhortations to excellence with justifications for his own treatment of the men he calls, alternately, "the cats" and "my family." Though discipline is his law, strife is not only likely but essential: "Any time a cat becomes a nuisance, that's the cat I'm gonna want." The matter of the rejected track is still on his mind: "Don't mean to degrade nobody. People do something they think is good. But you're gonna hear the difference. Get that hard sound." Frequently he dwells on the nature of the sound of which he is forever in pursuit: "Hard. Flat. Flat." One feels James Brown is forever chasing something, a pure hard-flat-jazz-funk he heard once in his dreams, and toward which all subsequent efforts have been pointed. This in turn leads to a reminiscence about Grover Washington Jr., who, apparently, recently presented James Brown with a track James Brown didn't wish to sing on. "He should go play smooth jazz. We got something else going. James Brown jazz. Nothing smooth about it. If it gets smooth, we gonna make it not smooth." Still musing on Grover Washington Jr.'s failings, he blurts, "Just jive." Then corrects himself, looking at me: "Just things. Instead of people. Understand?"

Throughout these ruminations, the members of James Brown's band stand at readiness, their fingers on strings or mouths a few short inches from reeds and mouthpieces, in complete silence, only sometimes nodding to acknowledge a remark of particular emphasis. A given monologue may persist for an hour; no matter: At the slightest drop of a hand signal, these players are expected to be ready. There's nothing new in this. The Hardest-Working Man in Show Business is one of the legendary hard-asses: His bands have always been the Hardest-Worked Men in Show Business, the longest-rehearsed, the most fiercely disciplined, the most worn-out and abused. Fuck-ups, I'll learn, will be cold-shouldered, possibly punished with small monetary fines, occasionally humiliated by a tirade. These men have been systematically indoctrinated into what begins to seem to me less even a military- or cult-style obedience than it is a purely Pavlovian situation, one of reaction and survival, of instincts groomed and curtailed. Their motives for remaining in such a situation? That, I'll need more time to study.

"I'm an old man," James Brown says. "All I can do is love every-body. But I'm still going to be a tough boss. I'm still going to give them hell. I got a family here. I tried to meet everybody's parents." At this, he suddenly squints at Damon, the guitarist, and says, "I don't know your people." Permission has apparently been granted to reply, and Damon corrects him. "Yes, you met them in Las Vegas. Just briefly." Then James Brown points to his son, saying cryptically, "I don't know where this cat's coming from." Daryl dares a joke (which it dimly occurs to me was perhaps the point): "But you do know my people."

"That's what I'm talking about," says James Brown, irritably. "Love." He poses a question, then answers it: "You go to the blood bank, what do you want? Human blood. Not baboon."

Throughout the afternoon, even as the band begins to record, these ruminations will continue, as though James Brown's mind is on permanent shuffle. Sometimes the subject is the nature of his art. "Jazz," he states simply at one point. Or he'll segue into a discourse on his relationship to hip-hop: "I'm the most sampled and stolen. What's mine is mine, and what's yours is mine, too." At this, the band laughs. "I got a song about that," he tells me. "But I'm never gonna release it. Don't want a war with the rappers. If it wasn't good, they wouldn't steal it." Thinking of his influence on contemporary music, he mentions a song by Alicia Keys with a suspicious riff: "Sometimes you find yourself meeting yourself." Yet he's eager to make me know he's not slagging Keys: "I don't want to scrape nobody." Later, in a moment of seeming insecurity, dissatisfied with something in his own performance, he blurts, "The minute they put up that statue I was in trouble."

Much of the afternoon is spent working on an arrangement of a medley comprising another Sam and Dave song, "Soul Man," and one of James Brown's own most irresistible and enduring classics of the early seventies, "Soul Power." James Brown tinkers with the guitars, indicating the desired tones by wailing in imitation of a guitar, as well as by issuing what sound like expert commands: "Diminish. Raise nine. Flatten it." Of Damon's solo, he requests, "Go psychedelic." It seems to be the nature of the guitarists—Keith, Damon and Daryl—that they are the center of the band's sound but also the source of considerable problems.

A horn player—a large, slightly hound-doggy saxophonist named Jeff Watkins—interjects. Raising his hand like a schoolboy, he suggests, "They might have it right, sir. They just didn't play it with conviction." To the guitarists, Jeff says, ever so gently, "Play it like you mean it."

They do, and James Brown listens, and is persuaded.

"I'm wrong," the Godfather says, marveling. "Play it like you mean it—I like that, Jeff." James Brown's deadpan is perfect: It is as if he's never heard that particular phrase before.

Now he coaches his bass player, an aging, willowy, enigmatically silent black man named Fred Thomas, on the bass line: "Ding-dong, ding-dong." Again, he emphasizes: "Flat. Flat. Hard." Fred Thomas does his best to comply, though I can't hear any difference. James Brown turns to me, urgently, and introduces me to Thomas. "It's all about 'Sex Machine,'" he says. "This man's on more hits than any other bass player in history." I nod. Of course, it will later occur to me that one of the most celebrated partnerships in James Brown's career was with the future Parliament-Funkadelic bassist Bootsy Collins—and anybody who cares at all about such things can tell you that Bootsy was the bass player on "Sex Machine." Fred Thomas was, in fact, Bootsy's replacement, which is to say he's been in the band since sometime in 1971. Good enough. But in this matter we've at least briefly entered what I will come to call the James Brown Zone of Confusion: James Brown now puts his arm around Fred Thomas. "We're both cancer survivors," he tells me gravely.

Suddenly, James Brown is possessed by an instant of Kabuki insecurity: "I'm recording myself out of a group." This brings a spontaneous response from several players, a collective murmur of sympathy and allegiance, most audibly saxophonist Jeff's "We're not going anywhere, sir." Reassured, James Brown paradoxically regales the band with another example of his imperious command, telling the story of a drummer, a man named Nat Kendrick, who left the room to go to the bathroom during the recording of "Night Train." James Brown, too impatient to wait, played the drum part himself, and the recording was completed by the time Nat Kendrick returned. "Go to the bathroom, you might not have a job."

The two-inch tape is now in place, and James Brown and his band attack "Soul Man/Soul Power" once again. "It's about to be as good as it was yesterday," he says, reminding them again of the Ramada rehearsal. "We're not recording, we're just having fun." Indeed, everything suddenly seems to come together. "Soul Power" is an unbearably funky groove when taken up, as it is now, by a James Brown who sings it as though he's never heard it before, with crazy urgency and rhythmic guile, his voice hopped up on the crest of the music like a surfer riding a curl. In a vocal improvisation, James Brown shouts in Gatling-gun time with the drums: "Food stamps! Welfare!"

This take sounds better by far than anything that's gone before it, and James Brown, seated on his stool at the microphone, looks half a century younger now. At the finish, he rushes from his stool directly to where I sit and slaps me on my knee. "That was deep, Mr. ROLLING STONE!" he exclaims, then dashes from the room. The band exhales a burst of withheld laughter the moment he's through the door. "Food stamps!" several of them cry out. "Never heard that before." His son Daryl says, "Damn. I almost dropped my guitar when he said that." They seem genuinely thrilled and delighted now to have me here as a witness and go rollicking out the door, into the room where James Brown, ever impatient, is already preparing to listen to playback. They've done it, cut a classic James Brown funk jam! Never mind that it is a classic that James Brown already cut in 1971!

The laughter and conversation cease as Howard is commanded to roll the tape. Midway through the first time he's heard the tape, James Brown's head sinks in weary dissatisfaction: Something's not right. When it ends, after a single beat of total silence, James Brown says soberly, "Let's do it again, a little slower." And so the band trudges back in, in dour, obedient silence.

During the playback session, guitarist Keith leans in and whispers to me, "You've got to tell the truth about what goes on here. Nobody has any idea." I widen my eyes, sympathetic to his request. But what exactly does he mean?

Someday, someone will write a great biography of James Brown. It will, by necessity, though, be more than a biography. It will be a history of a half-century of the contradictions and tragedies embodied in the fate of African-Americans in the New World; it will be a parable, even, of the contradictions of the individual in the capitalist society, portentous as that may sound. For James Brown is both a willing and conscious embodiment of his race, of its strivings toward self-respect in a racist world, and a consummate self-made man, an entrepreneur of the impossible. This is a man who, out of that shack in the woods of South Carolina and that whorehouse on Twiggs, mined for himself a career and a fortune and a legacy and a statue; who owned an airplane; who has employed hundreds; whose band begat many famous and lucrative careers; whose samples provided, truly, the foundation for hip-hop; who had his photograph taken with presidents and whose endorsement was eagerly boasted of, first by Hubert Humphrey, then Richard Nixon; who was credited with single-handedly keeping the city of Boston calm in the twenty-four hours after the assassination of Martin Luther King Jr., a man who owned radio stations, controlling the very means of control in his industry; and who did all of this despite the fact that no likelihood except desolation, poverty and incarceration may seem to have existed.

He's also a martyr to those contradictions. That James Brown should succeed so absolutely and fail so utterly is the mystery. For no matter his accomplishment and the will that drove it, he has no fortune. No plane. No radio stations. The ranch home that he so proudly bought for himself in a mostly white suburb of Augusta was claimed by the IRS in lieu of back taxes. Unlike those whose fame and money insulate them from scandal, James Brown has been beset: divorces, 911 calls, high-speed road chases ending in ludicrous arrests and jail sentences. This great exponent of black pride, of never dropping out of school, of making something of yourself, found his way, relatively late in life, to the illegal drugs not of glamour and decadence but those of dereliction and street life, like PCP. With their help, he nearly destroyed his reputation.

The shadow of his abuse of musicians and wives, disturbing as it may be, is covered in the larger shadow of his self-abuse, his torment and unrest, little as James Brown would ever admit to anything but the brash and single-minded confidence and pride he wishes to display. It is as though the cape act is a rehearsal onstage of the succor James Brown could never accept in his real life. It is as though, having come from being dressed in potato sacks for grade school and in the drab uniform of a prisoner to being the most spectacularly garbed individual this side of Beau Brummell or Liberace, James Brown found himself compelled also to be the Emperor With No Clothes. What his peculiar nakedness reveals is the full range of the torment of African-American identity. Oblivious to racism, he was also its utter victim; contemptuous of drugs, he was at their mercy. And the exposure of his bullying abuse of women might seem to have made squalid hypocrisy of his calls for universal love and self-respect.

For my part as a witness, if I could convey only one thing about James Brown it would be this: James Brown is, like Billy Pilgrim in Kurt Vonnegut's *Slaughterhouse-Five*, a man unstuck in time. He's a time traveler, but unlike the HG Wells-ian variety, he lacks any control over his migrations in time, which also seem to be circumscribed to the period of his own allotted lifespan. Indeed, it may be the case that James Brown is often confused as to what moment in time he occupies at any given moment.

Practically, this means two things. It means that sometime around 1958—approximately the year he began voyaging in time, if my theory is correct—James Brown began browsing through the decades ahead—sixties, seventies, eighties and perhaps even into the nineties—and saw, or, more correctly, heard, the future of music. This, if my theory is correct, explains the stubbornly revolutionary cast of his musical efforts from that time on, the way he single-handedly seemed to be trying to impart an epiphany to which only he had easy access, an epiphany to do with rhythm, and with the kinetic possibilities inherent but to that point barely noticed in the R&B and soul music around him. From the moment of "Night Train"—the track, oddly enough, during which Nat Kendrick went to the bathroom and James Brown had to play drums himself—onward, through one radically innovative track after another—"Out of Sight," "I Got You," "Papa's Got a Brand New Bag," "Cold Sweat," etc.—James Brown seemed less a musician with an imperative either to entertain or to express his own emotional reality than one driven to push his musicians and listeners to the verge of a sonic idea, and then past that verge, until the moment when he became, more or less officially, the inventor of an entire genre of music called funk: "Sex Machine," "Super Bad," "Hot Pants," etc. That sonic idea has never been better expressed than by critic Robert Palmer: "The rhythmic elements became the song. . . . Brown and his musicians began to treat every instrument and voice in the group as if it were a drum. The horns played single-note bursts that were often sprung against the downbeats. The bass lines were broken into choppy two- or three-note patterns. . . . Brown's rhythm guitarist choked his guitar strings against the instrument's neck so hard that his playing began to sound like a jagged tin can being scraped with a pocket knife." Another way of thinking about this: James Brown seemed to hear in the interstices of soul and rhythm & blues—in the barked or howled vocal asides, in the brief single-chord jamming on the outros, in the drum breaks and guitar vamps—a potential for discarding the whole of the remainder of the music in favor of a radical expansion of these interstitial moments, these transitional glimpses of rhythm and fervor. James Brown was like a filmmaker who gets interested in the background scenery and fires the screenwriter and actors, except that instead of ending up with experimental films nobody wanted to watch, he forged a style of music so beguilingly futuristic that it made everything else—melody, lyrics, verse-chorus-verse—sound antique.

This time-traveler theory would best explain what is hardest to explain about James Brown, especially to younger listeners who live so entirely in a sonic world of James Brown's creation: that he made it all sound this way. That it sounded different before him. This time-traveler theory would explain, too, how in 1973, right at the moment when it might have seemed that the times had caught up, at last, with James Brown's sonic idea, that the torch of funk had been taken up and his precognitive capacities therefore exhausted, James

Brown recorded a song, called "The Payback," that abruptly predicts the aural and social ambience of late-1980s gangsta rap.

My theory also explains the opposite phenomenon, the one I so frequently witnessed in Augusta. If the man was able to see today from the distance of 1958, he's also prone to reliving 1958—and 1967, and 1971, and 1985—now that 2006 has finally come around. We all dwell in the world James Brown saw so completely before we came along into it; James Brown, in turn, hasn't totally joined us here in the future he made. That's why it all remains so startlingly new to him; why, during one playback session, he turned to Mr. Bobbit and said, "Can I scream and moan? I sound so good, I want to kiss myself!" He spoke the phrase as if for the first time, and that may be because for him it was essentially occurring to him for the first time, or, rather, that there is no first time: All his moments are one. James Brown, in this view, is always conceiving the idea of being James Brown, as if nobody, including himself, had thought of it until just now. At any given moment James Brown is presently reinventing funk.

This theory also neatly explains what I call the James Brown Zone of Confusion: Fred Thomas as the bass player on "Sex Machine," and so on. It's hard, for a man of James Brown's helplessly visionary tendencies, to know what happened today, yesterday or, indeed, tomorrow. All accounts are, therefore, highly suspect. Nat Kendrick may in fact have gone to the bathroom during the recording of "Think" or "I'll Go Crazy." Nat Kendrick may not, indeed, have gone to the bathroom yet.

The faster James Brown thinks, the more fiercely his hipster's vernacular impacts upon itself, and the faster he talks, the more his dentures slip. So, though transcribing James Brown's monologues as they occur is my goal, much of what he says is, to my ears, total gibberish. As today's session begins, James Brown is recalling members of his band who've passed. "Jimmy Nolen gone. What about the tall cat?"

Hollie, apparently, knows who he means by "the tall cat," and replies, "Coleman? He's alive." This leads James Brown into the subject of health, primarily digestive health. He speaks of dysentery while on tour in third-world countries: "Doing number one and number two at the same time" and exhorts the band: "Maintain yourself." To me: "Olive oil. I always tell them, 'Bring olive oil on the road.'" I don't ask what the olive oil is for. This reminds James Brown of the dangers of the road, generally, especially of exotic locations, which he begins to reel off: "Jakarta. Cameroon. Peru." He recalls, "We were in communist Africa. . . . At the end of the show there were baskets of money . . . protected by machine guns, though. Got confiscated for the government." He recalls the Zairian dictator Mobutu Sese Seko attempting to keep him and his band from departing when George Foreman's injury delayed the Foreman-Ali boxing match: "We got out. We got paid. One hundred grand." James Brown seems torn between bragging of munificence—painting himself an "ambassador to the world" who paid his own way to Vietnam to entertain the troops—and bragging of his shrewdness in always getting paid in cash, even in circumstances of maximum corruption and intrigue: promoters dying mysteriously, funds shifted through Brussels.

Shrewdness wins, for the moment, as he switches to tales of his gambling prowess, though he seems initially most keen on Mr. Bobbit's confirming a time when he came within a digit of winning a million-dollar lottery. "Yes, sir, you almost hit that pot," agrees Bobbit. James Brown then tells of playing craps on the road. "I won enough from the Moonglows to buy myself a Cadillac. Them cats was so mad they stole my shoes. Wilson Pickett, all these guys, I look so clean, they don't think I can play. I was a street man even though I had a suit on." But his stake in being thought of as the luckiest man alive is compromised by an eagerness to divulge his secret: "shaved dice," which always came up the way he wanted them to. Later this day, I ask several members of the band whether James Brown is babbling for my benefit. Not at all, they explain. "He's making us ready for the road," Damon tells me, reminding me that on Monday, James Brown and his band are heading to Europe for a month of shows. "He knows it's going to be hard. He wants us to remember we're a family."

When, what seems hours later, work at last begins for the day, it will be on two different fronts. First, James Brown records a ballad that trumpeter and arranger Hollie has written and arranged in his off-hours. The ballad, it turns out, has been lurking in the background for a while, with Mr. Bobbit and several band members gently inducing James Brown to give it a chance to be heard. Today, James Brown has—impetuously, suddenly—decided to make use of it. Hollie, given this chance, hurriedly transposes the changes for the guitarists and hands out sheet music. The simple ballad is swiftly recorded.

James Brown then goes into a small booth, dons a pair of headphones and, in the space of about fifteen minutes, bashes his way through a vocal track on the second take. Audibly, James Brown is inventing the melody and arriving at decisions about deviations from that melody (syllables to emphasize, words to whisper or moan or shout, vowel sounds to repeat or stretch) simultaneously, as he goes along. With uncanny instincts married to outlandish impatience, he is able to produce a result not wholly unlistenable. Understand: This is a matter of genius but an utterly wasteful sort of genius, and after we listen to the playback, and James Brown is out of range of the band's talk, Hollie and Keith agree that if James Brown were to regard the track he just recorded as a beginning—as a guide vocal to study and refine in some later vocal take—they might really have something. But they also seem resigned to the fact that James Brown considers his work on the track complete.

Next, James Brown writes a lyric, to record over a long, rambling blues-funk track titled "Message to the World." For anyone who has ever wondered how James Brown writes a song, I have a sort of answer for you. First: He borrows Mr. Bobbit's bifocals. James Brown doesn't have glasses of his own, or left them at home, or something. Second: He borrows a pencil. Third: He sits, and writes, for about fifteen minutes. Then he puts himself behind the microphone. The result is a cascading rant not completely unlike his spoken monologues. Impossible to paraphrase, it meanders over subjects as disparate as his four marriages, Charles Barkley, Al Jarreau, a mixture of Georgia and Carolina identities he calls "Georgia-lina," the fact that he still knows Maceo Parker and that Fred Wesley doesn't live very far away, either, Mr. Bobbit's superiority to him as a checkers player, the fact that he believes himself to have both Asian and Native American ancestry, and, most crucially, his appetite for corn on the cob and its role in his health: "I like corn, that's a regular thing with me. Gonna live a long time, live a little longer."

Afterward, we gather in our usual places for playback. Late in the eleven-minute song, James Brown issues a universal religious salute: "Salaam-aleikum-may-peace-be-unto-you, brother. . . . Believe in the Supreme Being!" As these words resound, James Brown glances at me and then abruptly commands Howard to roll the tape back to that point: There's something he wishes to punch in on the vocal. Hustling into the booth, when the tape arrives at the brief pause between "brother" and "believe," James Brown now wedges in a brief but hearty "shalom!" Re-emerging, he points at me and winks. "Shalom, Mr. ROLLING STONE!" James Brown has pegged me as Jewish. So much for being invisible in this place. He has apparently tampered with the spontaneity of his own vocal, merely in order to appease what he imagines are my religious urgencies.

Indeed, he now fixates on me, for a short while. During this same playback session, while deeply engaged in transcribing what I've heard around me, my head ducked to the screen of my Powerbook, I notice that James Brown has begun singing, a cappella, a portion of the song "Papa Was a Rolling Stone." I continue typing, even transcribing the lyrics of the song as he sings them: "Papa was a rolling stone / Wherever he laid his hat was his home. . . . " Odd, I think: This isn't a James Brown song. Then I hear the band's laughter and look up. James Brown is singing it directly at me, trying to gain my attention.

"Oh," I say, red-faced, as I look up at him. "Sorry. I forgot my new name."

"That's all right, Mr. ROLLING STONE," says James Brown. "I was just missing you."

Roosevelt Johnson, known always as R.J., sits with me and explains his role, a role he's occupied since he was nine, forty-two years ago: "Hold the coat." Excuse me? "Hold the coat, hold the coat." R.J. expands, then, on the basic principle of life in the James Brown entourage: You do one thing, you do it right and you do it forever. It is the nature of traveling with James Brown that everyone treats him like a god: "The people that show up in every city, they all fall back into their old jobs, like they never stopped. The doormen stand by the door, the hairdressers start dressing his hair." R.J. is being modest, since his responsibilities have grown to a performing role, as the second voice in a variety of James Brown's call-and-response numbers ("Soul Power," "Make It Funky," "Get Up, Get Into It, Get Involved"), replacing the legendary founding member of the Famous Flames—James Brown's first band—Bobby Byrd. R.J. sounds uncannily like Byrd when he sings—or "raps"—Byrd's parts in the classic songs, and in concert R.J.'s ebullient turns often draw some of the mightiest cheers from the crowd, who nonetheless can have no idea who he is. Yet for him, his life is defined by his offstage work: "Someday I'm going to write a book about my life, called *Holding the Coat*."

(Hearing this, Cynthia Moore, one member of James Brown's backing singers, the Bitter Sweets, interrupts: My book's gonna be called *Take Me to the Bridge, I Want to Jump Off.*)

The greatest exemplar of the Entourage phenomenon is, of course, Danny Ray, the little man with the pompadour and the voice familiar from so many decades of live introductions. Danny, from Birmingham, Alabama, joined James Brown in the fifties, when they met at the Apollo Theater. He joined as a valet. And, though he has become nearly as recognizable a voice as James Brown himself, he is still a valet; indeed, his concern for the band's clothes obsesses Danny: He is the human incarnation of James Brown's lifelong concern with being immaculately dressed. Valet, and master of ceremonies, Danny Ray is also the proprietor of "the cape routine"—i.e., he comes onstage to settle the cape over James Brown's shoulders when he collapses onstage, and he receives the cape and takes it away when James Brown has shrugged free of it.

R.J. and Danny Ray briefly allude to another responsibility that tends to devolve to valets: wrangling James Brown's irate girlfriends. Danny Ray cites a few vivid episodes: "Candace. Lisa. Heather. The one from Las Vegas that came to his house carrying a .357. She said, 'What is your intention?'" It is R.J. who finishes the story, laughing: "Brown said, 'My intention is for you to get on the plane, go back to Las Vegas. Get out of here.'"

Keith and Damon, the guitarists, ask me if I'd care to join them at a bar. We arrange to meet in Jeff the saxophonist's room at the Ramada. It is here that I learn Jeff's nickname: Sizzler. Sizzler is named for how there's always something aromatic burning in his room—a candle, incense or "something else." And, sure enough, Jeff's room is a haze when I arrive to find Keith and Damon there, along with Hollie, drummer Robert "Mousey" Thompson and George "Spike" Nearly, the second percussionist. Here, safely distant from either James Brown's or Mr. Bobbit's ears, I'm regaled with the affectionate and mocking grievances of a lifer in James Brown's band. I think I'm beginning to understand what story it is Keith feels has never been told: The glorious absurdity of the band's servitude.

"We're supposed to follow these hand signals," Keith explains. "We've got to watch him every minute, you never know when he's going to change something up. But his hand is like an eagle's claw—he'll point with a curved finger, and it's like, 'Do you mean me, or him? Because you're looking at me but you're pointing at him.'"

They take turns imitating James Brown's infuriating mimed commands to them during live shows. "It's like rock-paper-scissors," jokes Damon. Each of the band members, I gradually learn, has a spot-on James Brown impression available. Each has memorized favorite James Brown non sequiturs: "Sixteen of the American presidents were black," or the time he asked an audience for thirty seconds of silence for a fallen celebrity he called "John F. K." To these men, James Brown is both their idol and their jester, their tyrannical father and ludicrous child.

Jeff tells me of going on the *David Letterman* show for a three-minute spot. "We didn't discuss what we were doing until we got out there. Sound-checked a totally different song. I didn't know I was doing a solo on TV until he waved me out front."

Hollie, the longest-enduring among them there, says, "I don't think there's another band on the planet that can do what we do."

Damon adds, "I like to call it Masters of the Impossible."

Yet they hurry to make me understand their vast reverence and devotion—for you see, they're also the luckiest musicians on earth. Keith tells me, "Brown told us, 'You got it made. You cats are lucky, you're made now.' Eleven years later, I get it. The man hasn't had a hit for twenty years, but we'll work forever. We're going to the Hollywood Bowl, Buckingham Palace, the Apollo Theater, it never stops. We could work for a hundred years. You play with someone else, you might have two good years, then sit for two years, wondering if anything's ever going to happen again. With James Brown, you're always working. Because he's James Brown. It's like we're up there with Bugs Bunny, Mickey Mouse. There's no other comparison."

"Listen," says Jeff. "There's something we want you to hear." I've been corralled into Jeff's room for a purpose: the unveiling of the secret recordings of James Brown's band. The frustration these musicians feel at having no voice in composition or arrangement has taken its toll, a certain despair about the prospects for the present recording sessions. James Brown, they complain, just won't let his band help him. Yet these frustrations have, in turn, found an outlet.

Sizzler fires up his iTunes, connected to a fair pair of desktop speakers, and there, seated on a Ramada bedspread, I'm treated to an audio sample of What Could Be, if only James Brown would allow it. The songs are original funk tunes, composed variously by Damon, Mousey, Jeff and Hollie, and recorded, under cover of darkness, in hotel rooms while the band travels, or while they assemble, as now, for official sessions. The songs are tight, catchy, propulsive numbers, each with one foot in seventies funk and another in a more contemporary style. They have the added benefit of being something new.

No one has dared tell James Brown that this music exists. He might fire them if he knew. In this, the band's wishful thinking tangles with its sense of protectiveness of the boss's feelings. For James Brown, it seems, has had so many important musicians outgrow his band—Bootsy, Maceo, Pee Wee Ellis and Fred Wesley—that his passion for control has outstripped his curiosity about what his present roster might have to offer him. Anyone showing signs of a life of their own, musical or otherwise, tends to be the target of elaborate and vindictive humiliations. "It's abandonment issues," says Keith. "Has to do with being abandoned by his parents." James Brown will deliberately schedule mandatory rehearsals to clash with weddings or funerals. Keith tells me, "At the Apollo, the first time my wife was going to see me play, he sat me down offstage, didn't let me go on."

The funniest of the secret recordings is a song called "Pimp Danny," which, unlike the others, consists not only of live instruments played directly into laptop computers but of samples of old James Brown records. By pasting together various introductions to shows over the years, the band has created a track where Danny Ray takes the role of lead vocalist, saying things like, "I like to feel dynamite, I like to feel out of sight! I like to feel sexy-sexy-sexy!" "Pimp Danny" also samples the voice of Bobby Byrd and a drumbeat from Clyde Stubblefield, one of the great drummers from James Brown's sixties band. In this way, "Pimp Danny" is not only a celebration of Danny Ray, who seems in many ways the band's talisman-in-servitude, but a kind of yearning conflation of the legendary past eras of the band with its present incarnation. And there's a plan: Fred Wesley, James Brown's trombonist and bandleader throughout the sixties and seventies, has promised to come to the studio tomorrow to record a few trombone solos, for old times' sake. (Everyone comes back.) The band wants to try to sneak Wesley back to the Ramada so he can add his horn to "Pimp Danny."

Many sizzles later, Keith and Damon and I have made it to the Soul Bar, where loud rap is on the soundtrack, which spurs a brief rhapsody from Keith: "You hear a Chuck Berry song, a Jerry Lee Lewis song, it's an oldie. It's got no relevance. James Brown comes on, it's got relevance. Some rapper has a hit, it's got a little piece of him in it. He hears himself everywhere. His relevance sustains him." Keith and Damon go on some more about what they'd do if only they could seize control of the sessions. "James Brown should go out like Johnny Cash did," they say. Keith says, "We're like a blade of grass trying to push up through the concrete."

Now, to note that James Brown is self-centered or egotistical or pleased with himself is hardly an insight worth troubling over. That James "I want to kiss myself" Brown dabbles in self-adulation hardly makes him unique in the history of art. James Brown's subjugation of his various bands' musical ambitions to his own ego, to his all-encompassing need to claim as entirely an extension of his own genius every riff invented by anyone within his orbit, is, needless to say, a cause of much dispute. To put it simply: The James Brown sound, its historic sequence of innovations, depends on a whole series of collaborators and contributors, none of whom have been adequately acknowledged or compensated. Yet the more I contemplated the band's odd solicitude toward James Brown's ogreish demands, the more completely I became persuaded that James Brown is re-enacting an elemental trauma: the abandonment by his parents into a world of almost feral instability and terror. One doesn't have to look far. His own 1986 autobiography, *James Brown*, bears the dedication "For the child deprived of being able to grow up and say 'Momma' and 'Daddy' and have both of them come put their arms around him."

This is a child who ate "salad we found in the woods" in his first years, a child who was sent home from school—in the rural South—for "insufficient clothes" (i.e., potato sacks). This is a teenager who was nearly electrocuted by a pair of white men who whimsically invited him to touch a car battery they were fooling with. This is a man who, during his incarceration in the 1980s, long after he'd drowned his nightmare of "insufficient clothes" in velvet and fur and leather and jeweled cufflinks, was found to be hiding tens of thousands of dollars in cash in his prison cell, an expression of a certainty that society was merely a thin fiction covering a harsh jungle of desolation and violence, and if James Brown wasn't looking out for James Brown, no one was.

His, then, is a solipsism born of necessity. When it most mattered, there was nobody to jump up and kiss James Brown except himself. His "family" is therefore a trickle-down structure, practically a musical Ponzi scheme, and anyone willing to give him his best is going to be taken for as long a ride as he can take him on. Gamble with James

Brown, and he will throw the shaved dice, until, like the Moonglows and Wilson Pickett, you are forced to understand that you are dealing with a street man. And much as in the cases of Duke Ellington or Orson Welles, James Brown's ability to catalyze and absorb the efforts of his collaborators is a healthy portion of his genius.

And discipline is good for the child, after all. When James Brown sings, as he does, of corporal punishment: "Mama come here quick / Bring me that lickin' stick" or "Papa didn't cuss, he didn't raise a whole lot of fuss / But when we did wrong, Papa beat the hell out of us," it is with admiration, and pride. Though his band consents to call itself his family, the structure bears at least an equal resemblance to jail—which is where James Brown was more likely to have absorbed his definitive notions of authority. So when his musicians begin to bristle under his hand, they find themselves savaged for their "betrayals"—for daring, that is, to risk subjecting James Brown to further experience of abandonment. This explains what I encountered in Augusta: The band James Brown has gathered in 2005 is the vanishing endpoint of his long struggle with Byrd, Maceo, Bootsy, Pee Wee, Wesley and all the others: a band more inclined to coddle his terror than to attempt to push him to some new musical accomplishment, however tempting it might be.

James Brown is in his mid-seventies, for crying out loud. What more do you want from him? What's really special about James Brown is how undisguised, how ungentrified, he remains, has always remained. Most anyone else from his point of origin would long since be living in Beverly Hills, just as his peers in the R&B and soul genre of the fifties and sixties smoothed down their rough edges and negotiated a truce; either went Motown, meeting the needs of a white audience for safe, approachable music, or else went jazzily uptown, like Ray Charles. Whereas James Brown, astonishingly, returned to Augusta, site of his torment, and persistently left the backwoods-shack, backwoods-church, Twiggs Street-whorehouse edges of his music raw and on view. His trauma, his confusion, his desperation: those are worn on the outside of his art, on the outside of his shivering and crawling and pleading onstage. James Brown, you see, is not only the kid from Twiggs Street who wouldn't go away. He's the one who wouldn't pretend he wasn't from Twiggs Street.

Today is Fred Wesley day, and everyone's excited. The studio is more populous than before: For unclear reasons, today is also family day. James Brown's wife, Tommie Rae Brown, a singer who is a part of the band's live act, has brought along their five-year-old son, James Brown II. Then appears James Brown's thirty-one-year-old daughter, Deanna, a local radio talk-show host. Deanna has, variously, sued her father for royalties on songs she claimed to have helped write when she was six years old and attempted to commit her father into a mental institution; lately, they're on better terms. Also on the scene is another son, whose name I don't catch, a shy man who appears to be in his early fifties, and with two sons of his own in attendance— James Brown's grandsons, older than James Brown II.

These different versions of "family," with all their tangible contradictions, mingle politely, deferentially with one another in the overcrowded playback room, where James Brown and Fred Wesley are seated together in the leather chairs. Wesley, his red T-shirt stretched over his full belly, is a figure of doughy charisma and droll warmth, teasing and joshing with the children and with the room full of musicians eager to greet him. His eyes, though, register wariness or confusion, as though he's trying to fathom what is expected of him here, a little as though he fears he may have wandered into a trap.

James Brown, startlingly, has abandoned his three-piece suits today for an entirely different look: black cowboy hat, black sleeveless top, snakeskin boots and wraparound shades. What we have here is the Payback James Brown, a dangerous man to cross. I wonder whether this is for Wesley's benefit, or whether James Brown just woke up on the Miles Davis side of the bed this morning. James Brown is giving Wesley a listen to "Message to the World," plainly hoping to please him. Wesley nods along. The two of them slap hands when the song comes to James Brown's references to Maceo and to Wesley. The smile James Brown shows now is by far the warmest and most genuine I've seen from him.

Next James Brown commands Howard to play an instrumental track for Wesley, a shuffle that James Brown calls "Ancestors." Wesley listens closely to "Ancestors" once through and then says simply, "That makes all the sense in the world, Mr. Brown. Thank you very much." He fetches his trombone, in order to lay a long solo over the shuffle. I gather that, once again, a track is to be unceremoniously slammed together before my eyes.

The entire band, as well as the many family members, lingers to gaze through the sound room's long glass window at Wesley as he plays. Wesley makes a rollicking figure there, his red T-shirt and gleaming trombone spotlit in the otherwise darkened studio. The band members I've come to know seem both exhilarated and tired; these long sequences of not playing are wearing on them, but Wesley is a genuine inspiration. Hollie, meanwhile, is troubling over the track's changes, trying to anticipate the next crisis: "Ask him if he wants me to transpose that keyboard, just so he'll be in D."

Wesley concludes and re-enters the playback room. Next, James Brown enters the studio to lay a "rap" over the top of the track. The moment the boss leaves for the soundproof chamber, the band members laugh with admiring pleasure: "Damn, Fred, you come in here and just start blowing, man!" They're thrilled at his on-the-spot facility. "Just went with those changes, never heard them before. I told him, 'It goes up a half-octave'—*bam*!"

Wesley laughs back: "What could I do—damn! Shuffle in F."

Now we listen as James Brown begins what he calls "rapping," a verbal improv no one seems to want to call a sheer defacement of

Wesley's solo. The spontaneous lyrics go more or less like this: "Fred Wesley. Ain't nothing but a blessing. A blessing, doggone it. Get on up. Lean back. Pick it up. Shake it up, yeah. Make your booty jump. Clap your hands. Make your booty jump. Dance. Ra-a-aise your hands. Get funky. Get dirty. Dirty dancin'. Shake your boo-tay. Shake you boo-boo-boo-boo-tay. Plenty *tuchis*. Plenty *tuchis*. Mucho. Mucho grande. Shake your big booty. Mucho grande. Big booty. Cool-a. *TUCHIS*!" On delivering this last exclamation, an exhilarated James Brown rushes from behind the glass and, rather horrifyingly, in a whole room full of colleagues and intimates, points directly at me and says, "*Tuchis*! You got that, ROLLING STONE?"

I say, "That'll go right into the piece, sir,"

James Brown then makes a shape in the air and says, "South American boo-tay." We all laugh, at the helpless insanity of it, at the electricity of his delight. "Jewish boo-tay," he says. "Jewish boys and Latina girls get up to a lot of trouble!"

Unfortunately, James Brown demands that we listen to "Ancestors" five times in a row—which we do, as usual, in a state of silent reverence, heads nodding at each end to the track. James Brown makes a "*tuchis*" joke every time the song resolves on that word, as if surprised to find it there. Then, heart-crushingly, he asks for a playback of "Message to the World"—the eleven-minute rant. A few band members have gradually crept out, but most sit in a trance through all the replays.

Next we listen to Hollie's ballad, recorded the day before. James Brown tells his wife the ballad's lyric is dedicated to her (the innocuous sentiments are along the lines of "If you're not happy, I'm not happy either"). At this, James Brown's wife gets nervous, and in a quiet moment I overhear her asking Damon exactly what it says.

"For me?" she asks again.

In irritation, James Brown says, "For all wives." This seems to put an end to the subject.

Afterward, in front of us all, James Brown's wife urges him to consider breaking from his work for a snack. His blood-sugar level, I learn, has been a problem. "I put a banana in the fridge for you," she says. This information displeases James Brown intensely, and the two begin a brief, awkward verbal tussle.

Mr. Bobbit leans in to me and whispers, "A rolling stone gathers no moss." Taking the hint, I go and join Wesley and the band, most of whom have tiptoed out of the playback room and are hanging out in the kitchen.

There, an ebullient Wesley is teasing a rapt circle of admiring musicians for having the audacity to kvetch about how hard the James Brown of today rehearses his band. "Y'all don't know nothing about no eight-hour rehearsal," he tells them. "Y'all don't got a clue. Y'all don't know about going to Los Angeles, nice bright sunshine, sitting there in a dark little studio for eight hours, all those beautiful women, all the things we could do, stuck rehearsing a song we've been playing for fifty years, going, '*Dun-dun-dun*' instead of '*dun-dun-doo*.'"

Seizing their chance, the cats confide in Wesley about "Pimp Danny" and how they hope Wesley will contribute a solo. "So is that why I'm here?" Wesley replies warily, as if sensing a conspiracy of some kind. "I'll play trombone on anything," he explains to me. "You know the story about the $200 whore? Guy says he's only got fifty dollars, she says, 'That's all right, I'll fuck you anyway.' 'Cause she just likes to fuck. That's me: I like to play."

Suddenly, Mr. Bobbit has arrived with a vast delivery of takeout food: several gallon buckets of Kentucky Fried Chicken, assorted sides and a few boxes of doughnuts, too. These are spread on the table, and James Brown emerges from the playback room and joins us. The blood-sugar issue, it appears, is to be addressed, and not by the banana in the fridge. Mrs. James Brown and James Brown II are now nowhere to be seen.

James Brown, still in his black hat and shades, fills a plate with chicken and plunks himself down between me and Wesley. "You gotta talk to this guy," he says, indicating Wesley. "That's twenty percent of your story, right there."

Wesley demurs: "People always try to tell me that, but I'm always saying, there couldn't be nothing without The Man. It all comes through him. You need someone who thinks unbounded. I used to be contained within the diatonic scale. He'd tell me something and I'd say, 'It can't be written down, so it can't be played.' He'd say, 'Play it, don't write it down.' It took me years to understand. Now I'm a teacher."

James Brown and Keith begin reminiscing, plainly for Wesley's sake, about having to teach the Black Eyed Peas' bass player how to play a James Brown bass line. Usher's people, too, needed a tutorial. James Brown and Keith laugh at how slow others are to get it—the guitarist who said, "That's the wrong chord," and James Brown's reply: "How can it be wrong, when it's never been played before?"

Following this five o'clock lunch break, James Brown leads the Bitter Sweets in some more vocal arrangements, leaving the band and Wesley sitting on their hands. Though James Brown's energy is phenomenal, as the evening drags toward seven the general belief is that nothing further will be accomplished here today. Jeff says, wonderingly, "I never even took my horn out of my case today. Checked my e-mail, smoked a twist, ate some Kentucky Fried Chicken." Yet it is on this cue, seemingly as if he has gleaned the risk of mutiny, that James Brown sends the Bitter Sweets home and calls instead for the band—the whole band.

James Brown's mood has turned again. He's so determined, he's almost enraged. "Got to be ready," he chastises while they assemble. James Brown has decided he wants to play his organ but snaps at Howard and snaps at Jeff as the amplifier cables get tangled and, briefly, unplugged. He also castigates Fred Thomas, who he claims has missed a cue: "You want to play bass? Then play." Next he rages at Mousey, who, trapped in a separate booth, can't watch the hand signals. James Brown actually steps in and briefly plays the drums for Mousey, ostensibly showing him how it's done—shades of Nat Kendrick! The silence in the room, during these attacks, is suffocating. I can't help thinking of the present band's embarrassment in front of Wesley, and of Wesley's embarrassment in front of the present band. Here's living proof of every complaint they've wished to register with me.

The tinkering preparations and ritual outbursts at last conclude. James Brown takes his place behind the keyboards, looking ferocious in his shades and sleeveless top. He leads the band through an endlessly complicated big-band jazz-funk piece, which, after three or four false starts, he runs for a perhaps fifteen-minute take, long enough for him to request, by hand signals, two Fred Wesley trombone solos, a bass solo from Fred Thomas and three organ solos from himself. During his own solos—his famously atonal and abstract keyboard work is truly worthy of Sun Ra or Daniel Johnston—James Brown looks fixated, and again appears to have shed thirty years. At the end of his last solo he directs the horns to finish, and laughs sharply: "Takes a lot of concentration!" He turns to me and slaps me five. Fred Wesley turns to the ashen Fred Thomas and, perhaps trying to put a chipper face on what they've been through, says, "Playing that bebop, damn."

I rendezvous with the band in England ten days later, for a performance in Gateshead. The players are in another kind of survival mode now, keeping themselves healthy under punishing travel conditions, while trying to stay in the mood to put on The Show. Donning their red tuxedos, the guitarists point out details they can guess will amuse me. "Danny Ray had jackets made without pockets," says Damon. "He doesn't want to see any lines. So I don't have any place to put my picks onstage." I obligingly examine his tux—sure enough, no pockets. Damon explains that he has no recourse but to stack a supply of picks on an amp, where they invariably vibrate off, onto the floor.

I ask them how the tour's been to this point. Damon, while not critical of the previous week's shows, says, "He needs to warm up on tour, too. Think of all the bits he has to remember. If he screws up, you notice." Damon recalls for me a night when the floor was slick and James Brown missed his first move, and as a result "lost confidence." Lost confidence? I try not to say, "But he's *James Brown!*" It is somehow true that despite my days in his presence, my tabulation of his foibles, nothing has eroded my certainty that James Brown should be beyond ordinary mortal deficits of confidence. And with this thought I discover that a shift has occurred inside me. I wish for the show tonight to be a triumphant one, not for myself, or even for the sake of the band, but so that James Brown himself will be happy.

I'm wanting to take care of him, too.

It's as if I've joined the family.

Bumbling along with the red-costumed tribe in the tunnel to the stage, I find myself suddenly included in a group prayer—hands held in a circle, heads lowered, hushed words spoken in the spirit of the same wish I've just acknowledged privately to myself: That a generous deity might grant them and Mr. Brown a good night. I still haven't seen Mr. Brown himself. Now I can hear the sound of the crowd stirring, boiling with anticipation at what they are about to see. As the players filter onstage into their accustomed positions, bright and proud in their red tuxes, to an immense roar of acclaim from the Gatesheadians, I settle into a spot beside Danny Ray.

When the band hits its first notes and the room begins to ride the music, a kind of metamorphosis occurs, a sort of transmutation of the air of expectation in this Midlands crowd. They've been relieved of the first layer of their disbelief that James Brown has really come to Gateshead: At the very least, James Brown's Sound has arrived. After the band's long overture, Danny Ray, every impeccable tiny inch of him, pops onstage. He says, "Now comes Star Time!" and the roof comes off. Under Danny Ray's instruction, the crowd rises to its feet and begins to chant its hero's name.

When James Brown is awarded to them, the people of Gateshead are the happiest people on Earth, and I am one of them. Never mind that I now know to watch for the rock-paper-scissors hand signals, I am nevertheless swept up in the deliverance of James Brown to his audience. The Sun God has strode across a new threshold, the alien visitor has unveiled himself to another gathering of humans. I see, too, how James Brown's presence animates his family: Keith, fingers moving automatically on frets, smiling helplessly when James Brown calls out his name. Fred Thomas bopping on a platform with his white beard, an abiding sentinel of funk. Hollie, the invisible man, now stepping up for a trumpet solo. Damon, who, during Tommie Rae's rendition of "Hold On, I'm A-Comin'," can be heard to slip a reference to "Lady Marmalade" into his guitar solo.

The show builds to the slow showstopper, "It's a Man's Man's Man's World." The moment when James Brown's voice breaks across those horn riffs is one of the greatest in pop music, and the crowd, already in a fever, further erupts. When they cap the ballad by starting "Sex Machine," it is a climax on top of a climax. The crowd screams in joy when James Brown dances even a little (and these days, it is mostly a little). Perhaps, I think, we are all in his family. We want him to be happy. We want him alive. When the James Brown Show comes to your town—when it comes to Gateshead, UK, today, as when it came to the Apollo Theater in 1961, as when it came to Atlanta or Oklahoma City or Indianapolis anytime, life has admitted its potential to be astounding, if only for as long as the Show lasts. Now that James Brown is old, we want this to go on occurring for as long as possible. We almost don't wish to allow ourselves to think this, but the James Brown Show is a precious thing that may some-day vanish from the Earth.

Now James Brown has paused the Show for a monologue about love. He points into the balconies to the left and right of him. "I love you and you and you up there," he says. "Almost as much as I love myself." He asks the audience to do the corniest thing: to turn and tell the person on your left that you love him. Because it is James Brown who asks, the audience obliges. While he is demonstrating the turn to the left, turning expressively in what is nearly a curtsy to Hollie and the other horns, James Brown spots me there, standing in the wings. The smile he gives me is as natural as the one he gave Fred Wesley, it is nothing like the grin of a statue, and if it is to be my own last moment with James Brown, it is a fine one. I feel good.

DAVID KASTIN

NICA'S STORY
THE LIFE AND LEGEND OF THE JAZZ BARONESS

As if heralding the passing of a mythic hero, a tremendous clap of thunder is said to have echoed across the night sky above New York at the moment of Charlie Parker's death. While those who had been following his precipitous decline could hardly have been shocked at Parker's untimely demise, even some of his most fervent admirers were startled at its rarefied setting. A half-century later, the story of Charlie Parker's final days in the hotel suite of a Rothschild heiress not only remains one of the cornerstones of Bird lore, but it has also been enshrined in the lesser-known legend of the enigmatic figure who reigned for four decades as New York's "jazz baroness."

During the last few months of his life, Charlie Parker had suffered the loss of his infant daughter Pree, separated from his wife, hocked his horn, attempted suicide, been sued by his own band for breach of contract, and checked himself in to Bellevue Hospital for acute depression. He had been off heroin for most of this period, but was typically drinking more than a quart of alcohol a day. Although Parker's now infamous Birdland performance on March 5 had disintegrated into chaos, George Wein decided to hire the saxophonist to play his Storyville club with a pick-up band of local musicians. A few days later, Bird prepared to set out for Boston, hoping to put his career back on track, but he never made it to the gig. On March 12, 1955, a stormy Saturday night in New York City, Charlie Parker died at the age of 34.

For Bird aficionados, Parker's death was fraught with bizarre discrepancies and unanswered questions that immediately gave way to conspiracy theories. Why, for example, did his body lie unclaimed in the city morgue for three days? Why were there two divergent cause-of-death statements? Why was he initially identified as "John Parker, age fifty-three?" And why did rumors of a fatal blow suffered at the hands of a famous jazz drummer persist within bebop's inner circles?

But, when news of his death broke on Tuesday morning, the headlines in many New York newspapers prompted a very different question: how did bebop's troubled genius come to meet his fate in a Fifth Avenue hotel suite overlooking Central Park that was the residence of an English baroness?

Of the various New York papers taking note of Parker's death, it was the *Daily Mirror* that provided the most colorful coverage, beginning with the classic hard-boiled headline—"Bop King Dies in Heiress' Flat"—that appeared above its front-page logo. Aside from the misidentification of Parker as a "53-year-old" saxophonist and the race-conscious reference to Parker's wife, Chan, as "a lovely fair-skinned brunette," the page-3 story presented a reasonably accurate account of how Bird had taken ill soon after he arrived at the "swank Fifth Ave. apartment of the wealthy Baroness," how "Dr. Robert Freyman [*sic*], of 9 E. 79th St." was summoned to treat the saxophonist, and how he died a few days later while "watching a TV show."

Even the more sober account buried inside the *New York Times* gave prominence to the lofty ambience of his demise ("A Be-Bop Founder and Top Saxophonist Is Stricken in Suite of Baroness," read its subhead). After describing Bird's place in the jazz pantheon ("Mr. Parker was ranked with Duke Ellington, Count Basie, and other outstanding Negro musicians") and pinpointing the location of his death as "the apartment of the Baroness de Koenigswarter in the Hotel Stanhope, 995 Fifth Avenue," the *Times* went on to identify its occupant as "the former Kathleen Annie Pannonica Rothschild of the London branch of the international banking family of Rothschild."

So, while initial reports of Parker's death may have sparked readers' curiosity about what had brought him to that Stanhope suite, before long they began to wonder what *she* was doing there. In the following weeks, gossip columns and scandal sheets launched a barrage of speculation about the answer to both these questions.

The first to weigh in was Walter Winchell. On March 17, his syndicated column, "Walter Winchell of New York," carried a blind item about Parker's death that was charged with racial paranoia and sexual innuendo: "We colyumed about that still-married Baroness and her old fashioned Rolls Royce weeks ago—parked in front of midtown places starring Negro stars. A married jazz star died in her hotel apt . . . Figured." Some of the era's celebrity pulps, exploiting the murky circumstances of Bird's death, even hinted at "fowl play." An *Expose* magazine story, titled "The Bird in the Baroness' Boudoir," drew on its deepest reserves of purple prose to paint the innocent jazzman as the victim of an exotic (and perhaps ethnically suspect) seductress: "Blinded and bedazzled by this luscious, slinky, black-haired, jet-eyed Circe of high society, the Yardbird was a fallen sparrow."

The tabloid spotlight soon turned toward other titillations, but the short-lived attention of the media had already taken its toll. After hearing the news reports linking his estranged wife to the fallen Bop King, the Baron Jules de Koenigswarter (who was then serving as head of the French Government Tourist Office in New York) initiated divorce proceedings. Meanwhile, the management of the Stanhope Hotel, which had grudgingly tolerated her eccentricities and "unsavory" visitors, made it clear she was no longer welcome. After holding out for a few months, she climbed into her silver 1953 Rolls Royce convertible, drove across the park to a spacious apartment at the more accommodating Hotel Bolivar, and, seemingly undaunted, resumed her singular role within New York City's insular jazz subculture in relative anonymity.

In 1960, her fifteen minutes of infamy long past, Nat Hentoff wrote a lengthy profile for *Esquire* titled, "The Jazz Baroness," heralding de Koenigswarter as the "most fabled figure on the New York jazz scene," and the subject of "more fanciful speculations . . . than anyone in jazz since Buddy Bolden." For the next three decades—until her death in 1988—she continued to be among the most vibrant (and controversial) figures in what Hentoff called "inner councils of jazz." Today, "the baroness" or "Nica" (as she is variously known to the cognoscenti) has taken her place as one of the legendary figures within the larger mythos of the music.

Although most contemporary jazz fans still identify her as "that Rothschild heiress in whose hotel suite Charlie Parker died," Bird was only one of a score of jazz giants who were the beneficiaries of her unwavering friendship and generosity. In fact, since 1964—when *Time* magazine devoted a sizeable portion of its cover story on Thelonious Monk to their intimate (but ambiguous) relationship—Nica has become more closely associated with the brilliant (but inscrutable) pianist/composer who would also die in her home. Yet even jazz fans unfamiliar with her life and legend would no doubt recognize at least a couple of the dozen-or-so musical tributes written for her over the last 50 years by the likes of Horace Silver ("Nica's Dream"), Kenny Durham ("Tonica") and Monk himself ("Pannonica"), just as a handful of bebop diehards—and hardcore Nicaphiles— would be able to conjure up their own Hirschfeldesque image of the baroness, fashioned out of little more than a cascade of black hair, an outsized cigarette holder, and a golden flask.

Born in 1913, Kathleen Annie Pannonica Rothschild was the youngest daughter of Nathaniel Charles Rothschild, prominent member of the British branch of the international banking dynasty. While Charles (as he was known) had succeeded his father as senior partner in the family business, he was, like so many members of the extended Rothschild clan (including Nica's siblings Miriam and Victor), even more devoted to the pursuit of his scientific interests. According to Niall Ferguson's two-volume history, *The House of Rothschild*, Charles was a "dedicated amateur botanist and entomologist who published 150 papers and described 500 new species of flea."

In fact, it was on one of his collecting trips to Hungary that he met his future wife, Rozsika von Wertheimstein, a local beauty, celebrated sportswoman, and member of the country's Jewish elite. Their lavish wedding, held in Vienna in 1907, not only attracted throngs of Rothschilds from across the continent, but also a small cell of Communist conspirators who attempted (unsuccessfully) to blow up the synagogue where the ceremony was held.

After returning to England and starting a family—Miriam was born in 1908, Elizabeth a year later, and Victor a year after that—the young couple assumed their familiar niche in the upper echelons of British high society. During their childhood, Pannonica and her siblings lived in a rarefied world of country estates and London mansions, of private zoos and private railway cars, of governesses and formal gardens, all run with clockwork precision to the uncompromising standards of the formidable Rozsika. In the interview with Hentoff (one of a handful she ever granted), Nica recalled her mother's intimidating presence with a mixture of pride and anxiety. "She was altogether remarkable. She dug everything, had tremendous, dynamic charm, and could captivate you in two seconds; but everything I did seemed to be wrong." For much of her childhood Nica's father suffered from a neurological condition that was a side effect of the Spanish flu, and in 1923, after a protracted physical and mental decline, he committed suicide.

While Rozsika may have had the most profound role in shaping her personality, it was Charles who had chosen to name their daughter for the vast ancient sea that once inundated central Hungary and whose fertile plain now supported an array of indigenous butterflies that he avidly sought for his collection. In this way, "Pannonica" both symbolized her father's entomological passion and paid tribute to the land of her mother's birth. Although their daughter would later rebel against her family's claustrophobic rigidity and social pretensions, she would also come to embrace the name (or its abbreviation, Nica) as an affirmation of her heritage and identity.

In 1956, when Thelonious Monk taped a solo version of his recently composed homage to the baroness, simply titled "Pannonica," the usually taciturn pianist described the origin of his haunting ballad in a rare spoken introduction: "It was named after this beautiful lady here," he explains. "I think her father gave her that name after a butterfly that he tried to catch. I don't think he caught the butterfly." Two years later, when Jon Hendricks put lyrics to Monk's music—to create a song he titled "Little Butterfly"—Hendricks directly addressed the intangible essence of its subject:

> *Delicate things such as butterfly wings*
> *Poets can't describe, 'tho they try*
> *Love played a tune when she stepped from her cocoon,*
> *Pannonica, my lovely, lovely butterfly.*

And, like that elusive butterfly, Nica spent her life evading every attempt to pin her down.

At 16, Nica was sent off to a finishing school in Paris operated by three lesbian sisters ("all wore wigs and made passes at the girls," she told Hentoff) who took turns instructing their wealthy charges in the requisite social graces. Upon completing her Parisian polishing, she and her sister, Elizabeth (known as Liberty), embarked on a yearlong Grand Tour of Europe that included a visit to Germany where, despite their Rothschild pedigree, they experienced at first hand the rising tide of anti-Semitism. After returning to London, the 18-year-old Pannonica was formally presented to King George V and Queen Mary (whose circle of intimates included her mother, Rozsika), and she threw herself into the swirl of debutante balls and coming-out parties.

While there was something redolent of the 19th century permeating this period of Nica's life, her modernist sensibility—which would flower fully in the 1950s when she embraced bebop's radical restructurings and breakneck tempos—first manifested itself in an attraction to the headlong speed of finely crafted automobiles. Virtually every jazz memoir in which she makes an appearance contains at least one vivid account of the baroness behind the wheel.

During the last 30 years of her life, Nica was the owner of a silver 1957 Bentley S1 Continental Drophead Coupe (dubbed the "Bebop Bentley") whose top speed of 120 miles per hour made it the fastest four-seat production car in the world. In fact, she had traded in her '53 Rolls because she had been losing late-night street races with Art Blakey and Miles Davis. In the chapter "Cattin' with Nica," from his riveting autobiography, *Raise Up Off Me*, the bebop pianist Hampton Hawes recalls driving down Seventh Avenue in Nica's new Bentley (along with Thelonious and Nellie Monk). It was three or four in the morning when Miles pulled alongside in his Mercedes-Benz, "calling through the window in his little hoarse voice . . . 'Want to race?'" After agreeing to the challenge, the baroness turned to her passengers "to tell us in her prim British tones, 'This time I believe I'm going to beat the motherfucker.'"

Decades earlier, however, Nica had transcended all such terrestrial concerns by taking to the air. She had learned to fly at 21, and it was on an early jaunt across the English Channel to Le Touquet Airport that she met a fellow enthusiast ten years her senior. The dashing Baron Jules de Koenigswarter, a mining engineer, was then working as head of financial studies for the Bank of Paris. Although they had been living in France for over a century (his father was President of the Court of the Seine), the de Koenigswarters traced their ancestry to Austria, where the family title had been acquired in 1870.

Three months after they met, the equally fast-moving baron, a widower with a young son, proposed marriage. When Nica left France—without committing herself—to join her sister Elizabeth on a trip to America, de Koenigswarter pursued her across the Atlantic. On October 15, 1935, the couple married in a civil ceremony at New York's City Hall. For six months the newlyweds traveled around the world before taking up residence in Paris. By 1939, when the Germans invaded, the family—which now included Nica's two young children as well as her stepson—was living in a chateau in Dreux. Barely managing to get out of France before the borders were closed, the baroness fled first to England and then to America. Meanwhile, the baron made his way to Brazzaville, where he joined de Gaulle's Free French forces.

Ironically, it was about this time that Nica's older brother Victor also achieved baronial status, having inherited the family title following the death of their Uncle Walter in 1937. The family business, however, was another matter. After his graduation from Trinity College, Victor accepted a fellowship in the zoology department of his alma mater. Turning his back on the world of high finance, he began a long and distinguished career in academia. But, as Niall Ferguson suggests, it was Victor's exposure to Cambridge's left-wing intellectual climate (along with the passion for science inherited from his father) that had ultimately dissuaded him from assuming his rightful role as scion of the house of Rothschild.

While at university, Victor joined a circle of radical idealists that included Anthony Blunt and Guy Burgess. His long-term friendship with them—and later association with Kim Philby—would eventually lead to the enduring accusation that Victor was the mysterious "Fifth Man" in the clique of communist conspirators commonly referred to as "the Cambridge spies." In fact, with the looming prospect of a war against fascism, Victor had joined the British secret service, and it was at his recommendation that Blunt was recruited into MI5, where he would function as a Soviet mole for decades. Although Victor would periodically proclaim his innocence, in 1986, when he publicly challenged the government to clear his name, he had to be satisfied with Prime Minister Thatcher's terse—and artfully opaque—official statement: "We have no evidence that he was ever a Soviet agent."

After the war, Victor returned to Cambridge as assistant director of research in the zoology department, but eventually he did go on to pursue various business interests; and finally, in 1975, he returned to the fold as chairman of N. M. Rothschild and Sons. Through it all, however, he not only continued to play a shadowy role in Britain's permanent government, but he also became the subject of yet another round of even more insidious rumors. Often identified as a key figure in that never-ending mythic saga known as the "Jewish Conspiracy for World Domination" over the years, Victor would be blamed for such nefarious acts as providing classified material for the Israeli atom bomb and participating in the assassination of JFK. He was also the person who introduced his sister to jazz.

A skilled amateur pianist, Victor's own interest in jazz had been sparked by a series of recordings Teddy Wilson had made with the Benny Goodman Trio in the 1930s. Not long afterwards, when Goodman brought his band to London, Nica joined her brother in the audience, and, when Victor persuaded Wilson to give him a couple of private lessons (at $5.00 each), she was allowed to listen in. "Afterward he'd play for me," Nica told Max Gordon, owner of Village Vanguard. "He brought me some records, and I learned about a shop in London where I could buy some more."

Not one to sit out the war in safety, once Nica had secured her children in the United States, she immediately signed up to accompany a cargo of medical supplies bound for the Free French forces. After rejoining her husband in Brazzaville she made her way across North Africa and Egypt working as a decoder, translator, and radio broadcaster. She then signed on with the War Graves Commission as a private second class, serving as an ambulance driver in Italy and Germany (for which she was awarded the Medaille de la France Libre). Meanwhile, her husband was distinguishing himself in major military campaigns throughout Northern Africa, Italy, and France. The baron, who ended the war with the rank of lieutenant-colonel, was cited for numerous acts of heroism and rewarded with the Croix de la Liberation and the offer of a position in the diplomatic corps. In 1946 Baron de Koenigswarter was appointed counselor of the French Embassy in Oslo, Norway, a post he held for three years, before being transferred to the embassy in Mexico City.

Following their move to Mexico, Nica continued to fulfill her duties both diplomatic and domestic (she and the baron would have five children together), but she had also begun to chafe at the constricting requirements of both of these roles. During this period, the baron—a man of stringent standards with little appreciation for music (least of all jazz)—would occasionally express his frustration at his wife's habitual tardiness for dinner by breaking her records. The fact is that, by marrying an ambitious Jewish banker of aristocratic heritage with deeply traditional values, Nica found herself trapped in a world of rigid social conventions (and strict time schedules) similar to the one she had sought to escape in her own family.

By the late 1940s, the baroness had begun taking frequent respites from the escalating marital discord in New York City where—through her connection to Teddy Wilson—she gained immediate entrée into the jazz community. It was on one of her New York getaways that Wilson insisted she hear Thelonious Monk's newly released recording of his now-classic composition, "Round about Midnight." Although Nica was scheduled to fly back to Mexico, she went out, bought a copy of the record, and, as she explained to Hentoff, "started playing it, missed the plane, and stayed in New York three more months."

In 1953, when the baron was appointed to head the French Tourist Office in New York, the couple separated and Nica took up residence in an antiques-filled penthouse at the Stanhope Hotel, where she lived on an annual trust fund estimated at $200,000. One of the few descriptions of the apartment appears in Hampton Hawes's autobiography; it is his first visit to the baroness's pad and the pianist is suitably impressed: "A lot of paintings and funny drapes, a chandelier like in an old movie palace, Steinway concert grand in the corner. I thought, This is where you live if you own Grant's Tomb and the Chase Manhattan Bank."

Just as the world war was ending overseas, on the home front a fierce battle was raging in the world of jazz as a corps of young jazz insurgents was beginning to challenge the swing era mainstream. Having devised their rhythmically complex and harmonically advanced music in late night jam sessions at Minton's Playhouse and Clarke Monroe's Uptown House, Charlie Parker, Dizzy Gillespie, Thelonious Monk, the drummer Kenny Clark, and the young guitar genius Charlie Christian were soon making inroads onto 52nd Street, New York's midtown jazz mecca, and putting their new sound onto disc. By the time the baroness settled into her new life in New York, the battle lines had been drawn and the ongoing skirmishes among opposing musicians (and fans) were being avidly covered in the still-thriving jazz press.

Never one to sit on the sidelines no matter what the conflict, the baroness immediately cast her lot with the modernists. Before long she had developed personal relationships with a widening circle of jazz innovators including Art Blakey, Horace Silver, Gigi Gryce, and Sonny Rollins, all of whom were now making regular appearances on "the Street" (and each of whom would soon be involved in recording a musical tribute to her). She even considered trying her hand at managing Blakey's new band, the Jazz Messengers. "I thought I could help him and his men become more employable," she told Max Gordon. "I invested in six matching, blue tuxedos. I thought that would help them get jobs. I was out of my mind."

More to the baroness's chagrin, however, the one musician she most wanted to hear was not able to perform in the jazz clubs that lined both sides of 52nd Street. Although Thelonious Monk is widely credited with laying the foundation of the bebop movement—"Monk is the guy who started it all," Blakey once asserted—for two long years after Bird's breakthrough discs Monk had been unable to get a recording contract. And, while others were regularly including his distinctive compositions in their live performances, Monk's unorthodox piano style and uncompromising aesthetic vision conspired to keep him from getting his own gigs. Then, a 1951 drug arrest—resulting in the loss of his "cabaret card"—shut the door firmly on the possibility of Monk getting work in any club in New York State.

In 1954, however, Monk received an invitation to perform at a French jazz festival. When Nica heard the news she immediately hopped on a plane and flew to Paris. In addition to attending his concert at the Salle Playel, she arranged to meet Monk through the auspices of the formidable pianist/arranger, Mary Lou Williams, who at the time was a member of Paris's expatriate jazz community.

For the next eight days, Nica spent every minute she could with Thelonious, and it was the start of an unwavering, if unlikely, friendship that would end only with the pianist's death in 1982.

In the months following their return home, the relationship deepened and Monk became a familiar presence in Nica's Stanhope suite. On one of his visits to the baroness during this period, Hampton Hawes recalls hearing "a low rumbling sound, the whole place shaking with it"; peeking through a doorway he saw "a body layed [*sic*] out on a gold bedspread, mudstained boots sticking out from a ten thousand dollar mink coat." It was then that Nica came rushing up "finger to lips as if I'm about to wake a three-week-old baby from its afternoon nap, 'Shhh, *Thelonious* is asleep.'" A few months later, Bird would also seek the aid and comfort of the baroness, but by that time it was too late.

Virtually everything we know about Parker's final days (including that portentous clap of thunder) derives from an interview the baroness did with Robert Reisner for his 1962 book *Bird: The Legend of Charlie Parker*, a compendium of ornithological anecdotes and tributes from a couple of dozen of Bird's colleagues and acquaintances. It is here, for example, that Nica sets forth one of the most fabled passages in the sacred text of Bird lore. It comes during her account of Dr. Freymann's initial examination of the ailing saxophonist. "Do you drink?" the doctor asks Parker (who had been consuming prodigious quantities of alcohol for months). "Sometimes," Bird responded with a wink, "I have a sherry before dinner." Along the way, however, the baroness also takes pains to highlight the platonic nature of their relationship ("we did have a wonderful friendship going, nothing romantic").

Nor was she the only one who has felt it necessary to set the record straight. Hampton Hawes's memoir, known for its searing honesty, also makes it clear that the unique bond she forged with the jazz community had little to do with mid-century stereotypes of race and gender. "I suppose you would call Nica a patron of the arts," he writes, "but she was more like a brother to the musicians who lived in New York. . . . There was no jive about her, and if you were for real you were accepted and were her friend." When asked about the woman who had inspired his composition "Nica's Dream" (now one of the most famous jazz standards), Horace Silver spoke with great warmth of her generosity to the entire jazz community. "She loved the music and she loved the musicians," he told me. "She was a beautiful person," explaining that his tune was a "tribute to her because she was so good to us."

When Hentoff asked the baroness directly about her motivation, the unaffected candor of her response cut through the welter of psychohistorical theories and racial ruminations; it also suggests how her own experiences had prepared her to recognize the essential message of all jazz. "The music, the music is what moves me," she told him. "It's everything that really matters, everything worth digging. It's a desire for freedom." However, there is also little question that—like the beboppers she idolized—she too paid a price for her freedom.

Having sacrificed marriage and social status in exchange for a precarious place in an often-demonized subculture, Nica had to endure not only the scorn of the mainstream, but hostility from some within the jazz world itself. Accused of everything from naïveté to "murder" (Charles Mingus, for one, is said to have publicly accused her of being responsible for Bird's death), the most pervasive criticism leveled against her had to do with her response—or lack of it—to the heroin epidemic that decimated so many of the giants of the bebop era. In the parlance of contemporary addiction theory, Nica was seen as "an enabler." As the wife of one jazz club owner put it, "One couldn't say she isn't a good friend, but I would say she's not a good friend to have for someone who needs some lecturing rather than permissive acceptance."

Suspicions about Nica's role in the bebop era's drug-ravaged jazz scene also taint a fictional portrait of the baroness that appears in

Julio Cortazar's 1967 short story, "The Pursuer," a *roman-à-clef* about the heroin-addicted alto saxophonist, "Johnny Carter." Although she is depicted as both deeply attuned to the music and "absurdly generous," it is the enigmatic and amoral "Tica" (a.k.a. "the marquesa") who bears the brunt of the blame for the hero's downfall ("I'm sure as can be," says the story's narrator, "that the marquesa was the one who got the junk for him").

While, in fact, she is no more complicit than the other members of Carter's inner circle, it is Tica's unique ability to emerge unscathed from the wake of his self-destructiveness that makes her an object of their resentment ("Tica's doing very well," says one. "Of course, it's easy for her. She always arrives at the last minute and all she has to do is open her handbag and it's all fixed up"). Although most of the story takes place in Paris, Carter finally does return to New York, where he dies in the marquesa's apartment ("he died happy and without knowing it was coming. He was watching TV, and all of a sudden slumped to the floor"). After chancing upon the Cortazar story, the pianist/composer Joel Forrester recalls rushing to Nica with his discovery only to find she had already read it—in Portuguese. "And does it show a likeness?" he asked. "Well, vaguely," the baroness responded.

In her defense, Nica insisted that she had often tried to persuade musicians to "kick," but with little success. "I used to think I could help," she told Hentoff, "but no one person can. They have to do it alone." What she could do was provide a safety net (something for which Hampton Hawes, among others, had reason to be grateful). As he explains in his autobiography, Nica had "a number you could call from anywhere in New York and get a private cab. If I was sick or fucked up I'd call the number and the cab would come and carry me direct to her pad."

In 1956, Nica was comfortably ensconced in the Hotel Bolivar on Central Park West. Her Steinway was tuned up and the late-night jam sessions were in full swing again. Although Monk was still coping with the creative and financial restrictions imposed on him by the loss of his cabaret card, he was again a regular visitor to the baroness's suite and his composition, "Ba-lue Bolivar Ba-lues-are"—composed at her piano during this period—is yet another nod to Nica's hospitality.

One night when Monk was on his way to the Bolivar, he suffered his first serious psychological breakdown and underwent his first hospitalization. Although no official diagnosis was made during Monk's brief stay in Bellevue, this initial episode of sudden acute disengagement would be repeated with increasing frequency for the rest of his life. Periodically, during times of psychological stress, Monk simply shut down and entered a state of near-catatonic silence. Yet there is evidence that, even during these periods, on some deep level he was supremely conscious of the world around him. "He disconnects sometimes," Harry Colomby, the pianist's long-time manager, has explained, "then all of a sudden he comes up with something so profound it scares you."

With Monk's wife Nellie working full time to help support their two young children—a son, also named Thelonious (nicknamed "Toot"), and a daughter, Barbara (known as "Boo Boo")—Nica was gradually becoming not only a source of emotional and financial assistance, but, with Nellie's blessing, almost another member of the family. "They were like the Three Musketeers," Monk's son recalled. "Nica knew he was in love with Nellie, but that was OK because she loved him anyway."

Although Colomby continued to work his day job as an English teacher at Far Rockaway High School, he had taken on the manager's mantle because of his deep appreciation for Monk's genius, and, though such lofty sentiments were hardly the norm in the hard-nosed New York jazz scene, Colomby's stubborn persistence was now beginning to pay off. As one old-school booking agent put it,

"Well, if you have nerve enough to be Thelonious' manager, I guess I'd have nerve enough to try and book him."

So, with Nica working behind the scenes to foot the legal fees, Colomby engineered the return of Monk's cabaret card and secured a gig for the pianist at an East Village hang out for poets and artists called the Five Spot. Thelonious Monk's Five Spot debut on July 19, 1957, turned out to be one of the most significant cultural events of the decade. For months Monk kept the place packed with dedicated jazz fans, fellow musicians, and curious celebrities, and, of course, the baroness's Bentley was conspicuously parked out front almost every night.

Unfortunately, Nica was experiencing some familiar difficulties of her own during this period. It had not taken long for her to wear out her welcome at the Hotel Bolivar and a brief sojourn at the Algonquin did not turn out much better (although she managed to stay long enough for Monk to compose his timeless musical love letter, "Crepuscule with Nellie," there). At this point, it seemed the only solution was for her to get a place of her own. What she came up with was a two-story modernist house set high above the Hudson River in Weehawken, New Jersey, that had originally been built by the film director Josef von Sternberg. She quickly moved in her books and impressive record collection, parked her Bentley in the driveway, and placed her Steinway in front of a wall of glass that looked out across the river to the midtown Manhattan skyline.

She also got a couple of Siamese cats. Given free run of the house—and the freedom to reproduce—they eventually numbered as many as 100, thereby providing the residence with its official nickname: the Cat House. No doubt enjoying the double entendre, the baroness even designed her own "Cat House" stationery that she would use for the rest of her life. With no hotel managers to worry about, Nica immediately set about establishing her new home as a venue for jam sessions, an informal jazz salon, and a haven for penurious pianists. In addition to Thelonious Monk, among the others who found refuge there were Barry Harris and the brilliant (but fragile) bebop master, Bud Powell.

Powell had returned to America in 1964 after a difficult three-year hiatus in Paris during which he had been befriended by the young French jazz aficionado, Francis Paudras (a relationship that forms the backbone of Bernard Tavernier's film *'Round Midnight).* As soon as Nica heard that Bud was back in New York, she invited him (and Paudras) out to Weehawken. "In the days that followed," Paudras writes in his book about Powell, *Dance of the Infidels,* "each time we saw Nica was a veritable delight. Nothing was too good for us. Every thoughtful gesture was made with utter discretion, as if it was perfectly natural. Once and for all, I was certain that she was the great lady of jazz." But soon Bud Powell would test even Nica's vast reserves of good will.

Upon learning that Powell was staying with Ornette Coleman in an unheated basement flat, Nica insisted that he move into her house. Although he had something of a feline phobia, Powell braved the prowling cats and made himself at home. In doing so, however, he also discovered the wine cellar where the baroness stored the shipments of Mouton Rothschild that she received annually from her family's French vineyards. After one late-night binge, Powell—whose delicate psychological equilibrium was upended by the consumption of even modest amounts of alcohol—stole off into the night.

For the next two days, Nica drove Paudras across the city, hitting every nightspot and jazz haunt from Brooklyn to Harlem. "Nica spent a fortune that night," Paudras recalled. "She knew everyone and often, before leaving a place, she would leave a little money for someone in trouble." Finally, alerted by a newspaper article about Powell's disappearance, a policeman found the pianist collapsed in a Greenwich Village doorway and got word to Paudras. Again Nica got into her Bentley, drove through the Lincoln Tunnel into Manhattan, slipped a roll of bills to the sympathetic cop, and brought Bud back to Weehawken. Although he had been scheduled to return to Paris with Paudras a few days later, Powell never made the flight. A 1965 comeback concert at Carnegie Hall ended in disaster and, a year later, the man who is generally recognized as the definitive pianist of the bebop era died at the age of 41.

Although many in the jazz community feared that Thelonious Monk would soon share the tragic fate of Bud Powell and Charlie Parker, the 1960s turned out to be the most productive and successful decade of his career. Following the return of his cabaret card, pent-up demand for the celebrated pianist resulted in a deluge of nightclub bookings, festival appearances, and world tours (on which he picked up many of the exotic hats that would become his trademark). In 1962, after being signed to a long-term contract by Columbia, the most prestigious of the major labels, Monk proceeded to re-record his entire catalog of classic compositions and release solo albums featuring his own idiosyncratic interpretations of jazz standards and popular songs. Finally, on February 28, 1964, Monk, the ultimate outsider, achieved the ultimate seal of mainstream approval—the cover of *Time* magazine, a distinction then shared by only three other jazz musicians.

While there were still a couple of smirking references to Monk's "mystical utterances" and an offhand depiction of the pianist as "a perfectly normal neurotic" it was the baroness—prominently featured in both the text and photos—who continued to be haunted by the lurid and superficial stereotypes of the past. Introduced as Monk's "friend, mascot and champion," Nica is reduced to a cartoon character, an "honest-to-God-Baroness" who pulls up "in her Bentley with a purse crammed with Chivas Regal" and then disappears back "home to Weehawken where she lives in a luxurious bedroom oasis, surrounded by the reeking squalor of her 32 cats." So, as Monk was being inducted into America's cultural pantheon, the baroness became permanently relegated to the role of "mascot," just another of his eccentric accoutrements, like one of his weird hats.

While jazz fans were gratified by the overdue acknowledgement of one of the music's masters, African-Americans celebrated the fact that one of their culture heroes had been honored by one of the most potent symbols of mainstream culture. This feel-good consensus, however, proved not to be unanimous. Before long, a scathing deconstruction of the *Time* cover story (titled "The American Way") had appeared in the radical black publication the *Liberator*. Analyzing the Monk profile from a Marxist perspective, Theodore H. Pontiflet found that "[b]ehind the facade of the genius recognized" there lurked a more fundamental socio-economic reality: "Thelonious Monk is earning a living with his talent, but is also being cruelly exploited."

Both *Time* and Columbia Records were taken to task for seeking to "fatten their pockets" at Monk's expense, but it was the baroness who bore the brunt of Pontiflet's critique. For, in the cover story's depiction of Nica as Monk's patroness and benefactor, he finds yet another example of the emasculation of the black male. "She serves as a bitter insinuation to both black and white Americans alike," he declares, "that a rich white woman is the black jazzman's salvation." Not that he liked the portrait of Nellie ("mockingly portrayed as a devoted wife and maid') any better. As he saw it, "The article tries to convince us that black women are in the background, reduced to the domestic chores of getting her man dressed for the performance and serving him ice cream in bed." For Pontiflet, *Time* magazine's ultimate message is clear: the pianist's success was a devil's bargain in which "Monk and Nellie remain as pure as honey," with the baroness simply an inevitable part of the deal—"the bitter part of the sweet."

In ten years the baroness had metamorphosed from the "luscious, slinky, black haired" sexual seductress who lured Bird to her deadly lair into a castrating surrogate mother without whom Monk, the "black genius," is "made to seem helpless." Although she had just turned 50, the dramatic shift in Nica's persona had less to do with her own transition to middle age than with the rapid transformation of America's racial politics.

Charlie Parker's death in 1955 had coincided with the advent of the civil rights era when the struggle against segregation raised the lurid specter of old taboos. By 1964, when the Monk cover hit the stands, the black power movement had forged a separatist stance that was challenging the traditional values of white liberalism. In fact, the Afrocentric consciousness that was reflected in the *Liberator* piece had already been roiling the world of jazz for a couple of years.

During the late 1950s, jazz performers had begun to address America's escalating racial turmoil directly in works such as *The Freedom Suite,* a 1958 album by Sonny Rollins, "Fables of Faubus," a bitterly satiric composition, by Charles Mingus (released a year later), *We Insist! The Freedom Now Suite* by Max Roach (issued in 1960), and the heart-wrenching elegy, "Alabama," by John Coltrane (composed after the 1963 bombing of the Birmingham church in which four young black girls were killed). A small, but vocal faction of musicians and critics had also become engaged in a campaign to claim jazz as an exclusively black art.

As part of this effort, some of the more extreme proponents of musical separatism were pressuring black bandleaders to hire only black sidemen. Dubbed "Crow Jim" by its opponents, the phenomenon emerged in the early 1960s as a subject of heated debate in the increasingly fragmented jazz community. Yet, despite Monk's oft-quoted statement that he had originally conceived bebop as music that *"they* couldn't steal because *they* couldn't play it," the pianist flatly dismissed attempts to convert him to anyone else's ethnocentric orthodoxy. Harry Colomby recalls that during this period Monk once confided to him: "You know, a lot of guys are telling me I should have a black manager, but I don't believe in that bullshit."

For a while Monk continued to record regularly and to headline jazz festivals from Helsinki to Tokyo. By the late 1960s, however, the periodic episodes of disconnection and withdrawal from which he had suffered for over a decade had begun recurring with increasing frequency and severity. What had once been occasional respites at Nica's Weehawken home gradually stretched into weeks, and then months. Monk eventually took over a second-floor room as his own, often spending extended periods of time lying in bed fully dressed simply staring off into space.

It was during this period that the baroness befriended a young pianist/composer named Joel Forrester after hearing him play at a New York jazz club. Having already recruited a retinue of massage therapists and spiritual healers in a determined attempt to break through Monk's self-willed silence, Nica invited Forrester out to Weehawken, hoping that his inventive compositions would engage Monk's interest. On each occasion, Forrester (who went on to co-found the respected jazz/new music band, the Microscopic Septet) would sit down at the Steinway grand placed just outside Monk's bedroom and begin playing.

Although Monk never came out of his room, if he liked something he heard he would slowly nudge open the door. "The things he couldn't tolerate," Forrester remembers, "were not only repetition of ideas, but anything that was glib or where I attempted to show off"; then the door would abruptly close again.

During the early 1970s Monk somehow managed to make a handful of appearances with a new band that included his son, Toot, on drums. He also briefly joined an all-star aggregation featuring Dizzy Gillespie and Art Blakey for an international tour organized by the jazz impresario George Wein. Perhaps rejuvenated by his old bebop cohorts, Monk's performances were cited by a number of reviewers as the highlight of their shows. Yet, upon his return, he again took up residence in the baroness's Weehawken home and took to bed. In 1976, Monk made his final public appearance when he accepted an invitation from Barry Harris (who was also rooming at Nica's) to sit in at his Carnegie Hall concert. According to Harris, Monk walked on stage, sat down at the piano, and played the entire show. "I got paid," Harris recalled, "and didn't have to play at all." As far as anyone has been able to determine, Monk never played the piano in public again.

Meanwhile, the legend of the jazz baroness had filtered down to a new generation of bebop devotees and mainstream fans, and a kind of underground subculture of Nicaphiles was beginning to emerge. Take the case of Robert Kraft, a young pianist who had recently arrived in New York (after graduating from Harvard) to try his hand in the music game. By the end of the decade, he had formed a band (Robert Kraft and the Ivory Coast), developed a book of original compositions, and been signed to RSO Records. He also continued a personal tradition he had begun in college of sending annual birthday greetings and Christmas cards to Thelonious Monk c/o the baroness's Weehawken address.

One night Kraft showed up at Tracks, a small New York nightspot where Toot was performing, and there, sitting together at a nearby table, were Nellie and the baroness herself. After introducing himself, Kraft mentioned an article on Monk that he'd just written for *N.Y.C. Jazz,* a free music guide distributed in clubs and record stores. Kraft sent Nica a copy of the piece, and in turn received a letter of acknowledgement on her personal "Cat House" stationery.

While Kraft's brief encounter with the baroness might simply have served as the basis for an entertaining anecdote, it turned out to be the prelude to a warm transcontinental friendship that lasted until her death in 1988. But, as it turned out, it was Monk's death that would prompt Nica to write him a letter of her own, one that provides a poignant coda to the story of Kraft's longstanding (albeit one-sided) correspondence with the legendary pianist.

Although he would soon be moving to Los Angeles, Kraft was still in New York on February 17, 1982, when word spread that Thelonious Monk had died following a stroke he had suffered a week earlier. Like many Monk acolytes, Kraft attended the memorial service at St Peter's (the so-called "jazz church"), and afterwards, while walking alone through Central Park, began writing a musical farewell to the departed master titled, "The Night Monk Returned to Heaven" (the song appears on the album *Bodies and Souls*, by the vocal ensemble Manhattan Transfer). A couple of weeks later, a letter showed up at Kraft's apartment with a Weehawken return address. "I received a letter out of the blue, from the baroness," Kraft explained, "saying, 'Dear Robert Kraft, I wanted to let you know that while cleaning out Thelonious's room, behind his headboard, I found all your cards and letters.'"

In L.A., Kraft made a gradual transition from the stage to the executive suite, and, as the years went by, his epistolary relationship with the baroness continued to deepen. He would write her about his latest album, or his marriage, or the birth of his sons, and she would send back congratulations and encouragement. As Kraft described it, "She responded as a kind of doting grandmother." Her letters—written on "Cat House" stationery in brightly colored felt-tipped pen—now hang, framed, in his Los Angeles home. In fact, the only time he remembers her completely closing down the lines of communication was when he proposed writing something about her.

For the past 25 years Kraft has been developing a story set within the bebop-era jazz underground. Initially conceived as a stage musical, loosely based on the relationship between Thelonious and Nica, it later evolved into a straight dramatic screenplay and, at one point, a full-blown Hollywood biopic about the baroness. Although it never went into production, Kraft does recall a casting meeting at the Creative Artists Agency in the early 1990s at which Meryl Streep was suggested for the Nica role.

Kraft—who is currently President of Fox Music, Inc.—likens the baroness's role in American music to the one Peggy Guggenheim had in the world of mid-century modern art.

> Here a hand reached down from the clouds to say, "Come up to the penthouse with me . . . I'll treat you like a king, like the court of the Medici." There's something really magical, and maybe fabulously traditional about a rich patroness, a traditional role from another era that was hard to fit into a forties mentality.

He suggests that, in assuming this role, Nica was neither self-aggrandizing nor entirely selfless.

> She made an unbelievable connection to the music; it inspired her. She had—under the thin disguise of a cynical, jaded, sophisticated, "Eurotrash" baroness—a great charitable spirit, an understanding artistic spirit that connected to the music and the artists and just said, "This makes my life worthwhile."

Through it all, Nica continued to make her nightly forays to New York jazz clubs from the Village Vanguard to the West End Cafe. The disc jockey, Charlie Parker scholar, and jazz raconteur Phil Schaap—who was booking shows at the West End during this period—remembers Nica holding court there on as many as 100 occasions, reminiscing with old friends like the bass player Sam Jones (who had played with Monk in the early days) or the tenor saxophonist Big Nick Nicholas (whom she had known back in the early '50s when he ran jam sessions at Harlem's Paradise Club). "She was genuinely liked by all those jazz musicians," Schaap told me recently. "She had a sense that led her to the greats," he went on, "and [they] trusted her implicitly."

Schaap also recalls how accessible the baroness was and how gracefully she would "disarm and put at ease" those who might be intimidated by her title or her legend. And, while the baroness continued to reject requests for formal interviews about her life (and was, as Schaap put it, "completely private about Monk"), informally she spoke with complete candor about her exploits in the jazz world and was even willing to "rehash the old Stanhope business."

In 1988, Nica entered the hospital for an operation. While access was supposedly limited to the immediate family, Joel Forrester managed to charm his way past the team of vigilant nurses. Although Nica was impressed, she revealed that he was not the only one who had been able to accomplish the feat, pointing to the enormous vase of flowers that Clint Eastwood had brought on his own recent visit. A longtime jazz fan, Eastwood had recently produced a Monk documentary titled *Straight, No Chaser* (which contains some rare footage of the baroness), and was also in the process of completing *Bird*, a Charlie Parker biopic that featured several scenes with a glamorous Nica character (including one that vividly recreated the account of Parker's death she had given to Robert Reisner).

Although her surgery had initially been deemed a success, on November 20, 1988, Nica died of heart failure at Columbia-Presbyterian Medical Center. Two weeks later a memorial for her was held at St Peter's Church (as had been done for Thelonious Monk six years before). In addition to Nica's children, the space was filled with musicians, jazz world insiders, and assorted Nicaphiles, while the musical segment of the service was provided by Barry Harris, the last in the line of pianists who had found refuge in her Weehawken sanctuary. Mourners also included both Thelonious Monk's widow, Nellie, and his son, T.S., who offered a moving eulogy to the woman he had known since childhood.

During the course of a long phone interview for this article, T.S. spoke of Nica with undiminished exuberance and pride. He began by recounting stories she had shared with him about her own childhood, conjuring up a fairy-tale world of life in the Rothschild household. She described the visits she had made with her father to the vaults of the Bank of England (during which the guards playfully challenged her to pick up one of the gold bars), and told him about a visit to her home by Albert Einstein (who delighted Nica and her siblings by performing after-dinner parlor tricks).

He also recalled tagging along on some of Nica's late-night missions of mercy. In the early 1960s, when he was about 10 years old, his father was booked into the Five Spot for an extended engagement.

> We'd drop him off at the club, and then me and Nica would go off in her Rolls Royce and go up to some street in Harlem to save somebody. I was with her all the time: going to *this one's* house to bring him some food, or we had to run around all day because *he* didn't have a horn but Nica was going to buy him a horn.

Based solely on what he personally witnessed, T.S. firmly believes that Nica was "one of the greatest artistic benefactors in the history of the world."

But he now realizes that her contributions went far beyond the material support she provided. "Nica's story is so integral to the *emotional* survival of so many of the musicians," he told me. "What she really provided was the belief in them; she really believed in them. She brought a credibility that musicians really needed and appreciated." T.S., a drummer and bandleader who has recently emerged as a dedicated and eloquent spokesman for America's jazz heritage, feels that the respect she received in turn from jazz musicians also had a deeper source. "Nica really, really knew the music. That's one of the things the musicians loved about Nica—that she really *knew*, as if she was a musician herself."

In 1997, more than 40 years after she had been unceremoniously evicted from her Stanhope suite—and about a decade after her death—Nica made a belated return to the elegant Fifth Avenue hotel when Andre Balazs took over the Stanhope's first-floor restaurant/outdoor cafe. Now best known for his own chain of fashionable boutique hotels, Balazs decided to name his new enterprise "Nica's at the Stanhope" in honor of the hotel's notorious former resident. Although Balazs sold the restaurant a few years later, and it has since gone through a couple of other incarnations, for many of her admirers, Nica's symbolic reinstatement represented a posthumous vindication, as well as confirmation of her legendary status. Nor was it the only such sign.

Two years later, for example, the dancer/choreographer Thomas DeFrantz, an associate professor in M.I.T.'s Department of Music and Theater (and archivist for the Alvin Ailey American Dance Theater), debuted his new experimental dance/theater piece titled *Monk's Mood: A Performance Meditation on the Life and Music of Thelonious Monk.* In our interview, DeFrantz described the work—which includes puppetry, high-tech video and sound elements, and DeFrantz's own blend of tap and modern dance vocabulary—as "an emotional narrative taking place in his [Monk's] head." In addition to exploring the story of the composer's creative life, the piece probes the complex dynamics of Monk's relationship with Nellie and the baroness.

While DeFrantz initially used the term "seduction" to characterize the nature of Nica's role in the piece, he explained that, rather than embodying the temptation of sexuality, she represents "the enticement of another way to be." He explained that, by providing affirmation from an elite world of high culture, Nica offered a taste of "the stuff the world has to offer, which may have been especially enticing to Monk." Asked to address the issue of Nica's own motivation, DeFrantz suggested that "Nica's iconoclasm was a way for her to do her own thing, and ultimately to be an artist herself," and that through her deep commitment to Monk, Parker, and the other black jazz musicians she befriended—"because she was willing to take things to the end," as he put it—Nica "was able to gain entrée to their world."

In gaining full-fledged membership into the insular and hermetic jazz fraternity, Nica achieved what has been the ultimate fantasy of jazz fans from the music's earliest days. In the final analysis, perhaps this is the primary reason that—a decade and a half after her death—she remains both an icon and an archetype for bebop aficionados and jazz buffs around the world. Currently, for example, jazz clubs named "Pannonica" keep alive the legend of the jazz baroness in France, Japan, and the Netherlands—just as many of the compositions that bear her name continue to be staples of the jazz repertoire and new generations of jazz vocalists sing her praises in cover versions of "Little Butterfly," Jon Hendrick's fervent 1959 homage.

While Nica's story has found a permanent place in the oral tradition that continues to serve as the primary repository of jazz history, it is one that remains virtually unknown to the public at large. Although this may simply be the shared fate of those who populate the chronicles of all marginalized subcultures, there is some evidence that, at least in part, the baroness's Garboesque persona may have been the result of a self-conscious strategy to cultivate the kind of aura of mystery that becomes a legend most.

In a letter declining my request for an interview, Nica's youngest daughter, Kari (who was born in 1950), explained that, by refusing all such appeals, she and her siblings were merely honoring their mother's own longstanding policy. "The reason that so few know about her contributions to jazz," she wrote, "is that she had a very firm view about any publicity. The view was expressed many times, not only to all her children, but also to jazz musicians, journalists and

writers. She valued her privacy and that of her family." On the other
hand, Joel Forrester recalled that, in a conversation with his wife,
Mary, about her own rejection of the increasingly avid inquiries from
the media, Nica had admitted that she preferred instead "to have all
manner of things imagined about me."

It was also Forrester who perhaps came closest to unlocking the
moral of Nica's story when I first invited him to consider the "Big
Question" that's always been at the heart of the life and legend of the
jazz baroness: What had really motivated her to abandon a life of
privilege and prestige to cast her lot with a handful of black jazz
mavericks who—even within the jazz world itself—had been both
accused of musical heresy and dismissed as ridiculous? "It's not a
vexed question, I don't think," he wrote me. "Simply put: she followed her heart."

As he continued his explanation, he managed to elevate Nica effortlessly into the modern jazz pantheon with which she felt such a
special connection. "True self belief is rare," he proposed:

> she would have heard it in Bird's tone, in Monk's generous
> translations of his temporal moods. These were her masters
> and her peers; how honor them unless she could match
> them in self-belief? Could she expect to be reviled? To
> arouse hatred and suspicion? To appear absurd? Worse, to
> lose much otherwise dear to her? Oh, without doubt. But a
> Nica without her resolve would have long since departed
> from memory; while the Nica who was really as weird as all
> that . . . lives on and will while *that beat* stirs human hearts.

ERIK DAVIS

ALWAYS COMING HOME

JOANNA NEWSOM

Last February, in Los Angeles, Joanna Newsom took to the stage at the ArthurBall and performed, for the first time in their entirety, the five loonnggg songs that make up her new album *Ys*. Many folks present were already chest-deep in the cult of Joanna, a fandom that made 2004's *The Milk-Eyed Mender* a leftfield indie hit and that turned Newsom herself into the sort of music-maker that inspires obsessive devotion as well as pleasure. At the time I admired *Mender*, but was, as of yet, no acolyte. I dug a handful of songs, but like many listeners, I found the eccentricity of Newsom's voice sometimes rather grating. I also feared that the outsider waif thing was just an underground pose stitched together with lacy thrift-store duds and an iPod stuffed with mp3s of the Carter Family and Shirley Collins.

My bad. The performance I saw that night was preternatural: a young artist stretching beyond her art towards something even more essential, simultaneously in command of her craft and caught in the headlights of her own onrushing brilliance. The song cycle she played was to *Mender* what, I dunno, *Astral Weeks* is to *Blowin' Your*

Mind, or what *Smile* is to *The Beach Boys Today!* She sang of meteorites and bears and ringing bells, of her and him and you, and she played not for us, it seemed, nor for herself exactly, but for the very presences her music conjured. Her songs were not performed so much as drawn from herself like nets dredged from the sea, heavy with kelp and flotsam and minnows that flashed before darting back into the deep. When she occasionally stumbled and lost her way, the material itself would pick her up again and carry her forward.

None of us standing there in that rapt crowd had ever heard music like this before. Newsom's wild child ballads seemed loosed from some location heretofore unseen in the realms of popular song, a secret garden lodged between folk and art music, or an unnamed island lying somehow equidistant from Ireland, Senegal, and California's redwood coast. The music fluttered and leapt, and though there were few obvious refrains, the patterns she played circled round some magnetic core of return, at once familiar and strange. Yes she was genius. But *genius* has become a throwaway word, a thumbtack of muso claptrap that marks the person rather than the source that lies behind the person. And this music was all source. And yet, it was she and not the source we heard—this charming young harper with the arresting voice and the awkward stage patter and the lacy thrift-store duds.

Sorry to keep the tankards of Kool-Aid raised high, my friends, but Newsom's album is also pretty dang nifty: the cult disc of the decade, like the aforementioned *Astral Weeks* or *In the Aeroplane Over the Sea*. She is not alone this time but supported on the album by Van Dyke Parks, the sometimes Brian Wilson collaborator who feathered four of Newsom's five songs with vivid and sprightly arrangements. The orchestration adds another dimension to Newsom's already evocative ramble through memory and desire, a journey that goes in turns intimate and cryptic, like the alchemical meanderings of a deep dream.

Faced with music as singular as *Ys*, it seems almost churlish to try to pin the butterfly down. (Or is that a moth?) That said, there is no denying that the spirit of prog has moved across the face of its waters. The album, after all, has an allegorical Renaissance portrait for a cover, features oboes and French horns, and draws its odd, difficult-to-pronounce title from the Celtic folklore of France. (It sounds like *ees*, as in "Oui, Serge Gainsborough *ees* very heep.") And indeed you must return to Van Der Graaf Generator or *Trespass*-era Genesis to find this sort of dramatic and, sorry, *literary* fit between highly wrought lyrics and the dynamics of long, intricate, tempo-twisting songs. However, I would urge you even farther back, to the great songs on the great Incredible String Band records, which also embroider earth visions onto patchwork tunes that combine heavy insights and bucolic play. For though the landscape of *Ys* is not particularly psychedelic, its peaks are very high, from "Emily"'s invocation of the cosmic void to "Cosmia"'s final ascent through the moonlight.

Happily for all, Newsom approaches such high-fallutin matters with a demotic American spirit and a folk fan's love of homespun melody and pastoral grit—not to mention a canniness that makes her at once too young and too old for the truly pompous. *Ys* may be precious, but it is precious because the spirit behind it is rare. It does not rely on sentiment, nor does it make Great Statements. It is, rather, a Great Work: an organic but deeply intentional labor from start to finish, from the inspiration through the cover art, from the arrangements through the final, analog mixdown. Newsom gathered a stellar cast of characters around her, including Steve Albini, Jim O' Rourke, and Van Dyke Parks, who contributes some of the best work in his career. But it is Newsom's own visionary ambition that makes this record the very opposite of a sophomore slump. A lesser artist would have simply ridden the quirky crest of *The Milk-Eyed Mender*, but Newsom glimpsed a golden ring glittering on the far horizon, and she stretched beyond herself with pluck and hooked it good.

HOMESTEAD

The house that Joanna Newsom recently purchased is, well, rather Joanna Newsom. The building lies in the outskirts of Nevada City, an old mining town nestled in the western foothills of California's Sierra Nevada range. The place has a small circular driveway, rose bushes, and a broken fountain with two cherubs smeared with mud up to their necks. The one-acre property is fringed by sycamores and pines, and two massive ivy-swaddled conifers loom over the patio out back, dripping gobs of sap onto a weathered table. The firethorn bushes that cloak the breakfast nook and the porch haven't been trimmed in a while, deranging the otherwise orderly air of a proper British cottage. Past their plump clusters of golden berries, you can glimpse her old, worn-out pedal harp, peeking through the window like a stage prop.

Newsom answers the door with a smile and invites me in. She is dressed in a knitted brown skirt, a low-cut sleeveless shirt, chocolate brown knee-high socks and moccasins. The wide leather belt tugged snug around her waist looks a lot like the belt she wears in her portrait for the cover of *Ys*. The bangs are gone, and she's cute as a vintage button.

"I'm sorry. I just moved in and I haven't really been here much." There is not much furniture beyond a couch and, alongside her harp, a gorgeous Craftsman wooden stool inlaid with turquoise. There is handwritten sheet music scattered on the floor and one large decoration waiting to be mounted on the wall, a nineteenth-century funereal display scavenged from a San Francisco thrift store. "It was there for years," she says, "and finally I had to have it." Having spent the last few weeks obsessively listening to *Ys*, I can see why, so crisply does the thing reflect some of her major themes and images: inside the large glass case, two stuffed doves face off over clusters of dried wheat, neatly arranged over a fat and faded ribbon printed with condolences.

We settle down on the table outside and dig into the past. Newsom grew up around Nevada City, but she lived for years in the Bay Area, where she studied composition and creative writing at Mills before dropping out, writing some songs and recording them with her first boyfriend, the musician and producer Noah Georgeson. Even then, she kept returning to the nest on weekends, but feared the phenomenon an old Austin friend of mine referred to as *the velvet rut.* "It's a real easy place to get kind of stagnant in your head, to get overly comfortable and have the years pass by." Now that her career has taken off and she is constantly traveling, she decided to return to the place that, in her words, makes her feel happiest and most at home.

Newsom loves her property, but what she would really like is to live on a high hill above the south fork of the Yuba River, surrounded by forests and horses and the looming lordship of the distant Sierra peaks—which is just the sort of place she was lucky enough to actually inhabit growing up. Her folks, both doctors and mildly hippyish in the manner of some California professionals, moved up here from San Francisco in the early 1970s, to a hilltop property surrounded by vineyards and stables and dogs and chickens that wandered everywhere. At the time, the former Gold Rush hotspot was becoming a quiet center of freakdom, making it one of those rare places in America where a proximity to wild country did not mean having to live under the cowboy boot of rural conservatism. The Beat poet Gary Snyder bought land on the nearby San Juan Ridge, the minimalist composer and Pandit Pran Nath devotee Terry Riley settled down to raise a family, and spiritual communities like Ananda Village were popping up. Even one of the guys from Supertramp got a place, and built a guitar-shaped pool.

Say you were standing on the back porch of the Newsom homestead and taking it all in: "Looking out over the canyon that the Yuba River is in, you see the two sides of the canyon and then the Ridge, and behind that the higher foothills—the pass over Tahoe—

and behind that the Sierra Buttes, these amazing huge mountains. We would eat outside, watching it all through dinner: insane hot pink clouds that come down and do what they do and then everything gets purpley and then the bats come out and get all drunk on bugs and bump into each other and its insane and then the lights come on and the moon comes out and reflects against the snow on the Sierras." She pauses, recalling the scene. "It's really pretty," she purrs. "It's really nice to look at."

California's gold country is beautiful, but it is also haunted by history. Downtown Nevada City holds onto its past with a vengeance, with zoning laws creating the atmosphere of a pleasant Miner Forty-Niner theme park. But darker and more wayward tales make their claim as well. A network of underground tunnels once linked brothels to more reputable taverns, while the Maidu Indians who called the area their home not so very long ago are tragically conspicuous in their absence. A big chunk of the hill that Newsom grew up on is fenced-off, with a nearby sign marking it simply as "Indian Burial Ground." Newsom and her buddies never even snuck onto it. "Even when we were little there was a little bit of reverence," she says. "We just felt really bad." She also felt that the restive spirits and "bad juju" of the place might have caused the weird energy that seemed to descend on her childhood home in the mid-morning hours—"like there was this unbearably loud chatter but there was nothing." Though she heard and sensed plenty of spooky shit in her house, she never saw an actual apparition there—nothing like the uncanny woman in flouncy skirts and a weird button-up collar that she glimpsed one night while working after close in Café Mecca, a Nevada City java joint that had once been a brothel. "It could've been a crazy Nevada City lady," she admits. "But it is a bit of a mystery how she got through the locked door. I don't know. I'm sort of convinced I saw a ghost."

Such specters may be nothing more than figments in the mind, but even so, they are figments of something deep: the persistence of the past, and the layers of rich and sometimes traumatic memories that cling to buildings and rivers and burial grounds. Newsom's music is also full of figments, of old blues blurred anew. Her famous line from "Sadie"—"This is not my tune, but it's mine to use"—captures this twisted continuity of memory and transformation, of love and theft. Part of what makes Newsom sound "folk" is her palpable sense of such ties—not just to the foothills of the California high country, but to her family, her friends, and her harp, with its own traditions, classical and folk alike. And as her own music proves, this sense of roots does not mean theme-park conservatism or a lack of innovation—especially, perhaps, when those roots are in a rootless place like California, a restless, visionary landscape that's always ready to crack.

HARPER

One of the most transcendent musical experiences of my life unfolded years ago during an annual folk festival held in the small Estonian town of Viljandi. A parade of slick Euro-folk-pop acts occupied the larger stages, but my wife and I preferred the informal tents, which were packed with folks dancing trad to teenage polka groups or locals playing perfectly rendered old-timey dobro tunes. As evening settled and the haze of beer fumes and burned sausage thickened, we slipped into a small whitewashed medieval church to hear the Ansambli Sistrum, an ensemble of four women who play the kannel, Estonia's lovely version of the lap harp.

The Estonians are a Finno-Ugric folk, and in the *Kalevala*, the Finnish folkloric epic patched together in the nineteenth century, the great magician Väinämöinen fashions the first kannel (or kantele, in Finnish) from the jaws and teeth of a monstrous pike. The birds and the bears and all the beasts of the field come to hear Väinämöinen play the instrument, which is later lost in battle and buried at the bottom of the sea. And it seemed to me, that night, that the master musician who led the ensemble must have fished the damn thing out, because the brocade of sound she and her bad-ass crew of ice-babes plucked from their elven devices was absolutely spellbinding: ancestral, spiky, and cosmic, like Messiaen in Middle-Earth. I was gone. Then some idiot's cell phone went off and he gruffly took the call, right there in the church—an abrupt reminder, as if one were needed, that angels and elves do not exist in our annoyingly real world. But the spell had been real, too, or as real at least as the instruments that had briefly conjured it into being.

The instrument in question, of course, was also a kind of harp, an ancient instrument that is found in most musical cultures and is often associated with magic. Väinämöinen's kantele is only one of a number of enchanting harps from northern climes, including the Irish chief Dagda's ax, which, depending on the melody he played, could compel listeners to weep, giggle, or sleep. King David composed the holy psalms on a harp, while the ancient Greek hero Orpheus, source of the mystic Orphic mysteries and commander of the beasts, invented the harp-like lyre (one of these Greek lyres is embossed in the leather diary that forms the booklet cover for *Ys*). The cheesy Hollywood angels that unconsciously reverberate through our imaginations when we see or listen to harps are the cotton-candy dregs of this numinous legacy.

Though she is understandably ashamed to admit it now, Joanna Newsom was first drawn to play the harp because of the angels and fairies and other girly phantasmagoria that swirled around the instrument in her head. She was only five or so when she told her parents her desire, too young to really grapple with the instrument, but when she finally got her hands on a Celtic harp a few years later, her fascination had not abated. By high school, Newsom had switched to the more challenging and versatile pedal harp. The fantasies had fallen away, and a painstaking musical apprenticeship had begun. Though the expressive potential of the harp is in some ways hamstrung by the standard classical and Celtic repertoire, Newsom was lucky: her first teacher, Lisa Stein, taught her the basics of improvisation from the get-go. Soon the teenager was composing her own lush and melodic compositions along with practicing the usual etudes and cadenzas.

Newsom's playing was already inventive and technically strong when the teenager met an established harper from Berkeley named Diana Stork. The two were attending a ten-day music camp held annually in the Mendocino County redwood groves—a longhaired, down-home gathering of global folk fanatics that Newsom's mom started taking her to when she was nine. Newsom immediately distinguished herself from the other young harpers there. "You could sense she was on a real path with the harp," says Stork, who attributes Newsom's remarkable drive to inspiration rather than ambition. "She's not driven by other people, or by making it, or by professionalism. The harp is what drove her, her passion and love for her instrument."

What Stork taught Newsom was rhythm. In particular, she taught her some interlocking figures based on the kora, a stringed lute-like harp-thing made of calabash and cowhide that's used by the wandering West African bards known as griots. Like nearly all West African music—and like essentially no classical Western music—kora music is largely polymetric, which means that each hand is following a different meter, or rhythmic pattern. The basic pattern that Stork taught Newsom is two (or four) beats against three. Stork explained that, according to the African lore she had learned, the duple measure, thumping like a heartbeat, represents the earth, while the triple time follows the breath and represents the heavens. By playing these beats against and through one another, a single performer can unite earth and sky. Said performer can also get pretty funky, because it's the overlapping and constantly shifting slippage between the different meters that gives West African music—not to mention James Brown—that special spine-wiggling groove.

Newsom fell hard for this polymetric plucking. She loved its physicality, and the sense of substance and danceability it brought to the harp's fragile, quietly resonating strings. She took pleasure in training her brain and hands to follow two different pulses at once, and in exploring more complex metric possibilities. Soon she began working versions of these interlocking figures into her compositions. "It was like an opportunity to do something—not new, because I didn't make it up—but to use it in a new way," she says.

Newsom's kora "bastardizations" are used to great effect throughout *Ys*, especially in the consoling middle passage of "Sawdust & Diamonds" ("Why the long face?"), and in the shimmering high section that follows the duet with Bill Callahan towards the end of "Only Skin." Newsom points out that these shifting rhythms can disorient the mundane metronome in our minds, defamiliarizing our sense of where we are in a song. "That disorientation is really effective for creating something that you actually have to listen to," says the songwriter, who has no interest in *Ys* becoming background music. "When any element in the musical environment is tweaked in such a way that you don't feel like you know what's coming next, it can cause less of a passive listening experience across the board. I like the idea of not just plodding through songs with a regular beat and a regular chord progression. Maybe the lyrics are felt or received differently, as if the listener were in a sharper mental climate."

Newsom was keen to create this sharper mental climate because, while the lyrics on *Ys* can seem pretty opaque at times, they are anything but casual. On a personal level, the album is a highly focused and richly encoded reaction to a lot of heavy shit that went down in the young woman's life, a year of mortal-coil turmoil that spun itself, through a series of uncanny coincidences, into something like a single fateful story of loss and release. This back-story not only upped Newsom's ambitions for the lyrics, but also forced the epic length of the songs, most of which hover around ten minutes, with "Only Skin" reaching the absurd, Yes-worthy expanse of 16:53. "I needed to respond to certain things musically and lyrically," she explains. "And I knew that I couldn't fit any of that gracefully within a normal song length form. I thought it would be really vulgar actually, and not even worth trying."

Luckily, Newsom already had the chops. One of the reasons that she stopped studying music at Mills was her discovery that the long and melodic instrumental pieces she was writing were more akin to traditional songs than the more explicitly experimental or conceptual compositions that are encouraged in music departments. So she opted to follow the songs. Then, with the gems from *Mender* under her wide leather belt, she was able to stretch out again for *Ys*. "I luxuriated in those new parameters," she says. "It promoted a sort of ambition because, while I'm not making any definitive statement here, I imagine that I probably won't do another record of long songs again. So I really wanted to do well within that format. I really wanted to do right by my topic."

The emotional demands of Newsom's new material also made demands on her voice—certainly the most idiosyncratic aspect of her music, and the one most likely to compel certain listeners to want to throw her CDs out the window. Newsom is a bit touchy about negative press reactions to her voice, and particularly the idea that she is affecting its simultaneously weathered and childlike eccentricity. When Newsom recorded her first EPs—which she has now "officially blacklisted"—she had barely been singing at all, and *Mender* was recorded less than a year after that. "When I listen back to those first EPs, I'm like, well, that voice does sound fucking crazy.

There is no way around it. But I know exactly what space I was in. I was so sure that I didn't know how to sing that I was just going balls out. I was like: I'm going to sing my heart out, as crazy as it sounds, and I'm not going to care because there's no hope of sounding anything like what people consider beautiful. I sure as hell wasn't affecting anything. I mean, the institution of singing is inherently an affectation!"

When Newsom wrote her harp compositions, she would often score passages she could not yet play, forcing herself to strengthen her technique in order to make the music she was hearing in her head. She took a similar tack to the vocals on *Ys*. "There are certain passages that I literally could not sing when I wrote them," she says. The song "Monkey & Bear"—which begins with a stack of over-dubbed harmonies that sounds like the Andrew Sisters in Oz—was "basically unsingable." But relentless touring had already improved her voice, softening its sharpness and lowering her register, and with obsessive practice she brought her throat up to snuff.

Newsom's vocals on *Ys* are rich and mercurial—girlish and wizened, nurturing and needy, with Kate Bush highs and Billie Holiday lows and, yes, some trembling Björkish breaths. She seems at once to command and suffer through the tangled and shifting emotions of the songs, the rougher edges of her voice refined without losing any of their spunk. The performance reminds me of something Newsom said in 2004, when she told *Arthur* why Texas Gladden's rendition of "Three Babes" had allowed her to sing. "It wasn't just that she was from Appalachia, and that she sang in that tradition," Newsom said. "It was that she was *her*. *Her* voice, in and of itself, is magical. And rare." Such singularity is not easy—it must simultaneously be stumbled upon and cultivated, not disciplined so much as embraced and befriended. "My voice is not necessarily more trained," Newsom admits. "It's just more familiar. I inhabit it more. It's not like this thing I'm holding out from myself. It's a part of me."

SONGS

The south fork of the Yuba River begins in an icy lake high in the Donner Pass, and plunges through chiseled granite outcrops and forests of fir before snaking westward not far from Nevada City, where the river canyons are largely protected from development. During the summer, when she's around, Newsom visits the river every day to take a plunge and hang out with her friends. "It's really perfect," she says, "an amazing, life-giving, life-shaping force." As she describes her lazy afternoons, I am reminded of why people move themselves, and their kids, to the sticks: "There's this river with these incredible rocks and it smells so good and you just lie on them and absorb the sun and then swim in this perfect water and get out again and joke around and play and do weird silly games like walking along on the bottom of the river with a big boulder so you can stay on the bottom." Afterwards, when evening comes, Newsom and her pals might have a barbeque or head up to a *Twin Peaks*-worthy steak house on the Ridge called The Willo; then they might spend the night drinking or dancing or probably both.

Rough stuff. But Newsom's relationship with the Yuba goes deeper than such idylls. Towards the end of high school, when she was eighteen, Newsom went down alone to a wild spot along the river. After asking their assistance, she arranged some stones into a circle, and then sat down within the ring. She stayed in the circle for three days, fasting, facing the river. Her best friend and some pals camped a few miles away, bringing her water and small portions of rice while she slept. She had assigned herself things to do but abandoned them all. She just sat there and watched the river, and, even more, she listened to it.

"I was a completely different person before I went to the river, and a completely different person after," Newsom says. When she first got back the girl was a total wreck. She would start crying when she woke up and not quit until she slept. She stopped going to school. She'd pick up the local paper and read a headline like "Man Dies in Car Crash," and then the crash would be in her mind, and the man's bloody crumbled body, and his pain and dread and fearful exit from this world. "None of the calluses or borders or walls we put up to protect ourselves from going absolutely insane while experiencing life—none of those stood anymore. They had been worn completely away. I was like infantile and dysfunctional, a weepy, drunk mess."

The Joanna Newsom who tells me this, of course, in no way resembles a dysfunctional weepy mess. She is assured and centered and gracefully goofy—not to mention whatever breed of mastermind you'd have to be to craft something like *Ys*. But that raw and convulsive openness is in her as well. You could say that *Ys* is a balance of all these forces, a marriage of keen design and crazy sensitivity, of intention and play and what she calls "skinlessness." Like a diamond, the record gleams from many sides. "Part of the intention was to send a message upwards," says Newsom. "Another was to come to peace with certain things. Another was to find voice for this huge, gaping, wind-howling tunnel that I was looking into and just being like, *FUUUCKKK*. Not knowing any words for it."

Well, she found the words. At times her songs tap into a deep well of lyric lament, the same old blues that inform John Dowland or Skip James or Nick Drake or the obscure 70s she-folkies on Numero Group's recent *Wayfaring Strangers* comp. But though Newsom is a powerfully moving singer-songwriter, she is in no way a *confessional* one. *Ys* is no diary, no sloppy heart-to-heart. Its baroque and inventive architecture, like its layers of the orchestration, act as a distancing mechanism that transmutes the emotional turbulence that inspired the work in the first place. Newsom's language, for one thing, is intensely worked. Evocative and sometimes piercingly tender, her lyrics also reflect an almost obsessive attention to old-school poetic stuff like consonance, alliteration, prosody, and internal rhymes. In "Sawdust & Diamonds," when she sings "mute" near "mutiny," the words not only echo phonetically but advance the song's themes of expression and rebellion. Later on in the song, after invoking the puppetry of romance, she introduces the image of a dove:

> *And the little white dove,*
> *Made with love, made with love;*
> *Made with glue, and a glove, and some pliers*

The easy rhyme of dove and love reflects the hackneyed ease of the cliché, which she then promptly takes apart. The word *glove* is a splice of *glue* and *love*, held together, as it were, with pliers and glue. This wordplay is not just surface but sense: it reflects the provisional and patched-together quality that exists beneath our idealizations of love, as well as what Newsom calls the "the Frankenstein phenomenon" that emerges when that love actually creates a living being.

Newsom says that every line she wrote for the album is significant, that choosing a single word arbitrarily would have been like contaminating or physically erasing the memory of a person or a key event. That's a high bar. At the same time, most of the specific meanings of the lyrics are locked away from the listener in Newsom's memories or dreams or creative imagination. Those who get obsessed with these songs—and there will be many—will find that deep and repeated listening will begin to open up their voices and images, some of which Newsom admits filching from proper literature like *Lolita* and *The Sound and the Fury*. But they'll only reverberate so far—and that's the point. "The whole intention of making a record out of all this instead of having a conversation with a best friend is to create an artistic or musical work whose worth is completely separate from the story that I'm trying to tell." This is the paradox of *Ys*: far more than most records, it tells a story, but the story it tells remains hers and hers alone.

Just as Newsom had no desire to make *Ys* an open book, she has no desire to turn interviews into cheesy confessionals. For one thing, she doesn't want to strip away the rich ambiguity of the words by explaining too much about their origins. She also dreads the prospect of having a bunch of journalists asking the same personal questions, over and over. "That seems unbearable," she says, pulling her hair back behind her elven ears. But the questions—and the misunderstandings—have already arrived, such as the notion that *Ys* is a "breakup record." She spoke at length with *Arthur* partly because, besides the fact that she actually reads the rag, she hopes to lay certain matters to rest and be done with them.

"There are three specific stories on *Ys*, and maybe five specific characters," she says. "There were two major losses and the knell, the ringing knell of another loss which is continuing, an illness basically." The hammer blow that began this series of hard knocks was the sudden death of Newsom's best friend, "one of the loves of my life." Newsom got the call while she was driving between gigs, during the year when her career was first blowing up. "So mortality is huge on this record. And there's more than one type of death, of course, and that's where the turmoil of the relationship figures in, but not quite as largely as you might suppose."

The sense of loss that overshadows the opener "Emily" is the kind that comes to all strong families despite, or perhaps because of, their intimacy. The song is addressed to Newsom's kid sister, who is often gallivanting about the world but came home long enough to sing on the track. "In some ways this song is a tribute to her, and in other ways it was like a plea, a letter to her about some stuff that's happening close to home, and a reference to the fact that a lot of the little structures and kingdoms and plans we built when we were younger are just falling to fucking pieces." The song begins with one of these imaginative kingdoms:

The meadowlark and the chim-choo-ree and the sparrow
Set to the sky in a flying spree, for the sport of the pharaoh.
A little while later, the Pharisees dragged a comb through the meadow.
Do you remember what they called up to you and me, in our window?

Meadowlarks and sparrows are songbirds, of course, but the chim-choo-ree, as far as I can tell, is probably an outgrowth of watching *Mary Poppins* too many times. We are in childhood, then, that weird wonderland that Newsom can invoke with her voice and the sandbox detail of some of her lyrics. Newsom has rightly complained that the "childlike" reading of her songs on *Mender* caused some people to take her for a naïf and to ignore the dark undertow of her lyrics. For of course it is not the *innocence* of the girlchild that is interesting—it is the savvy, that imaginative swagger that can inspire young girls to, say, command huge ungulate mammals around a dressage ring. (Or demand to play harps.) Here this same imagination has made toys of the pharaoh and the Pharisees, figures poached from Bible lessons, brought to life on a lazy day. But these characters are also avatars of the darker themes to come on *Ys*, of confinement and judgmental hypocrisy.

Emily majored in astrophysics at UC Berkeley, which helps explain all the astronomical imagery that blazes through this song and occasionally explodes into cosmic epiphany. In one of the few conventional choruses on the album, Newsom transforms technical nomenclature—the exact difference between *meteorite*, *meteor*, and *meteoroid*—into a wisdom teaching about the void and the relativism of perspective. Newsom's dad is also an amateur starhound, and she remembers him teaching her, over and over again, how to find the dirt red bullet of Arcturus by following the ladle of the Big Dipper. In the song, Newsom maps these overlapping relationships—father to daughters, and Emily's studies to her dad's hobby—with the figure of the asterism, a technical term that describes star clusters whose borders overlap or exist within larger constellations—the Dipper, for example, is an asterism of Ursa Major, the Big Bear.

Asterism is also a twenty dollar word. I had to look it up, and most listeners won't even bother. "I always get shit for using these big words," Newsom admits, laughing. "And that's valid—they can be distracting and take away from pure simple meanings. But other times they truly seem to be the only word that says the exact thing I need them to say." Another mouthful in "Emily" is "hydrocephalitic listlessness," which describes an image of peonies in spring, so full of water that their heads loll like the drugged. Newsom pulls off this astounding phrase—which some maniac out there has already tagged as his myspace name—with a gorgeous, lilting leap into her upper register. An allusion to a malady that afflicts someone in Newsom's extended family, the line, like so many here, also does double-duty, evoking the album's heavy atmosphere of saturated nature, when ripeness is all, and therefore already gone into decay. *Ys* is a pastoral record in many ways, but its vision of nature is as much about inundation and rot as the "fumbling green gentleness" of organic life.

Lots of images echo throughout *Ys*—birds, clay, borders, lights—but the most forceful is water in excess. Of course, the image is itself saturated with possible meanings—the unconscious or sex or the inevitability of change—but it doesn't really matter because, on this record anyway, the levee definitely breaks. At the close of "Monkey & Bear," a story-song whose animal protagonists play out a fable that sets confinement against the call of the wild, the bear Ursula flees from her monkey mate and master and swims out into the sea. In an almost shamanic process of dismemberment, she sheds her limbs and shoulders, her gut and her coat, which she then uses to catch fish that finally feed her hunger. As the music heaves in shorter and shorter bursts, the song reaches a peak of climax and apotheosis, a split moment "when bear stepped clear of bear."

This weird, erotic catharsis clears the air for "Sawdust & Diamonds," the one song Newsom plays without accompaniment and the one whose lyrics most amaze. Though *Ys* is not a breakup album, it's fair to call "Sawdust & Diamonds" a breakup song, though one that shares few sentiments with, say, "Hit the Road Jack" or "There's a Tear in My Beer." Rather than express the anger or grief of the jilted, the song invents itself from the more complicated pain of one who leaves but still loves, whose heart is doubled over and turned against itself. The tension between containment and rebellion recurs, along with images that explode beyond sense with a visionary, dreamlike power—a bell falling down white stairs, a belfry burning sky-high, a pair of marionettes that couple before an admiring audience. In the end, the song is not about couples per se but the forces that move them, for good and ill. "You would have seen me through / But I could not undo that desire," Newsom sings over an aching repeated arpeggio. Then she turns and addresses her desire directly, repeating the word with a plaintive ferocity that's both resigned and supplicant.

"Only Skin" is the longest, most obscure, and least shapely of the album's songs, the one that detractors will most readily point to as evidence of Newsom's art-rock self-indulgence. I've listened to it tons, and it's grown on me, and the peaks are worth the valleys. It was the last song she wrote, and the one where, perhaps foolishly, she attempted to weave together all the various threads and "ghost characters" in her tale. "It was an attempt to encapsulate everything, and to find some measure of grace." Most revealing, perhaps, is Newsom's admission that the last few verses of the song—where the long-suffering female protagonist promises to do right by her darling—are the only place in the whole album where she just made stuff up, where the song steps away from poetic autobiography. "I was hoping for a good resolution, but I felt helpless and foundering at the end. And so I reached for this fiction, because I didn't know how to end the song in full truth. Otherwise, it would go on forever."

Ys ends where the story began: with the death of Newsom's best friend. "Cosmia" is a composed rather than wrenching elegy, and the most conventionally structured of the five songs. The engulfing waters of the rest of the album are here channeled into a river, a site of solitude and communion. In the long line of beasts and critters that inhabit the rest of the record—meadowlarks and monkeys and horses and hens—here Newsom calls in the moth, the final form of what William Blake called "animal forms of wisdom." After the singer gets the devastating news, she walks into a cornfield, and moths almost drown her. Later, she invokes the classic image of moths immolating themselves in the artificial sun of a porch-light—those attractive but dubious goals towards which so many of us so readily plunge. But here wild Cosmia, her form a thing of water and fire, flutters off on a farther flight, towards the possibility of a "true light" bright enough that it might even shine back down here, when the night comes in.

Like the whole record, "Cosmia" affirms life without offering a wisp of false consolation. "The thing that I was experiencing and dwelling on the entire time is that there are so many things that are not OK and that will never be OK again," says Newsom. "But there's also so many things that are OK and good that sometimes it makes you crumple over with being alive. We are allowed such an insane depth of beauty and enjoyment in this lifetime. It's what my Dad talks about sometimes. He says the only way that he knows there's a God is that there's so much gratuitous joy in this life. And that's his only proof. There's so many joys that do not assist in the propagation of the race or self-preservation. There's no point whatsoever. They are so excessively, mind-bogglingly joy-producing that they distract from the very functions that are supposed to promote human life. They can leave you stupefied, monastic, not productive in any way, shape or form. And those joys are there and they are unflagging and they are ever-growing. And still there are these things that you will never be able to feel OK about—unbearably awful, sad, ugly, unfair things."

We are getting near the heart of things, and so I ask her, wondering myself, if you can experience such gratuitous joy without the trauma of skinlessness.

"Maybe not. It's possible that if you are not open to one of those experiences you can't be open to the other. It requires a sloughing off of a particular sort of emotional callus, and you're probably shedding the same block, the same blunting mechanism in terms of joy and in terms of sorrow. And maybe you go through a million regenerations of that in your lifetime, feeling very blunted, and then feeling very exposed and oversensitive."

"So where are you now?"

"I may be rewarding myself with a nice long numbing bath," she laughs.

ARRANGING

Newsom is an impressively late riser, and though I showed up at three she still hasn't had her coffee. So she pulls on a brown knit cap and we bundle into her dusty Suburu Forester and head towards Ike's Quarter Café, a neo-creole joint in downtown Nevada City. Over the gorgeous, elegiac folk sounds of the forthcoming PG Six record, she talks about how clumsy and disorganized she can be, especially when she's performing. She invariably spills water on herself, and once slipped in a puddle of beer at the Swedish American Hall and landed on her ass smack-dab in front of the audience, ripping her dress. "I'm eternally indebted to any journalists who were there because not a single person mentioned the incident."

We arrive at Ike's and settle into an outdoor booth shaded by vines and trellises. Newsom's speaking voice is almost as variable as her singing one, and when we place our orders, as when she says "please" or "thanks" or "hello," the boopsy factor goes up a notch, which is particularly amusing when the order in question is a medium-rare cheeseburger with bacon and a side of horseradish cream. Though a strict vegetarian for years, Newsom is clearly one no longer, and as a fellow veggie backslider, I relax. (Both of us, it turns out, started eating meat again after having carnivorous dreams.) She wants to go hunting sometime with her uncle Dave, who occasionally makes the cover of hunting and fishing magazines and likes to bag wild turkeys in the area. "But I'm pretty sure that when it came down to the wire it would be too difficult for me emotionally, which makes me feel like a huge hypocrite."

Hypocrite or not, Newsom is capable of eating steak every day when she is on tour, just to ground herself amidst the chaos. "I'm not a good traveler," she says. "If I wasn't touring I would probably almost never travel. On tour, I just get so drained and bonkers and fragile. Totally cuckoo. Very small things seem insurmountable."

Things go much better when she travels with people she digs, like when her friend Jamie accompanies her on tour, or the time Newsom took a road trip with her boyfriend Bill, just as she was thinking about how to shape her new songs into an album. Bill is Bill "Smog" Callahan, a Drag City label mate who met Newsom on tour. (She made a guest appearance on his 2005 record *A River Ain't Too Much To Love*.) For the trip Callahan bought Newsom a copy of *Song Cycle*, which Van Dyke Parks released in 1968, when the musician was just about Newsom's age. Parks is best known for collaborating with Brian Wilson on the lyrics for *Smile*, but his single greatest work remains this art-pop head-trip through the American musical landscape. Newsom listened to it for three days straight. She was already thinking about fleshing out her songs with orchestral arrangements, and told her fella that she wanted to work with someone who scores like Van Dyke Parks. "Well, perhaps you should ask Van Dyke Actual Parks," he said.

So she did. The couple were already heading towards Los Angeles, and Drag City arranged for her and a harp and Mr. and Mrs. Parks to all meet up in a hotel room, where Newsom played him all five songs in one fell swoop. Newsom was hoping he'd agree to score one song, but Parks told her he wanted to take on the whole thing.

Parks may not have known what he was getting himself into. Newsom knows what she wants musically and is not shy about saying it. Of all of Parks' initial arrangements, only the score for "Monkey & Bear" worked for her out of the gate—which is perhaps not surprising, given that Parks' first paying gig in Hollywood was scoring "Bear Necessities" for Disney's *Jungle Book*. But all the other arrangements required an exhaustive back and forth between Newsom and Parks; even then, none of the arrangements for "Stardust & Diamonds" ever felt right, which is why Newsom decided to leave the song unadorned, an intimate clearing in the midst of a forest of sounds. After half a year of working remotely on their shared vision, Newsom went to Parks' home studio in LA to sift through the final written score bar by bar. "He'd leave the room to go to cook his family dinner and I would just in there combing through everything."

"I've never had a bigger challenge," Parks told the webzine *Bandoppler* about working with Newsom. "Or more joy in discovery." You can certainly hear the joy. In "Emily," which features his most innovative contribution to the album, the orchestration both echoes and tickles the lyrics—a long minor chord follows her mention of shadows, while a goofy banjo appears when she sings about her Pa. One point of friction that occurred during the recording sessions was Parks' desire to add electric bass and electric guitar. "I was like *Hellll no*," Newsom says. But Parks, who also contributed accordion to the album, went ahead and called in two great session players of the old school, Grant Geissman and Lee Sklar. "What they added was unbelievably important and grounding," Newsom says. "I'm so glad that Van Dyke insisted on that." Another bone of contention was

Newsom's insistence on recording the orchestra to analog tape, something that has probably not been done in LA since the Rodney King riots. Newsom always wanted an all-analog project, and rehearsed the familiar arguments with Parks: analog recordings capture more information than digital, and are richer and warmer-sounding to boot. Parks agreed with her, but also pointed out that analog was a pain in the ass. Newsom kept on it, though, and eventually got her way. "It was definitely difficult but a lot of the difficulties weren't things I, um, had to personally deal with."

I asked Newsom why she was so insistent about analog. "Just instinct," she says, her green eyes lighting up. "I just thought it would be so rad to do a fully analog all-orchestral recording. It would be so incredible to get to hear the vinyl version and put that out there. That was the dream driving me the whole time."

ANALOG

The hoary debate over analog vs. digital recording usually grinds through its fated moves over issues of technical fidelity and sensual perceptions like "warmth" and "sharpness." But the wrangle also has a more intangible dimension, one that's emotional, cultural, almost metaphysical. Analog and digital aren't just different ways of handling sound—they are different metaphors about how we mirror and model the world. The term analog comes from *analogy*—the undulating grooves on your vinyl LP (and, more complexly, the magnetic fields captured and reproduced by the metal filings on magnetic tape) are very much *like* the material undulations of sound waves in the air. Digital comes from digit: an abstract numerical representation of a single slice of flowing sound, sampled at such a rate as to closely approximate a continuous wave. Analog hugs more tightly to the ways of the earth, with its flows and inevitable physical decay. Digital, which hypes the eternal life of the perfect copy, tends to dematerialize and disincarnate—just compare an MP3 or DJ software to an old 78 or a pedal harp. Faced with our now commanding empire of the digital, some people don't just choose to make or listen to more analog recordings. They choose to live more analog lives.

Take, for example, one Joanna Newsom, who was born two years before the first Macintosh appeared and has followed up her Ike's cheeseburger with a pint of Anderson Valley ale. She owns a computer but doesn't get the Internet at her house and has to take it to a café for email. She uses the machine to make CD mixes for friends, but never plays music from it. She doesn't own an MP3 player. When Newsom moved into her new house, she noticed the perfect spot for a CD player, which she had never owned. But she opted against it. (She does play CDs in her car.) "I decided that a good choice as far as sanity goes was to just have analog sounds in the house. I do have a digital camera and I'm fine with that. But sound affects the brain and the mood so much. It seemed like a good thing to just rule out any possibility of a crispy mosquito of digital sound boring into your brain. Just rule it out of the home environment."

Newsom learned a lot about listening to music from her boyfriend Bill, for whom vinyl recordings are as much an invitation as a storage medium. "The way he listens to music is one of the most endearing and sweet things I've ever seen," she says, taking a sip of her beer. "He takes off his shoes, sets them down and gets comfortable. He kneels or sits in front of the record player, lifts the cover, reverently chooses a record, puts it on, closes the cover and just listens, start to finish. Whenever I go to see him and we listen to music like that, I register in myself how much better it feels than other ways of listening, which are like rushing to eat a meal because you're super-hungry. You need to eat, just like you need to listen to music, but it never feels good if you do it like that. So I am trying to set my life up in a way where I don't have to listen to music any way other than putting on a record and sitting and listening."

Newsom recorded her own performance for *Ys* with Steve Albini, who has recorded thousands of musicians and works strictly with analog. (Albini once offered this thunderous prophecy on the back of his old band Big Black's *Songs About Fucking*: "the future belongs to the analog loyalists. fuck digital.") Albini and Newsom met at LA's slick Village Recording Studios, where Todd Rundgren was recording Meatloaf in the studio next door. Still, Albini had to go through five tape machines before getting one to work, and that one he had to fix himself. "It was a really embarrassing scenario," says Albini. "It's not like we were in some cheap-shit chop shop. I've made records in people's living rooms that went better from a technical standpoint." Once he cobbled together a studio, Albini then faced the challenge of recording the harp. "It's a quiet instrument. It doesn't excite the room much, so you have to work close to it, but because it's physically large you can't just stick a mic up close to it." Albini wound up placing four small Crown GLM mics, which are about the size of a kitchen match, along the instrument's resonating belly. A nearby mic picked up the stereo image of Newsom playing, and a distant mic picked up the reverberant sound of the room. "It was fun," says Albini, who enjoyed working with Newsom, a woman he describes simply as "bad ass."

The album was mixed by another analog enthusiast, the guitarist and producer Jim O'Rourke. The mixdown took place at New York's Sear Sound, a legendary shrine to analog recording run by Walter Sear, a Joe Meeks-like figure who once sold synths with Robert Moog. This is what Newsom told O'Rourke she wanted: "I want the vocal and harp performances to feel central and grounded and close and intimate and still, as though they are taking place in a small space very close to the listener. I want the orchestra to feel hallucinatory and constantly shifting in space and I want it to be mixed in a way that relates to the story being told and the lyrics and the mood very closely." After slaving two 24-track machines together to accommodate all the tracks, O'Rourke did a rough mix by instinct before returning for detail work. He methodically went through each track, following it from beginning to end with a flying fader, constantly modulating, creating an ever-changing landscape of sound that accorded with the shifts and undulations of the songs. He also cut out sections of Van Dyke Parks' arrangements, arguing that the gorgeous details that the arranger and Newsom had so painstakingly worked out were not always in service to the songs, which sometimes demanded greater intimacy. Everyone knew that Parks' arrangements might be cut back in the mix, but they worked hard to find the right balance. "Hopefully he's happy with the results," says Newsom.

One day at the studio, O'Rourke told Newsom he had a vision for an ad for the record. "It's just a picture of you. Above it says *Music*, and below it says *Is Back*." O'Rourke was not kissing ass. In an email, he wrote that Newsom's record recalled and confirmed why he fell in love with music in the first place. "It's someone's vision seen all the way through—sweat lost, brain racked, soul searched, and fingers callused. I doubt we'll hear anything as brilliant in a long, long time."

After *Ys* was mastered at Abbey Road and chopped into digital bits, advance CDs were, as usual, sent out to music scribes. Newsom expected that the record would leak onto the Net, an inevitable phenomenon and not necessarily a bad one. But *Ys* did not leak—it surged through a broken dam. For reasons that remain unclear, the album wound up on the public download server of the indie tastemaker Pitchfork. Because the leak itself was newsworthy, or at least gossip-worthy, a certain category of websites—a category whose loathsome name begins with "b" and rhymes with *slog* and *bog*—went apeshit. The word (and the downloads) spread through muso sites and beyond, to places that would normally not give a fig for Ms. Joanna Newsom, who, needless to say, was not particularly pleased.

Newsom had exerted her creative control throughout the entire creation of the album, and now she had lost it. Though *Ys* probably gained more in publicity than it lost in future sales, that didn't matter to the artist, who is a quality-over-quantity gal, and does not really cotton to such a calculus. She wants her album to be taken whole, as the old-school Album it is: a thematic and developmental sequence of songs wrapped up in a nifty package with a gorgeous cover, a beautifully designed booklet for lyrics, and, ideally, a nice big gatefold sleeve. "I want anyone who has the record to feel like it's this little object of some worth or substance," she says. "So much stuff is throwaway nowadays and I wanted it to not feel that way. Ironically, of course, it leaked on the Internet, which is like the epitome of throwaway, or at least intangibility." Indeed, there was something almost mythic about the whole affair. It was as if the archons of the digital needed to visibly humiliate Newsom, with her brazen and well-publicized invocation of the old ways.

PORTRAIT

A week before I met Newsom, when I was trawling Joanna fansites for bootlegs, I sampled some of the chatter about *Ys* and discovered that the most controversial aspect of the album by far was the cover portrait of Newsom. Some bitched about the "Ren Faire costume," and others compared the image to the cover of a fantasy novel. These reactions are understandable but still pretty lame. A great Album requires a great cover, and Benjamin Vierling's painting—which looks like a Dürer by way of Millais, but more pop-surrealist—is pretty great. Luminescent, esoteric, and vividly detailed, it mirrors Newsom's moodier new material as much as the strange and playful embroidery of Emily Prince's cover complemented *Mender*.

In the portrait, Newsom sits stiffly in an old oak chair, wearing a plain brown maiden's dress, a broad leather belt, and a wreath of wheat and flowers in her loosely braided hair. She is framed by a horse skull, a blackbird, and more flowers, some of which—like the

poppy in her hair and the morning glories surrounding her chair—
are visionary plants. The color of the morning glories, which are
somehow growing out of the floorboards, echoes the hues of the sky.
The outside is within, they seem to say, just as the ordered, formal
composition is fringed with wildness. But the symbolic heart of the
painting lies in Newsom's hands. Like the skull on the wall, the
nicked sickle in her left hand is a *memento mori*, a reminder of death,
its lunar shape echoed by the airplane contrail in the sky, another image of impermanence. In her right hand, she holds a framed and
mounted specimen of the order *Lepidoptera*. At first I took the critter
to be a butterfly, which made sense, if for no other reason than the
fact that Newsom loves Nabokov. The butterfly also represents the
transformative emergence from a death-like state, and is a traditional
symbol of the soul (the Greek word *psyche*, or soul, also means butterfly). But after a round of late-night Google searching, I finally discovered that the thing is actually a moth—a *Cosmia* moth, to be
exact, pinned and framed and protected, after a fashion, from the
ravages of time.

I want to see this painting in all its original glory, and so, after
Newsom and I finish our Solstice ales, we drive over to Vierling's
studio in downtown Grass Valley, which lies close to Nevada City.
We arrive at St. Joseph's Hall, a ramshackle former convent and or-
phanage now given over to artist studios and the occasional concert.
Climbing the shadowy exterior stairwell, I am not surprised to hear
from Newsom that this place too is haunted.

Vierling's small studio is orderly and calm, and the 31-year-old
man, who Newsom pegs as an "old soul," is thoughtful, friendly and
gently reserved. The Newsom portrait is radiant. Its luminosity and
juicy detail are the result of a laborious and exacting process of ap-
plying alternate layers of egg tempera and oil, an old-school technique that took Vierling six months to execute. Too eclectic to call
himself a true traditionalist, Vierling is most directly inspired by the

Nazarenes, a nineteenth-century group of German mystical painters who rejected the mannered styles of their day and looked back to medieval and early Renaissance models. As Vierling wrote in an email, "The Nazarenes glorified medieval art because it embodied a paradox: the perfection of the ideal as God intended, in contrast with the entropic negation that all matter is subject to." This attitude—which Vierling rightly says is more Gnostic than Catholic—influences his own dogma-free approach to sacred art. "I believe that a painting has the ability to reflect back to the viewer the image of what exists behind the subject, the spirit behind Matter if you will. It is my goal to reveal what is eternal in the subject, be it an object or a person."

Vierling did not paint Newsom's face from life or from a photograph, but from an image in his mind he constructed after studying scores of photographs taken of the singer from various angles. Some fans have complained that the portrait does not really resemble Newsom, but having spent half a day with her, I would counter that her face itself is mercurial. (And, except for the wreath, she is certainly not wearing a costume.) The painting's most excellent likeness, though, is Newsom's hands, which are also Vierling's favorite part of the picture. They are strong and lovely and articulate. Like the music on *Ys*, Vierling's rendering brings together an expressive, spiritual exuberance with an almost clinical execution of detail and technique. That tempered balance is the key. "The alchemists called it the Magnum Opus, the great work," wrote Vierling. "I call it a painting. It might just as well be a song, a verse, or even digital code. It is what you invest in, nothing more or less."

MYTH

The last element of Newsom's magnum opus to arrive was its title. Newsom spent a long time fishing for a name that would encapsulate the spirit of the project. One night she dreamed about the title, a swirling reverie that featured the letters Y and S smashing together in unusual combinations. Afterwards she began searching for a single-syllable word that bluntly combined the two letters. At the same time, Newsom also finally got around to reading the fantasy novel on her nightstand, which happened to be her best friend's favorite book. She thought the novel might be cheesy, but she loved it. And one night, there it was: a passage about a seaside castle that had been raised "by the magic of the ancient folk of Ys."

Et voila—Newsom had found her title in the name of a lost city immortalized in the folklore of Brittany, a region that lies along the northwest coast of France. As Newsom read more deeply into the legend, things got a little spookier. Here, in a nutshell, is one version of the tale: Dahut, the blond daughter of King Gradlon, begs her father to build her a citadel by the sea. And so he does, creating a city that's protected from the waves by an enormous wall of stone whose one entrance, a gigantic bronze door, is opened by a key that Gradlon carries around his neck. Like a lot of seaside towns, Ys attracts horny sailors laden with goods, and Dahut makes a wicked pact with the powers of the ocean to make the already decadent city rich. The agreement is rather kinky: every night the princess takes a new sailor as a lover and places a black mask on his head. In the morning, when the song of the meadowlark is heard, the mask strangles the guy, whose body is then offered to the waves. Eventually Dahut meets her match: a haughty crimson-clad lover who persuades her to slip the key from around the neck of her sleeping father. The rake then opens the gates of Ys to the raging ocean, which swallows the city. Father and daughter escape on a magic steed, but daddy is forced to drop the princess into the sea and she drowns. In some tellings, she is then transformed into a mermaid.

Newsom saw so many parallels between this story and her own that it freaked her out. There were the themes of decadence and excess, of fathers and daughters and boundaries burst, not to mention details like the meadowlark and the heroine's underwater metamorphosis. Then Newsom stumbled across the clincher: according to Breton folklore, on calm days along the coast you can hear the sunken bell of the cathedral of Ys, tolling evermore, the same bell that sounds in Debussy's "La cathédrale engloutie." Later, as Newsom finished the fantasy novel, she stumbled across yet another uncanny echo of her own tale: a line that spoke of "that damnable bell," a direct sample, as it were, from "Sawdust & Diamonds."

"To me that seemed like the craziest coincidence," says Newsom. "It seemed like a confirmation, a chiming confirmation, that all was aa it should be." Such synchronicities had ghosted her throughout the project, as the interwoven stories of her convulsive year became even more bound together in her lyrical retelling of them. That, of course, is one of the gifts of the creative imagination: a sort of gratuitous grace that can shelter us from the gaping sky, an excess of meaning that is capable of redeeming the mess we're in without denying how fucked up it is. Many of us have sensed a secret logic working through our lives, and at first Newsom resisted it.

"I fought angrily against seeing particular types of poetic organization because it seemed awful to see my own life and these actual events in that way. But when you put forth an intention into the universe to speak a certain truth and narrate a certain period of your life, you start to see the sorts of symmetries that you are not usually supposed to be able to see until you are on your deathbed and your life flashes before your eyes. And you see exactly why everything happened. And even the most painful things you've ever been through can seem unbearably beautiful."

Rob Harvilla

SPANKMASTER AND SERVANT

On the Psycho/Genius Double Helix and XXX Appeal of Kool Keith

And now, some dating advice from Kool Keith. "The girls in New York gotta go back to the '80s, and socialism," advises Kool Keith, wearing a cream-colored cape accentuated by an enormous popped collar made from—you know, that might actually be tin foil. As though his head were a microwave pizza. Like one of those long, conelike appendages you lock around a dog's head to prevent it from licking itself. (There is, in truth, a constant danger of Kool Keith licking himself.)

Anyway, socialism. Pretty sure he doesn't mean *that* socialism. This speech is more Carl Weathers than Karl Marx. Kool Keith is onstage at the Bowery Ballroom—Saturday night, sold out, cape/conelike appendage, etc.—admonishing women for . . . something. Resisting the notion of casual sex with Kool Keith, in all likelihood. "How many girls wanna husband?" he demands, to general audience confusion. "Stop giving guys the *application*. Just *rent the room*."

Uh.

"Most guys work for UPS," Kool Keith continues. "He can't be takin' you every weekend to the Olive Garden." We laugh. The Olive Garden we understand. "To *Sizzler*." Hahahaha. "To *Applebee's*." Hahahahahahahaha.

We laugh at Kool Keith. *With* Kool Keith. *At* Kool Keith. Either way, though, sometimes we feel bad. Are we savagely mocking a deranged, profane, helpless man oblivious to his own depravity, in the style patented by Wesley Willis and, more telegenically, Flavor Flav? Or are we paying sincere homage to a fully lucid master of emotional and conceptual disguise?

The Bronx rapper is an enigma wrapped in several Day-Glo magnum condoms. You know him perhaps from 1996's *Dr. Octagonecologyst*, his alter ego Dr. Octagon's pornographic alien autopsy concept album, whose deep-space dystopian hits are held sacred by the don't-really-like-much-rap-but-I-like-this set (see "Blue Flowers") and whose skits make splendid outgoing voicemail messages. ("Oh shit there's a horse in the hospital!") Every year since, he's put out roughly 20 albums utilizing roughly 40 alternate personas (best overall concept: Black Elvis; best album cover: *Diesel Truckers*. Dig the leg warmers). His erratic behavior and scatological acumen (best title: *Spankmaster*) are as crucial to Keith's popularity as 50 Cent's bullet wounds are to his. Keith's *crazy*, you see. Every article on the guy is contractually obligated to note that he was allegedly once a Bellevue psychiatric patient; that might be bullshit, though. This year's *The Return of Dr. Octagon* is most assuredly bullshit—even favorable reviews dutifully note that this record has no remote emotional or musical connection to *Octagonecologyst* (the skits suck too), and is allegedly "unauthorized," released by a nefarious country music label that fraudulently acquired raw demos of Kool Keith raps and farmed them out to a German production team. Allegedly.

This is the sort of crap fans of this guy have to put up with. It's great. *Return of Dr. Octagon*, despite a few solid rants with regards to global warming and "All you motherfuckers tryin' to be Al Green," is not. The Bowery Ballroom crowd does not care. We're here for the stage banter. Also, to add to the uncomfortable Wesley Willis exploitation factor, we are white.

Overwhelmingly. (*How white are you?*) We're so white there's a pack of bearded dudes by the downstairs bar singing the chorus to "Brandy (You're a Fine Girl)" a cappella. "There's gonna be a Parcheesi tournament after the show—word is bond," notes magnificently dreadlocked opening act Mr. Lif, whose act gets steadily more theatrical—skits, extensive dialogue, costume changes, onstage deaths—with every show. By 2008 he'll be on Broadway. Kiki and Herb and Lif.

And Keith. After a terrible DJ interlude from longtime cohort Kutmaster Kurt, the walking microwave pizza emerges, multiple buddies in tow, and begins with a few bronzed oldies from his '80s group Ultramagnetic MCs ("Ease Back" knocks 'em dead). He moves into solo material. "Blue Flowers" takes a bow, original and remix back-to-back. And then the Richard Pryor banter starts. "Anybody out there got a drinking problem?" Keith asks. "Who got a bottle tucked under the bed right now?" Then Keith's crew hands out 10 to 20 pairs of thong underwear to random ladies in the crowd, stoking demand via onstage models who gyrate suggestively as Kutmaster Kurt cues up "Girl Let Me Touch You." As we segue into such career-spanning hits as "Spank-Master (Take Off Your Clothes)," the evening teeters on the brink of a full-blown orgy, but Keith pulls us back via more wacky banter on the subject of . . . baseball. "Who know Tom Seaver? What you know about Rod Carew? What you niggas know about Ron Guidry? Fuck you know about Vida Blue?"

The "rap" part of this rap show has more or less ground to a halt at this point—Keith indulges us with maybe 30 seconds' worth of highlights like "Backstage Passes" or (personal favorite) "Halfsharkalligatorhalfman" in between boastful interludes wherein he compares himself to *Jeopardy* champion Ken Jennings or details his writing routine: "I get me a *Yoo-Hoo*, I get a motherfuckin' *donut*, and I *get in they asses*." He interrupts the jape central to "I Don't Believe You" ("You live at home with your mom") to cut the beat and announce, "Let me elaborate." (Pregnant pause.) "A lot of people live at home with their mom." He also sells copies of one of his "rare" albums *from the stage, during the show*, for $20 a pop, noting that eBay's going price is $500. (I don't think so.) By the time his sermonizing has progressed to socialism and/or dating advice, half the crowd has left in understandable frustration and the other half is absolutely spellbound. Half the spellbound folks, in turn, probably consider him a diabolical genius, the other half a raving, hapless lunatic. At about 2:15 a.m., the show finally disintegrates. Keith announces he's going to Rio and flees the stage.

Two days later the Bowery Ballroom hosts a significantly more professional troupe: the Dears, ludicrously melodramatic Canadian indie rockers led by goth-operatic frontman Murray Lightburn (pffft), himself a nonwhite in a sea of "Brandy (You're a Fine Girl)"–lovin' whiteness ("This one's for the honkies," goes a rare bit of stage banter), battering us with arena-caliber light & sound & earnestness. Outstanding, ce. During the encore Lightburn (pffft) boasts that "We aren't hidin' shit," playing up his band's guileless, bleeding-heart honesty and chanting "We love you we love you we love you we love you" for 45 seconds or so. I'm increasingly fond of his band, but I don't believe him. I believe, however, that Kool Keith partakes of Yoo-Hoo before putting pen to paper and getting in they asses. Thus is the nature of showbiz. The sensitive, stylish rockers rip their hearts out, but we react with disbelief we're willing to suspend for a possibly mental rapper with too many aliases and backstories to count, onstage talking dirty and flinging underwear into the crowd, swaddled in a cape and a dog cone collar, concealed in costume. We just know he still ain't hidin' shit.

JODY ROSEN

G-D'S REGGAE STAR

How Matisyahu Became a Pop Phenomenon

When I first heard the Hasidic Jewish reggae vocalist Matisyahu, I assumed his was a novelty act with distinctly limited appeal, destined to cause a small sensation among *Heeb* magazine subscribers and other Jewish hipsters with an overdeveloped sense of irony and secret shtetl lust—the pangs of nostalgia that periodically cause assimilated Jews to yearn for the good old days of piety and poverty in the Russian Pale of Settlement. Anyway, silly me. Matisyahu is a hit with the *goyim*. The 26-year-old singer's 2005 album *Live at Stubb's* spent eight weeks at the top of *Billboard's* reggae chart, went gold, and continues to sell briskly. A single, "King Without a Crown," cracked the Top 40 and has made Matisyahu a mainstay on alternative-rock radio. Last week, Matisyahu released a new album, *Youth*, which seems likely to enter in the upper reaches of the Billboard 200.

In short, Matisyahu has become the most famous Hasid this side of the Baal Shem Tov, the movement's 18th-century founder. Whatever you think of the music, there's no denying the powerful novelty of the singer's shtick. The Top 40 has always been a pageant of excess, absurdity, and trans-ethnic pastiche, but there's not really a precedent for "King Without a Crown," which finds Matisyahu crooning, in a lilting pseudo-Caribbean patois, "I want *Moshiach* [the messiah] now," shouting out paeans to *"Hashem"* (Orthodox Jews' favorite term for God), and declaring "Me no want sensimilla . . . / Torah food for my brain." The video for the new single, "Play Media Youth," is like a bad *Saturday Night Live* skit come to life, with the tracksuit-clad young Hasid skanking across a Brooklyn rooftop, brown beard billowing beneath a homeboy's hoodie. What's next, an Amish boy band?

It all gets a little less surprising when you learn Matisyahu's back story. Turns out, he's a *Baal Teshuvah*, or penitent, a secular Jew who "returned" to the Orthodox fold—before he was Matisyahu, he was Matthew Miller, White Plains, N.Y., native and student at the New School University in Greenwich Village. Most tellingly, he was a dreadlocked Phish fanatic, from which we may infer that prior to discovering "Torah food," he had a rather different attitude toward sensimilla. His religious awakening occurred in college, after meeting a young Lubavitcher rabbi in Washington Square Park, where many impressionable young men have experienced spiritual epiphanies. Lubavitcher Hasidim are famous for their aggressive efforts to proselytize to non-Orthodox Jews, and Miller soon traded in jamband fandom for 21st-century shtetl life in the Lubavitcher enclave of Crown Heights, Brooklyn.

Well, you can cut off the Phish follower's dreads, put him in 18th-century garb, and immerse him in Talmudic midrash—but the pull of post-hippie music is strong. Soon Matisyahu was performing his sub-Eek-A-Mouse-style dance-hall toasting for fellow yeshiva students, and, after securing the blessing of his rabbis, he put together a backing group and started playing the jam-band-club circuit. The sonic stamp of that musical subculture is all over Matisyahu's music. Roots reggae is one of the cornerstones of Deadhead musical taste, and Matisyahu's is a deeply old fashioned roots sound, miles away from the hip-hop-derived digital futurism of today's dance-hall reggae. His band is perfectly tight, but the aesthetic is white-boy-jam-band reggae, with lots of guitar filigree, frequent show-offy solos, and a far thinner bass sound than you'll hear on any Jamaican dance-hall record. On *Youth*, producer Bill Laswell tricks out the spartan rock-trio sound with some electronic touches, but it's just window dressing.

As for Matisyahu's vocals: They're adequate. He's got rhythm—he can chant-rap double-time rhymes—and if he sometimes sings off-key, so do most dance-hall artists. But there's no getting around the phony Jamaican accent; when, in "Play Media Jerusalem," he sings "In-a de ancient days, we will return with no delay / Picking up de bounty and de spoils on our way," he sounds no less silly than Vanilla Ice did impersonating a gangsta.

The truth is, Matisyahu isn't really a novelty—his is the oldest act in the show-business book. Minstrelsy dates back to the very beginnings of American popular music, and Jews have been particularly zealous and successful practitioners of the art. From Irving Berlin's blackface ragtime numbers to Al Jolson's mammy songs—from jazz clarinetist Mezz Mezzrow, who passed as black, to Bob Dylan, who channeled the cadences of black bluesmen, to the Beastie Boys— successive generations of Jewish musicians have used the blackface mask to negotiate Jewish identity and have made some great art in the process.

Matisyahu is the latest in this line, and while his music is at best pedestrian, his minstrel routine may be the cleverest and most subtle yet. Matisyahu is like a thousand other white guys from the suburbs who've smoked a lot of dope, listened to some Burning Spear records, and decided to become reggae singers. But as a Hasid, he has a genuinely exotic look—that great big beard and the tzitzit fringes flying—and the spiritual bona fides to pull off songs steeped in Old Testament imagery. It's an ingenious variation on the archetypal

Jewish blackface routine, immortalized in *The Jazz Singer* (1927), when the immigrant striver Jolson put on blackface to cast off his Jewish patrimony and become American. In 2006, Matisyahu wears Old World "Jewface," and in so doing, becomes "black."

And there are more layers to Matisyahu's act. Musically speaking, Jewish reggae is not such a far-fetched idea; as many critics have pointed out, the plaintive minor-key melodies for which Jewish liturgical music (and Hasidic folksongs) are renowned are also staples of reggae. What's more, Matisyahu's appropriation of Jamaican music is really no more brazen than Rastafarians' appropriation of Jewish religious tropes. If a Caribbean islander can plunder Jewish scripture and call himself a lost tribesman of Israel, why can't a Jew sing a song to a one-drop beat in a phony patois? Lubavitcher Hasidim even have their very own Hallie Selassie-like demigod, the late Rebbe Menachem Mendel Schneerson, who many Lubavitchers regard as *Moshiach* himself.

And yet, despite the copious "*Hashems*" and what is undoubtedly the first reference to "*treyf* wine" ever to appear on a Top 40 album, there is very little distinctly Jewish content on *Youth*. The only invocation of the idea of Jewish nationhood—Judaism's organizing principle—comes in "Jerusalem," a nonsensical riff on the Bible's most beautiful poem of exile, the 137th Psalm.

In fact, *Youth* has a lot more in common with a couple of other contemporary American religiosities. The album is soaked in therapeutic language: it's more Oprah than Torah. "Young man—the power's in your hands . . . / Storm the halls of vanity, focus your energy," Matisyahu sings in the title track. That emphasis on self-actualization and uplift, combined with Matisyahu's ceaseless diatribes about the moral impurity of secular life, is reminiscent of nothing so much as Christian rock. It's a reminder that Orthodox Jewish fundamentalists share a lot with their Christian counterparts, including political priorities—and that there's no one quite so beloved of the

Left Behind crowd these days than Orthodox Jews, whose in-gathering in Israel is essential stage setting for the coming of the Rapture. As if to make explicit the burgeoning alliance, Matisyahu recently recorded "Play Media Roots in Stereo," a duet with evangelical rap-rockers P.O.D. It's a cruddy piece of music and, as politics, it can't be good for the Jews.

STRAIGHT OUTTA ISRAEL

Yoav Eliasi is getting lost in the Nickelodeon studios parking lot. He circles the lot in his black, suped-up SUV, looking for the back entrance to the studio set, and he is already ten minutes late. "It's OK," says Eliasi, "we are operating on Israeli time. Being late is like being on time."

"Why don't we park in front and then ask someone where to go?" I suggest.

"That would be suicide," retorts Eliasi. "If we went through the front, we would never make it in." In the next moment, I begin to grasp what he means. As we drive alongside a group of Israeli children, I am reminded of the black-and-white footage of The Beatles arriving for the first time in America. Girls begin shrieking for the man of their dreams, while the boys bang on the car and point imposingly. Eliasi is noticeably happy with this feverish reaction. After all, just a few years ago, he was a nobody—an ex-soldier with a passion for hip-hop. Now, Eliasi, who raps under the name Hatzel ("the

Shadow"), and his partner, Kobi Shimon, aka Subliminal, are two of the most popular musicians in Israel today.

Fans know their strong, right-wing lyrics by heart and apathetic youth across the land are now taking great pride in their Jewish heritage, thanks to the duo's pro-Israeli message.

"Oh, shit," says Hatzel, with a sense of relief, as we view the children frantically chasing the car in the rear view mirror. "I will never, ever get used to that."

A major cultural transformation is taking place in Israel, a small country known for its sentimental folk music and patriotic sing-alongs. Teens who once sat around campfires singing about sowing the land with almond-bearing trees are now hanging out on street corners, rapping about the kind of hoes not necessarily used for harvesting crops. When it comes to role models, the older generation speaks about Moshe Dayan, David Ben-Gurion, and Golda Meir. But ask the more progressive youths and they speak with great reverence of Tupac, DMX, and Jay-Z.

"They're living like they're in America," says Shlomo, who makes his living driving a cab. (There's a long-standing truism in Israel that if you want to know the direction in which the country is heading, ask a taxi driver.) "These kids are naive for thinking about a future in this rapping business, when there is no market for it. But I also have never seen anything become this popular in this country before. It makes sense though. Israelis love to talk a lot, and rapping is like talking, no?"

"Rapping is the language of the streets," says controversial underground rapper Rocky B. "And the government is no longer representing us, so we have to express our opinions this way." Rocky B, whose real name is Roi Assayag, is a lanky 26-year-old, with an impressively fluffy afro and a permanently glazed-over look. He is wearing baggy clothing, outdated glasses, and a mischievously goofy smile.

"Welcome to the ghetto," he says, as we walk up the poorly lit stairs into his Jerusalem apartment. A lone refrigerator stands in the hallway. "Excuse the mess," he says. "We don't clean that much."

Calling his home "a mess" is an understatement. Clothes are haphazardly strewn about and dirty bowls are resting in random places, some filled with cigarette butts. Rocky then introduces me to his deejay, Walter the Einstein Frog, real name Itay Drai. At 21, he sports a similar afro and sits lazily in his chair, as if a hint of wind could blow him over.

Rocky B is very proud of his potent lyrical content, but he beams with true accomplishment when we talk about Miklat, Hebrew for "shelter," a frequent gathering at a dingy Jerusalem bar that brings together Palestinian, Israeli (like Israel's first-recorded rapper, Sagol 59), American, and Russian rappers for a United Nations of hip-hop.

"The capitalization of this state . . . Arabs and Jews throwing rocks at each other in the streets . . . I needed to wake up, man," says Rocky B. "I found a book about the Black Panther movement in Israel. I saw then and I saw now, and decided that I was a Black Panther. We are in a state of emergency." With his new frame of mind, Rocky B then hooked up with a local deejay named Caress and put on a hip-hop show called "Car Bomb." Some reacted with horror and disdain, especially in a hostile environment where deadly car bombs are not uncommon.

"Of course people reacted negatively," says Rocky, "but I'm a terrorist. A lyrical terrorist just like Chuck D." This anti-establishment rapper's beliefs revolve around a distinction that is gaining popularity in Israel. It is ironic that a state once founded as a haven for Jews is becoming a refuge from Judaism. "Look, I do not see myself as a Jew. I am an Israeli," he says. "I am tired of this militant bullshit. I am tired of motherfuckers talking about being Jewish and shouting, 'Fuck Arabs!' like Subliminal and his crew."

"But isn't this emergence of Israeli Jewish pride just a different form of Black Power," I ask?

"There is a big difference because Black Power came from a movement of the underdog," says Walter the Einstein Frog. "And we are not the underdogs now. A guy like Subliminal says he is keeping it real, but he's not."

"I see a great deal of hypocrisy from the Jews here because we are making our own Holocaust," says Rocky, sounding genuinely annoyed. "But it is a slow Holocaust against the Palestinians."

I take note of the contradiction. Moments ago, Rocky spurned the yoke of religious affiliation. Now he uses "we," grouping himself with "the Jews." Appropriately enough, Rocky B's most lyrically powerful song on his album is called "Enemy." The first verse's narrative tells the listener that, *"I am the enemy of myself,"* and then ends with this rebuke: *"We are the enemies of ourselves."*

"But do you love being here?" I inquire. "You sound so frustrated and tired."

"Shit, yeah. This is my land. There is so much diversity here in Jerusalem. But to make connections in Israel between the ghettos is so hard. Hip-hop unites us and that is why it's getting so popular today."

Although Subliminal may consider himself a thug, his grandmother answers the door at his home when visitors come to meet him. I walk into Subliminal's house, which is in a quaint Tel Aviv neighborhood, and see nothing indicative of a rap impresario's lifestyle. If this were an episode of MTV's *Cribs*, it would be a very short segment—there is only so much one can say about the only ostentatious item in the room: a massive fish tank.

Subliminal's grandmother calls up to him, as if we are children meeting for a play date. I make conversation with the elderly woman, but my Hebrew is not that great and she doesn't seem interested. Hatzel slumps down the stairs to say that Subliminal is waiting in his studio. I follow Hatzel and recall his opponents' mudslinging directed at Subliminal for his wealthy family and their comfortable way of life. But I can't help considering this environment middle-class. The décor is unintentionally retro—an eighties aesthetic—with a pastel palette and unrestrained use of mirrors.

I am introduced to Subliminal and I suddenly understand why he is the envy of many, and the inspiration for more. He is tall but not intimidating. He smiles like a trustworthy car salesman (if there is such a thing), heartily and warmly. His perfectly trimmed goatee is precise in its angles and design. Like Hatzel, Subliminal wears baggy streetwear that boasts a brand name (Reebok is a sponsor), but unlike his sidekick's propensity for black, Subliminal chooses lighter colors like whites and powder blues, which makes for his good-cop image, in distinction to Hatzel's bad cop.

In his impeccable, nearly accentless English, Subliminal excuses the small, cramped studio that was once a bedroom. As I peruse his CD collection, noticing mostly commercial rap and some metal-rap hybrids like Biohazard and Body Count, Subliminal tells me how he met the Shadow.

"I was the freak in my side of town and Yoav was the freak in his side of town," says Subliminal. "We would go to the same clubs and just started hanging out."

"Yeah, but I'm from the bad side," interjects Hatzel. "I'm from the 'hood."

Haztel grew up in a very hard neighborhood in South Tel Aviv, where his father was shot dead while Haztel's two younger siblings watched. Furthermore, he had been kicked out of more schools than he could remember for being a juvenile delinquent and causing "a shitload of trouble." Hatzel jokes that he was a very confused child, and, at one point, even sported long, green hair.

They regale me with tales of "back in the day," when they were innovators and rebels creating their own sense of self and style. Initially, the pair made their own clothes because baggy clothing was not yet available in Israel. Subliminal insists that he thought he had invented "baggies" and only discovered otherwise when he visited England, as a teen. Slowly but surely, as others replicated their image, it became easier to identify other fellow outcasts.

When Subliminal was 15, he rallied these self-proclaimed pariahs and organized a crew called T.A.C.T. (Tel Aviv City Team), and together, they opened The Joint, a local club. At the time, no one knew Subliminal's age, not even his 27-year-old girlfriend. Months later, The Joint was burned down.

"We always had the hottest party in town," jokes Subliminal.

"The roof, the roof, the roof is on fire," chants Shadow.

Eventually, the T.A.C.T. crew emulated their American heroes and recorded music. They constructed a makeshift studio in the back of a clothing store and wrote their first song, "Yisroelim Atzbanim," or "Mad Israelis."

"This was the cornerstone of Israeli rap," says Subliminal. "We started the game. We were living in a gangsta paradise movie. We had our own club. We got into fights every day. We were hard-core." It's hard to imagine Subliminal this way, when moments ago his grandmother answered the door. Hatzel, on the other hand, emits a subtle aggression, like a faint scent only a dog could pick up.

"I used to be a base commander in the army," says Hatzel, with great pride. "I served for five years as the youngest base commander in Israel. I loved the army. I had a rough childhood and they fixed me up. The army taught me discipline, they taught me about responsibility."

I make a joke about how he'd have to kill me if he told me where he served while in the military.

"Maybe," he says. His expression is a serious one, so I drop the subject.

"Hip-hop is the greatest weapon you can have to tell our message," says Subliminal, whose flowing conviction and passion in being "street" is, according to his detractors, one of the greatest marketing acts in the history of great Israeli salesmen (of which there are many). "I love my religion and my tradition. I love Hanukkah and lighting the candles. This is my tradition, and this is who I am."

"He's a little bit religious, while I am not at all," says Hatzel. "This is why he is the light and I am the Shadow. But we do have one thing in common: we believe that this is the one place on earth for the Jews. And when I put down the gun, I picked up the mic to say that."

"And we're so tired of the left media calling us 'fascists,'" says Subliminal. "People confuse our message and say, 'Death to the Arabs.' One kid at a show was chanting, 'Death to the Arabs.' And I said to him . . . I stopped the show and I said, 'No, fuck you. Not 'Death to the Arabs,' but 'Life to the Jews.'"

Two years ago, Israeli filmmaker Anat Halachmi made a ninety-minute film called *Channels of Rage,* a documentary project that chronicles three years in the lives of Subliminal and his friends, as they grew from rambunctious ruffians into superstars. Sharing the focus of the film is Tamer Nafar, an extraordinary young man who was once Subliminal's close friend. Growing tensions led to a broken friendship, and the two men no longer speak. Subliminal claims that Nafar's nationality has nothing to do with it, but the documentary says otherwise. Not only is Nafar a fellow rapper, but he is also arguably the most popular Arab-language rapper alive today.

I take a taxi to Nafar's house in Lod, on the outskirts of Tel Aviv. The majority of the residents here are Israeli Arabs, or, as they now defiantly call themselves, "'48 Palestinians." The buildings in the neighborhood are crumbling and morose. Nafar tells me that his house is very hard to find so he will meet me at the gates of his complex. As we near our destination, I become progressively more nervous. As a fair-skinned Jew from New York, with an obviously Jewish name, I have reason for concern.

Yossi, the taxi driver, is a healthy-looking man in his fifties, with salt-and-pepper hair and a permanent smirk. I ask him his opinion on the *matzav*, the situation. "I have five kids," he says, "and there's not a minute in the day that I don't wonder where they are. Imagine living with this anxiety."

I tell him that I'm sure things will get better before they get worse. This is a line I toss off, knowing I cannot ensure its validity.

"We are seven people in my family," says Yossi, his smile disappearing for the first time. "And every one of us has been to one or more funeral this year. If it does not get better, then I fear my children will get used to death."

The cab arrives and I spot Nafar. He has an athletic build, not too skinny but not too muscular. His face is wise and looks older than the age of the person wearing it. With a constantly furrowed brow, Tamer gives the impression that he is meditating on the words about to leave his mouth. His nondescript clothing—a baggy, plain-white T-shirt and loose blue sweat pants—lack the brand names that seem to come with the style of hip-hop. His voice is relaxed and he has a delivery that comes with the confidence of "speaking the truth."

In the living room, Nafar's mother sits with her daughter, watching TV, as they enjoy dipping pita in the drippy yolk of eggs sunnyside-up. The women barely notice us as he makes introductions. They are too engrossed in the game show.

Nafar's room is bleak and depressing—very little natural light enters the bedroom, and if I believed in feng shui this room would have "bad vibe" written all over it. Posters of hardcore rappers paper the walls. A large poster of Tupac Shakur lurches over Nafar's bed and one of Notorious B.I.G. adorns his brother's wall (they share the room).

"Over here," Nafar says, "there is not east and west. We love them both." Nafar introduces me to his best friend and fellow rapper Mahmoud Jrere, who looks like an adolescent in need of a nap, with his half-closed eyes and puffy, hairless cheeks. Together with Nafar's brother, Suhell, the trio makes up the Arabic rap group D.A.M. Jrere explains that the initials stand for "Da Arabic MCs," then astutely points out that the word *"dam"* means both "eternity" in Arabic, and "blood" in Hebrew.

"We are all Palestinians. I just happen to be living in Israel," says Nafar.

"What do you want from Israel?" I ask.

"What I want? What I want?" says Nafar, leaning forward. "Hmm . . . well, let's say you have an Arab who is a lawyer. You have a Jew who is homeless. That Jew can be anything he wants. That Arab lawyer has already reached his limits. It's over for him. When people say, 'Death to the Arabs,' you Westerners say that's racism. Fuck that. That's not racism. I'm talking about deeper racism. I'm not talking about occupied settlements, I'm talking about occupied spirits. Our souls are occupied."

I notice that while I am strictly discussing the conflict between Arabs and Israelis, Jrere and Nafar talk about Palestinians and Jews.

"I hate that the Jews are ignorant about our people and our culture," says Jrere. "The Jews say that no one was here before they took over the land, but that's ignorant. My family has a 500-year history in Lod. Even if we ever do have a Palestinian state, we wouldn't move there.

"And Arabs outside of Palestine resent us. They think we're Arab Jews, that we're taking the Israeli identity. It's in our song, all the world is treating us as Israelis and Israel is treating us as Palestinians."

"Doesn't that limbo dishearten you?" I ask.

"That's the problem with you guys," Nafar says, identifying me as just another one of his oppressors. "You think we'll stop, but we use this as fuel. We have so much to say, we want to keep going. The second I have nothing to say, we talk about bling bling, and then it's pointless."

I bring up his old friend Subliminal and the documentary, and Nafar becomes noticeably uncomfortable.

"The movie is about how we started off as friends—we never were friends—and then how we became enemies," says Nafar. "But his music is commercial shit. He raps about the streets and then he makes commercials on TV for hot chocolate. He's a commercial. He's the P. Diddy of our land. He's a businessman."

We all begin to smoke apple-flavored tobacco from a *nagila*, or water pipe. After I take a puff, I notice that they seem to be more at ease. We joke about women (they don't have girlfriends), marijuana (they don't smoke), and movies (*Romeo Must Die* is a classic). The nagila, in a sense, becomes our peace pipe.

"Unlike Subliminal, we don't care about the big houses, the cars," says Jrere. "We want a coup. We are going through the same racism here in Israel that the blacks went through in the sixties."

"But this is not like the days of Che Guevara, Martin Luther King, or Malcolm X," adds Nafar, holding up *The Autobiography of Malcolm X*. "Racism was more blatant then. It's become much more sophisticated than making us sit in back of the bus." Nafar then plays a song called "Who Is the Real Terrorist?" and asks if it is the one who fights to get more land, or the one who fights for freedom? The most controversial line is "You rape the Arab soul and it got pregnant / Giving birth to a baby called suicide bombers." Jrere's favorite line from the song is "I am not against peace / Peace is against me."

Nafar stares at me squarely in the eyes. "Look, we are here to clear the ignorance. We are going to use beats until our hearts stop beating." He comes up with rehearsed-sounding lines like this all the time.

Nafar and Jrere want to show me around the neighborhood, so we take a walk around the bleak, poverty-stricken community. Children shyly approach Nafar to slap him five, or they wave enthusiastically from a distance, too shy to disturb their local hero. On a smaller scale, this is like the reception Hatzel and Subliminal received in the Nickelodeon parking lot.

"You're a celebrity here," I say.

"Well yeah," Nafar responds, smiling proudly. "I speak for them. I'm their voice."

Inside Nickelodeon's studios, I can hardly hear Subliminal and Hatzel's performance because the crowd's shouting drowns everything else out. All the while, the two Israeli superstars beam with satisfaction, arbitrarily pointing to random members of the audience, which inspires even more screaming. I leave the room because the noise is both deafening and overwhelming.

"How was that for a performance?" boasts Subliminal, as he wipes the sweat from his face with a towel.

I tell him that I'm impressed. And, in truth, I really am.

"In ten years," says a solemn Subliminal, "All those kids will probably be in the army fighting for our country. That's a sad thought to consider and I think about that every time I perform for them.

"But if I'm reaching them at a young age and inspiring them to be proud of their country, to truly love this land, then I'm doing my job. Hopefully, we won't need the army then, but realistically, with the way things are now, we probably will."

Jack Erwin, Sean A. Malcolm, Andréa Duncan-Mao, Adam Matthews, Justin Monroe, Anselm Samuel, Vanessa Satten

TOLD YOU SO

THE MAKING OF *REASONABLE DOUBT*

At first, people didn't believe.

Raised by a single mother in Brooklyn's rough Marcy projects, Shawn "Jay-Z" Carter hit the streets as a teenager and made money, a lot of money, selling drugs. But what he really wanted was a rap career. He hooked up with The Jaz (later Jaz-O), a local artist who had a deal with EMI Records, and cut guest appearances with the likes of Original Flavor and Big Daddy Kane. He made a demo tape and shopped around for a deal of his own, but labels weren't biting.

Never short on confidence, Jay got with fellow hustlers Damon Dash and Kareem "Biggs" Burke, and, using capital saved from the streets, founded a label, Roc-A-Fella Records, and set to work on a debut album. Recorded at the storied D&D Studios in Manhattan, with production from DJ Premier, Clark Kent, Ski, Jaz, Peter Panic and Irv Gotti, *Reasonable Doubt* was released June 25, 1996, through a distribution deal with Priority Records. The album didn't set the world on fire right away. It sold just 420,000 copies its first year out, peaking at No. 23 on *Billboard*'s album chart, and wasn't certified platinum 'til 2002. Nevertheless, it announced the arrival of Jay-Hova, the God MC, and its moments—"Dead Presidents," with the Nas sample that would play so prominently in the greatest rap battle of all time; "Brooklyn's Finest," where Jay trades verses with the Notorious B.I.G.; and the hit single "Ain't No Nigga," which turned a 16-year-old Foxy Brown into a household name—loom ever larger with the passage of time.

Jay's made seven more albums since, and sold over 20 million copies of them. A lot has changed. He and Jaz-O had a falling out, with back-and-forth snipes over credit and loyalty. Roc-A-Fella grew to be an empire, of course, one that would eventually span music, fashion, movies and liquor. Last year, Jay split from Dame and Biggs and took over Def Jam Records—and kept the Roc-A-Fella name for himself. People believe now.

On this 10th anniversary, *XXL* pays homage, revisiting the creation of a classic with those who were there.

—JUSTIN MONROE

1

"Can't Knock the Hustle"
(Feat. Mary J. Blige)
Produced by Knowbody
Coproduced by Sean Cane and Dahoud

KNOWBODY: I made the beat at my mama's house. It was probably like '94. You know, Dame lived in 1199, which is right across the street from where I lived at. I know there was air [in the mix] and everything. I want to go back to doing beats like that.

The whole time after we gave Dame the beat and after he picked it, from then on we called like every week like, "What's up? Can you find out what's up?" They'd be like, "He's writing." So I don't know if he was actually writing. Dame just told me, "Quit calling me."

SEAN CANE: I remember thinking if they really wanted to keep the beat. I remember I kept calling Dame. He was like, "Nah, he's writing to it." I don't know if it was just being that they were trying to stall, but they just kept saying, "He's writing to it. Getting Mary." We was excited. Before we got Mary, we put Veronica on it to reference the song. Veronica, the Spanish singer, she was on Hola Records. Mary came in the day of the mix to do her vocals. She just really came in to do her part.

When Jay went in to do the clean vocals, I was like, "I think you messed up on this one. I think you could do this part here [again]." I forgot whether it was on the "nigga" or the "player." I was like, "I think that part you could say it a little better." He was like, "Play it back." He's like, "You're wildin'." That was in Platinum Island. That's where it was mixed at. But it was recorded at D&D, where they paid niggas with the shoe box of money. It was either fives or ones. It was ones. We had to count it. Jay and Dame, they came with the shoe box of money. Their whole shit, coming with the logo, they was hungry. They was grinding. We sat at the studio with the shoe box of money, and it was three people counting the money. It wasn't a lot. It was less than 10 Gs, put it like that. That same day is the day they brought in the Roc-A-Fella logo. They came in with the Roc-A-Fella logo, and were showing it to Jay like, "Yo, what you think about this for the logo?"

2

"Politics As Usual"
Produced by Ski

SKI: I was riding in the car with my baby's mama. I had it on the oldies-but-goodies station, and I hear "Hurry Up This Way Again" by the Stylistics. I said, "Yo, this shit is crazy. If I sample this here, and chop it up right and let Jay hear it, he got to hear that shit and love it." That same day, she took me to the old record store, and I took it home that night and chopped it up and played it for Jay the next day. He was going crazy for it. A funny thing is, at the same time, Clark actually found the sample too and did it. But I think the one I did was just a tad bit hotter. No disrespect to Clark, the one I did was just a tad bit hotter. That's one of my favorite records to this day. I think that was the blueprint to what Kanye and Just are doing now, the whole soulful voice thing.

Jay was quick with the verses. Back then, he might have wrote two verses down on paper, but he never really wrote it down. I would sometimes glance down and see three words on his paper, but the nigga doing a whole song. I'm like, What's he rapping from?

When I got paid for these records on *Reasonable Doubt* I used to go to Dame's crib, and I remember them giving me a book bag just full of money. I used to just get on the train. If niggas knew I had thousands of dollars in a backpack . . .

CLARK KENT: It's crazy, 'cause the same day that Ski brought him that beat, I brought him the same beat like an hour later. Jay was like, "Dag, I think yours is a little better." 'Cause mines was pretty sounding, because I made it big and very clear. But Jay was like, "You know how we do it, and real is real. He gave it to me first." So he did his version instead of doing my version of the same thing.

Me being a music business guy, I was like, "Which one's better?" He was like, "Clark, that's not right to switch one. He came first. And Ski is our boy." So that's how it was. And not for nothing, it was no love lost, 'cause Ski is my nigga. So I was just like, "Go ahead, do it. You're right." That's the way we are. I don't even know if Ski knows it went down like this.

LENNY SANTIAGO: I remember Ski was doing a group—I don't know if this is supposed to be out there, but whatever—he was doing Camp Lo. That was his group. He was very heavily involved with them. And actually, one or two of the songs were Camp Lo's. "Feelin' It" and "Politics As Usual." I'm almost positive those were Camp Lo's. And Jay ended up hearing them, and was like, "Oh no, no, no. I *need* that." No disrespect to them, but he just felt it so much, and he recorded it, and it ended up being his record.

3

"Brooklyn's Finest"
(Feat. Notorious B.I.G.)
Produced by Clark Kent

IRV GOTTI: I did not want that record to happen. I was adamantly against it. I would call Jay every day like, "No, fuck that! Don't do this record." I said, "What I'm scared of is you doin' [a record] with Biggie and you comin' off like his little man. And nigga, we can't be owning *shit* if you his little man. You never gon' get that throne." But this nigga would call me and be like, "Nah, but Gotti, I'm tellin' you, I'm gonna show 'em. I'm gon' make people see that I'm that nigga."

Jay and Big had a lot of love, but at that particular time it was very competitive. Go 'head and listen to that record—"It's time to separate the pros from the cons / The platinum from the bronze . . . " Real talk, Big's goin' at Jay in that record. "You ain't harmin' me / So pardon me . . . " Trust me. He's goin' at him real tough.

LENNY SANTIAGO: I was doing promotion at the time, and we were at the video shoot for "Dead Presidents." If you remember, Biggie was in the video. And it was during a break, Damon was being Damon, and everyone was around talking—Jay, Big, Lil' Cease, D. Roc—and Damon approached Biggie, like, "What's up with that record? You gonna do something with Jay?" And Big was like, "Whatever, nigga. I'm waitin' on y'all. Whatchu sayin'?" Dame was like, "I'm sayin', though, we could do it right now." At the time, Jay was comin' up and Big was the shit. He had the biggest record out, Puff was doing his thing, and Bad Boy was on fire. So Dame was trying to put him to the test. And they kept going back and forth, and Big was like, "Man, listen, whatever, anytime, anywhere." So Dame called Clark Kent like, "I got Big right here, he wants to do that record with Jay, whatever, whatever." So that same night, they ended up recording the record. And Clark did the track, and it was a classic. It was just funny how it happened from being put on the spot.

BIGGS: Biggie came to the video for "Dead Presidents," and he was saying how much he liked Jay, the whole style. Dame was talking about it, and said, "Do a record tomorrow." Him and Dame was drinking. They drank like five bottles of Cristal, shot for shot. Dame threw up outside. Dame had told Biggie to call the next day at five o'clock. I remember being in the office, and at five o'clock the phone rings. We went to the studio, and we spoke to him. We had a date, and they went in and recorded. It was funny, 'cause they came in with a pad, and Jay pushed the pad to Biggie. They're both looking at the pad like, Go ahead, you take it. No, you take it. That's when they found out that both of them didn't write.

That day we went in, I think Jay laid down his whole part. Biggie lay down like a line or two, then he said he couldn't finish, he had to go home and finish it. We had Biggie come and smoke 60 blunts. But he came back and laid down a little bit more, left again, and then he came back and finished it. We had fun the first [session]. Afterward, we all went to see Bernie Mac at Radio City Music Hall.

DAME DASH: We didn't do all of "Brooklyn's Finest" in D&D. We had to come back to it, 'cause that didn't have a hook. Me and Clark Kent had to make up a hook. We had to hand it in like the next day. Me and Clark and Biggs was in the studio, then Biggs left, and we finally got it, me and Clark Kent. Clark was trying to get me on the hook. We took a rhyme from the song, "Jay-Z and Biggie Smalls, nigga, shit your drawers . . . ," and he was trying to get me to say it. I was like, "I'm not gonna do it." I got Clark to do it.

CLARK KENT: I just freshly came off of tour with Big. We were doing Junior M.A.F.I.A.'s [debut album], and he heard the beat and went crazy. He was like, "I want the beat." I was like, "Nah, it's Jay's beat." He's like, "You're always giving this guy everything." He wanted that beat real bad. I'm leaving the studio to go to D&D to track it for Jay, and Big's like, "Yo, I want to be on that record." So I was like, "Yo, just come with me." So I went upstairs, and I left him downstairs. I was like, "Big wants to be on that record. Why don't you put Big on that record? He heard the beat. He likes it." Jay was like, "I don't really know him like that." And Dame was like, "I ain't paying him, neither," I was just like, Ah, okay. So then I'm like, "If I get him to do it for free would you do it?" He was like, "Yeah, we'll try it." So I run downstairs. I go get Big, bring him upstairs, and they met each other the right way, properly. And everybody was like, "Well, if you're going to do it for whatever . . . " Jay changed the verses around right there, and was like, "This is where you go, right there. You ready?" Big was like, "I can't do this right now!"

Two months later, Big came back with his verses. Days later, I was mixing it, and there was no hook. We were supposed to do the hook when we were mixing it. And Jay says, "All right, you got to scratch something." I'm trying to find things to scratch and nothing's working. So I'm telling Jay, "Yo, y'all gotta come up with a hook." Jay and Big are there. We're at Giant Studios. Big goes, "I'll be back, I'm going to the store." And then an hour goes by, and he doesn't go back. Then Jay goes, "I'll be back." They leave me there and never come back. So it's like three in the morning, I decided to write a hook, and I performed the hook. That's my voice.

To me, that's the best collabo I've ever heard. You would never think that Jay's verses were done so far in advance. It feels like they did it together. Big and Jay were that talented, they could pick up on that line and go from that line.

I'd made the beat before for one of Damon's groups. He had a group called the Future Sound, and I remixed the record with the same beat. And Damon said, "Yo, that beat is hot, give it to Jay." So he says he produced it because he said give it to Jay. How ridiculous is that? But whatever, it's all good. And then the other day he told me I jerked him because I didn't give him publishing.

4

"Dead Presidents II"
Produced by Ski

SKI: When I first found the sample and I threw the Nas thing in there, I liked the record a lot. But it wasn't my favorite record. I really loved it after Jay got on it. That's what made me a fan of "Dead Presidents." It was an old jazz sample, Lonnie Liston Smith ["A Garden of Peace"]. And Nas ["The World Is Yours (Remix)"]. When Nas was hot at the time, Nas' voice was crazy. And when Jay threw in the lyrics, the first verse, the way he came on was bananas.

CLARK KENT: I heard the second version when I was on the road with Big. I was playing "Dead Presidents" over and over again. The first and the second one. I was like, "Big, my boy rap better than you." And he was sick, 'cause I kept telling him. Everybody was mad at me. On the bus, I was like the alien for even trying it. But after Big heard that, this is before they met to do "Brooklyn's Finest," he was like, "Clark, that dude got it. He got it. He got it." That let me know that I wasn't crazy.

5

"Feelin' It"
(Feat. Mecca)
Produced by Ski

SKI: It was me and Geechi Suede from Camp Lo, it was my hook and everything. Jay heard it and was like, "I want that record. I don't care what you do, I want that record." I didn't want to give it to him, but I had to because I knew he was going to be the man at the time. So I said, "Fuck it, take the record." It really was me and Suede from Camp Lo, the flow and everything, the way he was flowing on it. That's the way we was flowing on it. So he just took the whole thing. But you know, he killed it in his own way.

6

"D'Evils"
Produced by DJ Premier

DAME DASH: It was important that we had Premier. I had to chase Premier for a while. He called while I was on the highway going to Baltimore. I negotiated it. Premier, he kinda liked the way I got out of the Payday deal. He was like, "I like the way you laid that down." He liked Jay as a rapper, so he said, "I'll give you a certain amount of beats for a certain amount of money." And he made all those beats specifically for Jay.

DJ PREMIER: At the time, I was working at WBLS doing a hip-hop show every Friday from 8 to 10. Jay had given me a copy of his 12-inch for "In My Lifetime." And being that Jay had been around doing stuff for Jaz and Kane and everybody else, prior to doing his own thing, it was just like a no-brainer.

I was charging him $4,000 a track. I was already making 30 grand a song, which was a lot at that time. Being that Jay was so-called family, just on the respect note of what he'd done in the past, it was nothing. I knew they was building a house, and I had no problem with helping out.

Jay gave me the whole idea of what he wanted. He even gave me the scratch ideas. Once he described it, I'm very good at fitting the description of how he wanted the record to sound. When a song is described to me, I always put the DJ and the fan mentally into the direction of the track. Jay has always been real direct with what he wants. The description he gave to me, I totally painted that. I just put it down right off the top of the head up at D&D. Jay came in, heard the beat, and went in and knocked it out.

Jay is one of the few who don't like to listen to my opinion. But when we did "D'Evils," I was able to get him to go in there. 'Cause he's the type who is like, "Yo, it's right." I'm like, "Nah, you could fix this line." He's like, "Nah, it's good." You're like, "Dawg, it could be better." And then after a few minutes there's a little silence, and I'm like, "All right. It's your record, if you say so . . . " And then he'd be like, "I'll go back and fix it."

7

"22 Two's"
Produced by Ski

DAME: Mad Wednesdays. That's where we used to go perform a lot, Mary Davis' joint. "22 Two's" was like the crowd winner. There was never a beat with that. That's some shit he would perform that would kill the crowd every fuckin' time. Originally, the skit was supposed to be like a trial, but for some reason we couldn't execute that plan. The concept of *Reasonable Doubt* came from Jay. He was supposed to be on trial, like Jay's the illest beyond a reasonable doubt. To be convicted of something, you've got to prove it. If you listen to the skit, she says, "I know you got your trials . . . " She's supposed to be saying he's about to beat the trial. But we couldn't do it, 'cause Jay wouldn't come in and do the skits.

CLARK KENT: "22 Two's" was a freestyle that we used to perform at the same club like every other week . . . He did his thing where he kept using the number two in the rhyme. "Too much West Coast dick-lickin', doin' your best Jay-Z rendition . . . " You would see people counting how many twos he said. And if you listen to the rhyme, 22 times he says the word "two," so it's "22 Two's."

8

"Can I Live"
Produced by DJ Irv

IRV GOTTI: I caught [the idea for the sample] off the movie *Dead Presidents*. I was watchin' it. And you know the part when it comes on, and they drivin', and it goes [*mimics the beat from Isaac Hayes' "The Look of Love"*] "dun-dun-dah-duuuu . . . " If you look at *Dead Presidents*, the energy of that track, you can just feel the realness all over the track. So I gave Jay the "Can I Live" record, 'cause to me, it was like some real gangsta shit. I was just like, "Dive into it and do that shit that you do. Talk about the nigga you are and who these niggas ain't. Fuck rap. Shit, talk about the life." Like, Yo, nigga, you the illest nigga. Fuck the rap shit! You the nigga who really got all this money.

Jay actually wanted Nas on it. He just did one verse, and we was leavin' the second verse for Nas. But the Nas thing didn't happen. So we came back in, and he did the second verse. But you know, like most Jay records, it don't take him no time. You know what I'm sayin', it don't take him no time, and he spits that shit.

DAME DASH: Jay wrote the second verse of "Can I Live," but the rest [of the album] was memorized. We'd just be in the studio, talking fly shit, things that we was doing at the time, and Jay would come and make a rhyme, make a song of it real quick. Biggs came up with that line, "We don't lease, we buy the whole car." It was like a collaboration. At the time, Jay was like the ambassador of our life, of our movement. He was the spokesperson for everything that we were doing.

9

"Ain't No Nigga"
(Feat. Foxy Brown)
Produced by Big Jaz

DAME DASH: Jay was the one who hooked up "Ain't No Nigga" and brought Foxy in. That was Jay all day. Jay came up with the beat [a sample of "Seven Minutes of Funk" by the Whole Darn Family], and Jaz put it together. I remember I was at a club, and Jay called me like, "Come over here. I just made a hit record."

   I had to chase the fuckin' dude around forever [to get the sample cleared]. I had to talk to the dude personally. I think somebody had jerked him or something.

CLARK KENT: Everybody might have tried to loop the beat, but the only person to successfully do it was Jaz, because there was no drums on it. The way Jay wanted the intro to go, it had to go like that, for the beat to loop the way it did. Because there's no kick on the one, it's a little offbeat, and Jaz-O was the successful one. It was just everybody had a problem trying to make it, but Jaz-O was the one who made it right. It was offbeat because of the way that it started, but it's not offbeat the rest of the record.

A girl needed to be on that record. And if I remember, the girl who was going on the record was a chick named Black Widow. She was from the Bronx. She's actually on a Jay record that didn't get on the album. Anyway, she was supposed to be a rapper, and she was going to be—we just needed a girl's voice for the record. But Foxy's my cousin, so I was like, "I want my cousin." So I go to Brooklyn, and I get my cousin. And I'm like, "We're going to the studio right now, and we're going to be on this record." That's the way it went down.

JAZ-O: It was actually impossible to loop without hearing obvious flaws. So for the hundredth time—and, maybe for somebody hearing it for the first time, I will clear it up for them: I did produce that song. It was Jay-Z's idea to use "Seven Minutes of Funk," but he did not—and no one else did—put that beat together. Nor did they figure out the correct way and the correct pitch and the note to perform the hook on the song, which I performed along with a young lady named Khadijah Bass. Preemo and Clark Kent had tried it, and they had negative results. They both came to me saying, "We tried it, we couldn't do it." That has nothing to do with their production prowess, it's just, I'm a special case.

I had to chop it up into seven different pieces instead of actually making a sequence within the [Akai] MPC 3000. I chopped it up, and knew exactly where everything went. And I actually hit the drum pads for the whole five minutes. I hit the pads on beat for like six minutes. And when you hear the song, that's what's going on. There's no SMPTE [time code], there is none of that shit. It's just me, perfect timing, hitting everything when I'm supposed to hit it. I remember Busta Rhymes even coming to me asking me, "How you loop that like that?" He was bugging. I am very disappointed at the fact [that Jay] downplayed what I did so much.

FOXY BROWN: Jay picked me up from school—Brooklyn College Academy. I was in ninth grade. This was in '95. We stopped and got some Kum Kau—me, Jay and his cousin B-High. Kum Kau was our favorite spot, the best Chinese restaurant in the world. After that, we get to D&D Studios. I walk in, and you know I'm timid. I'm young, I'm 15. I'm like, "Jay, wow this is crazy!" But what I always had, and what Jay always talks about, is my fire, I always had fire. He'd tell me, "Yo, you're a *problem*. Show 'em why you're a problem."

We get to the studio now, Jay-Z locks me in the room. The Kum Kau is done, and we finished buggin' out. All right, time to go to work! Jaz-O is in there, and at that time, Jaz-O was poppin' a little. So we all in the studio, and this was before Roc-A-Fella and Jay's rapping was like 100 miles per hour. He locks me in the room by myself with half a pizza pie and a big bottle of Sprite. I had my notebook from school. And Jay is going, I hear him—mind you, Jay doesn't write—so I hear him, "I keep you fresher than the next . . . " We wanted to make a point of being realistic with our lives and what we really were as Bonnie and Clyde. "I keep you fresher than the next bitch / No need / For you to ever sweat the next bitch . . ." I hear the flow . . . "With speed" . . . I'm hearing his opening lyrics, and it's like he's trying to murder me! So he's rocking the verse and everybody is going, "Ohhhhhhhhh."

Jay was going off of the top of his head. He's looking at me, right, "Fresh to death in Moschino / Coach bag / Lookin' half Black and Filipino." Everybody thought I was half Black and Filipino after he said that.

I think, no, I *know* we were the first. . . . See, Big and Kim had it different. Kim was the female in the crew. I never was a female in the Roc. I was Jay's Bonnie. We were Bonnie and Clyde. Jay had his team of niggas, but I was his Bonnie, 'cause I was his partner. So when I hear Jay's verse, I'm like, "What up, boo? / Just keep me laced in the illest snakes / Bankrolls and shit . . . " I go rock in the booth. They think I'm gonna come out wit' some bullshit, right? Some girl shit.

So the rhyme is over, and I'm still going, "What, nigga! Yeah, Jay! I remember when you was doing yada, yada, yada." So, he comes in the booth and me and him are going at it. "Man, your mom's so . . . " Nobody knows this, but we have about 30 minutes extra of talking, me and him going back and cracking jokes on each other the whole 30 minutes. We falling out, I got Sprite coming out of my nose. Jay was like, "Nigga, when you was rockin' the [Reebok] 5411s scuffed up in the front!" I was like, "Oh, duke, when your Lexus ain't have no TVs!" We laughing. We fell out, bugging out. We all fell asleep in the studio. The next day, I hear [the track], I'm like, "Yo, this sucka is crazy!" Mind you, Big and Kim just had "Player's Anthem," which was a beast in Brooklyn. Now here we come.

After I finished that, I went back to school. I had a big test in the morning. I got up, went to school and they kept me posted on what was going on and what we're gonna do with the record. It just so happened that

"Ain't No Nigga" took off. [Funkmaster] Flex was frontin' on the record and shit I don't know what Jay had to do to convince Flex to play the record. He spins the record, and it became a beast. Automatically, I'm a star overnight.

IRV GOTTI: If you look at the "Dead Presidents" single, the B-side was "Ain't No Nigga" dirty and instrumental. They didn't even have a clean version, but they put it on there 'cause I was like, "This is a hit. You should put that record out." They eventually pressed up some vinyl with the clean version, and I said. "Yo, I know Flex. You need to call Flex about all of this shit, too."

So we go up to 1372 Broadway, which was where Hot 97 was. And how I used to get my records played was, I used to wait up there for fuckin' Flex, give him the record and say. "Yo, if you like the record, play that shit." Now, I also knew Flex liked cars. And Jay and them had Lexus GSs, so I said, "Yo, let's go up to Hot 97 and park up there." So we all parked up there with TVs in the headrest, wit' Jay's shit rimmed-out and everything. We was lookin' like we had a lot of fuckin' money. So Flex pulls up and comes across like, "What up, Irv?" I'm like, "Yo, what up, Flex? I wanna introduce you to my niggas and shit. This is Jay, Dame and Biggs, they Roc-A-Fella Records. You know, they the illest niggas on the street . . . " Blowin' 'em up like that.

I gave him the "Ain't No Nigga" record, and told him it's the illest record. Dame gave him the whole energy, and Flex said, "All right, Irv. I got you." That night he played the record like fuckin' 15 times. In my opinion, that night is when Roc-A-Fella Records was really born.

10

"Friend or Foe"
Produced by DJ Premier

DJ PREMIER: "Friend or Foe" just came out of nowhere. We'd just did the track, and when Jay heard it he just went in there and did the "Friend or Foe" verse. It just happened to fit. I actually didn't like the track at the time. I felt like I could make it a little funkier. But he was like, keep it just like it is. He said, "I want it pretty much to give me the window to speak it out the way I want to speak it." It was cleverly done, and it was witty. Even though he was stepping to somebody else about territory, it was real witty. It's regular ghetto-communication-slang-type shit. To anybody who understands the concept of hustling and people running certain blocks in their neighborhood, it was real self-explanatory. But the way he did it was like you were there at the conversation when he stepped to the guy. But he didn't do it by yelling and screaming and saying all these really loud words, he did it calmly. It's his calmness that made you say, If this is a real situation, I better get out of here 'cause this dude means business without having to yell at me. You could completely visualize it. And again, once his lyrics were put down, I had no complaints.

That's when I started to realize his MC skills had really started to rise up from what he had done in the past. I think the more he kept recording, the better he got. Because he was never on that level of incredible lyrics back in the days, compared to what he does now. He's one of the great ones. That was a sign that he was about to really take it to the next level. I mean, everybody was listening to Jay by that time, as far as the new person to hold down New York.

11

"Coming of Age"
(Feat. Memphis Bleek)
Produced by Clark Kent

MEMPHIS BLEEK: We was in the basement of Clark Kent's house in Brooklyn. We ordered a bunch of Wendy's and were sitting on a bunch of old crates of records. Clark played the beat. Jay had already written the rhymes, all I had to do is remember a sheet of paper. He used to write chicken scratch, so it took me a few hours to learn the rhymes. And then once we put it down, it came out; it was as hot as it was.

DAME DASH: That was a demo that was done in probably '93. That's how Bleek got down.

CLARK KENT: Jay had a song called "Coming of Age," and he felt like he needed someone young to be on it. So B-High, Jay's cousin, tells him about young Malik from Marcy. We go to Marcy, and we listen to Malik rap. We just kept telling him, "Rhyme." I think we might have had him rapping outside for four hours on a bench. Just keep rapping, keep rapping, until it was okay. His voice is good, and we believed he could say these rhymes. So we took him to my house, and let him say the rhymes.

He was a rapper, though I don't think he'd ever recorded. You have to understand, on that record, it wasn't confusing, because Jay told him what he was going to say. It was, "This is how you're going to do it." Jay stood right there when he was saying it.

12

"Cashmere Thoughts"
Produced by Clark Kent

CLARK KENT: With us, it was too simple. I simply made beats all day, Ski simply made beats all day and Jay simply rapped all day. If he was coming to do a record, he was finishing his record in 15 minutes. Jay'd come in, do his raps, and be gone. Like, "Okay, put it on a cassette, let me go listen to it in my car." And we'd have 20 or 30 songs on a cassette, listening to it in his car. It really wasn't a project. Some rappers be in the booth for two days recording one song. It was, Here's the verses, let's do it. And then you're done.

"Cashmere Thoughts" was done in my house. When it was first done, it was just one verse, just the first verse. Then I did all the talking like in between the verses and behind the verses. It was one verse, and then when it was time to mix it, he came up with another verse right then. So then we tracked it and did the verse and all the talking and all of that over again to complement the second verse.

13

"Bring It On"
(Feat. Big Jaz and Sauce Money)
Produced by DJ Premier

SAUCE MONEY: It was real simple. Jay called niggas to the studio, had a beat set up on the reel already, and niggas had to come in and write their verse. It wasn't really no rocket science. We was zoned out back then. Ten or 15 minutes [to write our rhymes] max, if that. Nine times out of 10 we already had something in mind. It didn't matter what beat you put up there, we had fuckin' rhymes for days. I already had my shit. I'm a dinosaur. I use a pen and pad. Everybody's a magician these days. I don't do it.

I picked the slickest shit I could think of. "We pattin' down pussy from Sugar Hill to the Shark Bar . . . " You know, real graphic, intimate. It was just like a vivid Picasso and shit. You could see everything. Metaphors was always something I was big on. Trying to say the slickest shit you could possibly say. You had to, fuckin' with Jay on the verse, 'cause you know he's going to come up with some shit. You don't want niggas to fast-forward your verse. Anytime I ever got on a record with that nigga, I was trying to get with him.

DJ PREMIER: "Bring It On" was pretty much just a collabo with the family. That's when Sauce Money was always around, and they was in the studio. Jay would be in the A Room with Ski pretty much every day, and I'd be in the B Room—the B Room has always been my room— and he'd go back and forth. He would just go in there with Ski, lay down something, come in there with me, lay down something, go back in the A Room. Like it was an everyday thing. Biggie was always there; that's when Nas was always around. Those were the best days. To this day, out of all his albums, *Reasonable Doubt* is the realest.

"Bring It On" was pretty much a record-as-we-go situation, because he was like. "Come on, let's do one more." I did that one off the head, he walks in the room, heard it, and he calls Sauce and Jaz-O. I already had the Fat Joe sample at the time already in there. I had the a cappella to the D&D record that we had done back when we did that D&D All Stars record. It just happened to sound good with that sample. So I just said I'm going to leave it in there and it's up to Jay if he want to keep it. He had no problems with it. Those were the good old days when there wasn't any back-and-forth drama with any artist. Nas was still around during that picture.

From there, Sauce came in and did his thing. Then Jay's verse was real dope on there. And then Jaz-O just closed it out. And like I said, those are the good old days when it was really fresh and everybody got along with everybody.

JAZ-O: We recorded this in the B Room at D&D. Originally, it was supposed to be Sauce and Jay on the song. At the time, because I didn't have a deal, and I refused to sign under management with Damon, I guess, I wasn't going to be on the song. But somebody made the decision to put me on the song. I had to write my verse on the spot. They already had their verses, which I started understanding after a while. And honestly, I hate to keep doing this, but that's what made me realize how much nicer I am than a whole lot of other people, 'cause they would even go so far as, "Let's put Jaz on a song, but let him write his shit now. We already got our shit." They kept coming in the room like, "Yo, we're running out of time, we're running out of time!" All this little bullshit. So when I finished [writing], I went in and in one run-through I was done. I was like, "Yo, I could do it better than that." Damon was like, "Nah, that's it." So what you're hearing on that song, that's my first take. That's how I've been treated. How you're going to treat the old man like that? What you're telling me is: I'm not the old man, I'm the best dude. In order for you to shine, you got to dull my shit. I've never seen a combination like [Sauce, Jay-Z and myself] in hip-hop or R&B, because there is always one person who stands out, who is the most talented. Sauce is very talented, Jay is very talented—that's one thing in any of my discussions. Whether I speak about them positively or negatively, I will never sit around and say, Oh, he's garbage, he's a no-talent bum. Because that's a lie. I still love them cats. You can't erase all that history, everything that happened, the camaraderie, the laughter, all that shit. You can't erase it. You also can't erase all the bullshit. And it's very disheartening for me.

14

"Regrets"
Produced by Peter Panic

BIGGS: I don't know if that was the daytime, but I remember we was getting drunk that day. It didn't ever matter. It was all cool. It was all family.

CLARK KENT: That was done in my house. We took it and tracked again in the studio. It's practically identical to what was done in the house. Dame, he knew how to keep the atmosphere live, 'cause he was just being Dame. Those cats were so cool back then. They were so cool, they didn't do anything extra. It was fun.

PETER PANIC: I made the beat in Clark's house using an SP 1200 and an [Akai] S950. We recorded it at D&D . . . At that time, I was the young'n in the crew, so me and Damon used to clash all the time. But we had a good amount of respect for each other.

Jay's whole crew was there. He did his verses on one take, straight down. I listened to it, and I was like, "That's dope, but I want you to do it again with a little bit more emotion." The whole room stopped and looked at me like "You're buggin'." But because I've been around Clark so much, and seen Clark produce Big and Junior M.A.F.I.A., and working with all the other artists that he's done—a lot of records before then—I knew. At that time, Jay's charisma level isn't close to what it is now. And without even thinking about it, he stopped, went back in and did it again. And then after that, I made him do ad-libs and add a couple of other things. And people were like, "Yo, you buggin' out, askin'!" 'Cause at that time, Jay's the dopest rapper. But that was one of the reasons why that record had so much emotion. I think I was one of the first people to ask him to do his rhymes again.

KRIS EX

THE HISTORY OF COCAINE RAP

ALL WHITE

How did you get all of your material shit?
Did you get it through rapping?
Everything through rap.
So all the ki's and stuff that, it's just rhyming?
I never had nothing to do with no ki's, no shit like that.
                                        —Nasir Jones, interview (1996)

Crack is wack.

It may be hard for younger readers to believe, but at one point, this was the predominant philosophy in hip-hop's musical output, if not in the life of the community. For instance, in 1983, Melle Mel released "White Lines (Don't Do It)," which was meant to serve as a cautionary tale. But, even then, a conflict existed. According to legend, the song began as a celebration of cocaine use, not an admonition, and Mel was rumored to be skied-out during its recording. Tellingly, the tune sounds like a powdered trip through the Alps, with its stentorian, adrenergic bass line, exhortations to "Get higher,

186

baby," and odelike chorus. Even the song's video—directed by Spike Lee and starring Laurence (then Larry) Fishburne—showcases a *Flashdance*-like interpretive dance troupe catching the sniffles in a dressing room, a highway of snow running down a topless girl's spine and into her ass crack, and an abundance of pretty neon splashes. It plays more like an advertisement than a PSA.

This can be seen as the beginning of rap's long and conflicted relationship with cocaine. Rappers DMX, the late Ol' Dirty Bastard and Field Mob's Smoke have all been involved in high-profile arrests in which they were discovered in possession of crack cocaine that was allegedly for personal use. Philly's Beanie Sigel, who has undergone counseling at a drug treatment facility, and Staten Island's Raekwon have rhymed in the past about doing hard drugs. But, overwhelmingly, hip-hop's tales have centered on the sale of narcotics, not the use.

In today's rap, it seems as if the world revolves around the trade of crack cocaine and all the highs and lows endemic to a marriage of unbridled aspiration and deep despair. From artists such as Lil' Wayne—who, having been under the wing of Cash Money Records since he was knee-high to a kilo, has no verifiable trafficking history to speak of—to Juelz Santana (he of the memorable moniker "Human Crack in the Flesh") and his Dipset ilk, cocaine rap is the choice of the new generation. Even an artist like Busta Rhymes, known mostly for feel-good party anthems throughout his long career, chose to play up his stint in the drug game for the run-up to his latest album, *The Big Bang*, and jumped on the beat from Rick Ross' "Hustlin'," bragging about "that inconceivable guap" he made selling *cocaina* during the Reagan era.

Authenticity, of course, is put at a premium in hip-hop. But while a number of today's iceman MCs have legitimate records of drug dealing, their rhymes relay the honest truth. Real or not, the stories told in the music don't often delve past the fiduciary gains of the drug trade. From form to function to focus, cocaine rap has fallen under the auspices of style and design: Flows trump subject matter, thrills beat insight, and the gaud gained is more important than the lives lost. The game has become trapped in the trap, and it's dope-boy tragic.

The illicit mythos created by snow-shoveling stars is so dominant over the current rap scene that artists such as OutKast and Little Brother are revered by many simply because they eschew crack narratives. Of course, such artists find themselves in a precarious position when faced with the topic so prevalent in the work of peers. While the so-called conscious rappers are often quick to criticize the genre as a whole—attacking the dominant stylistic sameness, the monotonous tunnel vision exhibited by the slinger-songwriters' one-dimensional subject matter—whether due to politics, free-speech beliefs, or an understanding of the complex realities of their colleagues, they're usually hard-pressed to call anyone out by name. In fact, by and large, it is the conscious artists who are making the best arguments in support of their supposed opposites. For every trap Republican rehashing Chuck D's overworn analogy about rap as the ghetto's CNN or paraphrasing Nino Brown's courtroom speech about Negroes' not owning boats, planes, or gun factories, there's an Immortal Technique or a Mos Def breaking down the drug trade on a macro level, tackling geopolitics, connecting cocaine rap to Afghan wars and South American revolutions. Undeniably, the emotional back story of a song like Lupe Fiasco's "Kick, Push II" articulates a stronger defense of Young Jeezy and Rick Ross than anything ever put to wax by, well, Young Jeezy or Rick Ross.

While it would be fallacious to use the mores of an entertainment medium to convey wholly valid observations of the Black experience, what crack rap implies about reality cannot be ignored. On his debut album, Jay-Z rhymed that, "All us Blacks got is sports and entertainment," and whether art has imitated life or life has imitated art, the statement seems to have been taken on as a mantra by a generation—with the idea that drug selling is a last, but viable, alternative. A more perilous option, but one much more feasible, at least in terms of finding actual employment. As the Clipse's Pusha T once rhymed, young Black males "only know two ways of gettin'—either rap or unwrap." Despite recent efforts by an artist like Killer Mike, who is fervently working to flesh out the Southern d-boy caricature into a full-fledged human being, the trap star remains mostly an optionless hero. "It's hard being young from the slums, eatin' five-cent gums, not knowin' where your meal's comin' from," the Notorious B.I.G. rhymed on *Ready to Die*. The idea that UPS was hiring, as Biz Markie once noted, seems to have evaporated from the list of choices. So has trade school, driving a cab, or getting a college education.

Perhaps most disturbing of all is that narcotics are no longer being presented as simply a way out of the ghetto, but as a practical road to real-life riches. On *Ready to Die*, Big was all too happy to leave the street life behind. "I'm doin' rhymes now," he stated. "Fuck the crimes now. Come on the Ave. I'm real hard to find now." But by his second album, perhaps due to a realization that the music industry is a one-sided relationship, with the artist as an underpaid whore, he'd revamped his image. Though he was, by all accounts, never more than a midlevel hustler, he emerged as a boss in his rhymes, boasting that he, "In '88, sold more powder than Johnson & Johnson." The underlying dispatch was that the Notorious B.I.G. was not simply the alias of Chris Wallace, but the cover of the Black Frank White, the Verbal Kint to a man who was not primarily a rapper, but a drug lord.

Jay-Z once rhymed that, "The plans were to get funds and skate off the set," but by the time Shyne dropped his first album in 2000, the shift to rap-as-drug cover was gearing up for a full run. "I really sell weight," the now-incarcerated former Bad Boy claimed. "I just happen to rhyme great."

The upgrade from crack to cocaine in rap speak hasn't only been about one-upmanship among artists seeking novelty. It's rooted in some grim realities. "Soft beat faster, so, nigga, fuck crack," according to one Young Jeezy rhyme. "It get you more time, anyway. And I ain't cookin' shit—you get more time, anyway." Translation: If you're looking for fast money, cocaine would be more profitable than crack because there's less preparation involved, and with the unequal sentencing guidelines dictated by federal standards, it would behoove you to invest your resources higher up the totem pole.

There are certain milestones in crack-hop that cannot be ignored. One is Jay-Z's *Reasonable Doubt*, which shifted the conversation from the grind of hand-to-hand sales to out-of-town trips and overseas connects. Another is Raekwon's *Only Built 4 Cuban Linx . . .* , a record that introduced an unbridled and lasting affair with organized crime through a mafioso lens (regardless of the fact that the Italian mob stayed away from narcotics for most of its reign, and when they did get into drugs, their operations were brought down with vigor). Yet the album that casts the largest shadow over the current landscape is undeniably the Clipse's 2002 *Lord Willin'*, a full-length that not only spoke about large-scale trafficking with eerie precision, but also *sounded* like the game—all peaks and valleys, with paranoid gilds and desolate shines.

In the wake of *Lord Willin'*, Crack Rap 2.0 has produced artists like Young Jeezy, who manages to reveal details of the trade—running out of rubber bands, product wrapped in duct tape hidden in dirty laundry—without ever indicting those around him, and Rick Ross, whose music captures the highs and expansiveness of the country's major drug port without ever reaching past generic descriptions of bricks and more cars, more clothes, and more money to blow.

As titillating and compelling as it can be, crack rap is a sinister conspiracy. The victims of the mutually exploitative drug trade are rarely regarded in rap's action-adventure version. Instead, they're treated like a lingering fraction of the equation, rounded up to the next thrill. Every real crack rock that is sold is sold to a real person, but what becomes of that person remains a punch line or, in some more magnanimous cases, scenery for tales told through a project window. Same for the collateral casualties of the violence that accompanies the drug game—not the snitches, not the rival dealers, not the bad guys in the Cowboys-and-Indians episodes spun on wax, but the thirteen-year-old spotter caught up in a turf war, the five-year-old girl that takes a stray bullet.

Rappers, though, cannot be held singularly responsible. We—magazine makers, record company movers and shakers, music buyers—have agreed that, when it comes to our entertainment, we value aesthetics and fantasy over responsibility and reality. We can deny this all we want, but the covers, releases, and charts don't lie. Cocaine is a hell of a drug. And we're all addicted.

ELISABETH VINCENTELLI

BULGARIAN IDOL

Kiev, November 2004. The streets are alive with the sound of protest, and three days after a rigged ballot, a local singer, Ruslana, expresses her support for opposition leader Viktor Yushchenko. As her press release put it, "Ruslana has announced hunger strike and decided to place a symbolic ribbon around her head upon the news from Ukraine's Central Election Commission to announce Prime Minister Victor Yanukovich the next President of Ukraine." But Ruslana isn't your average buxom Carpathian activist: her engagement on behalf of Ukraine actually started earlier that year when, clad in Xena-like leather and backed by an armada of brawny percussionists, she performed "Wild Dances" at the Eurovision Song Contest—and won. With that success, she followed in the hallowed footsteps of such glorious exponents of pop music as France's Serge Gainsbourg (author of the 1965 winning tune, "Poupée de cire, poupée de son") and Sweden's Abba (triumphant in 1974 with "Waterloo"). But with her activism, Ruslana, née Lyzhychko, also vividly embodied the dizzying conflagration of pop and geopolitics that is the Eurovision Song Contest.

Terry Wogan, who's been commentating the annual live event for the BBC since 1971, once mused, "Is it a subtle pageant of postmodern irony? Is it a monumental piece of kitsch? Is it just a load of old plasticene?" It's actually all of the above, with a few key elements Wogan somehow overlooked: nation-building ideals, behind-the-scenes drama, inane choreographies, conspiracy theories, costumes from outer space (or at the very least, outer Croatia), and of course songs that veer from blisteringly stupid to blisteringly brilliant and, just as often, hit both extremes. The ESC may well be the greatest invention in pop-music history.

Growing up in France, I faithfully watched the telecast every May. Later, I also discovered punk rock and baroque, German techno and Norwegian black metal; I went to the opera and underground clubs. You might say I expanded my musical horizons. Yet I never got tired of Eurovision. In fact, I started enjoying it *more* as American and English indie rock got increasingly self-referential, didactic, and joyless. The Eurovision contest is the exact opposite: it's so garish that it makes Telemundo variety shows look like outtakes from a Bergman movie, and you can always count on surprises, whether it's a singer suddenly flailing out of tune or one unexpectedly putting on the kind of electric performance that short-circuits TV sets from Dublin to Bucharest. Every time I think nothing can top a particular eye-popping display, another act is champing at the bit in the wings, waiting to get its chance to show the world that his or her country's pop stars can shine as bright as any others, or maybe just as bright as those from powerhouse Ireland. (Eire has won the ESC more than any other country: seven times, including three times in a row from 1992 to 1994.) As for the songs, yes, many are mind-bogglingly awful. But there are as many good songs as there are bad ones, and a handful every year regularly qualify as great pop. So while I can't deny my enjoyment is somewhat ironic at times, it is also deeply sincere because the ESC offers plenty of what pop is best at: outlandishness, disregard for bourgeois standards of good taste, music as community-building enterprise, and of course lots and lots of disco performed by divas of all genders.

Now living in New York, I buy Eurovision contest CDs by mail order, read Eurovision contest websites (which can sport some of the internet's most wickedly entertaining writing), and watch Eurovision contest broadcasts on videos mailed from France by my ever patient mother. And yet all this wasn't quite enough, so I finally broke down and decided to attend the actual event, which that year happened to be the fiftieth-anniversary edition. Which is how on May 17, 2005, I found myself on a Ukraine International flight to the host city of Kiev. An attendant named Stalina poured me a Coke. I knew I was pointed in the right direction.

Let's start by getting some pesky facts and rules out of the way so American readers—most of whom are sadly unaware of the Eurovision Song Contest—can follow. For the past half century, the ESC has been mixing cultural and political truisms faster than you can say "Lithuanian disco." Inspired by the Sanremo Music Festival, running in Italy since 1951, Eurovision was hatched in 1955 by the European Broadcasting Union (EBU), an umbrella organization gathering public broadcasters, in an attempt to foster cultural exchange between European countries via the international language of pop music. The idea was that each country would nominate a song to represent it in a pacific battle every year. So far, so UNESCO.

Combining musical performances and the judging thereof, the show—which is broadcast live to millions of viewers, not a single one of them in the U.S.—is split into two halves. First, the songs are performed, then there's a ten-minute intermission during which tele-voting takes place in each participating nation (people can't vote for their own country). The last hour of the contest is devoted to pure white-knuckle suspense as country after country calls in its points. To quote the EBU's official rules for Kiev, each nation gives "12 points to the song having obtained the highest number of votes, 10 points to the song having obtained the second-highest number of votes, 8 points to the song having obtained the third-highest number of votes, and so on down to 1 point for the song having obtained the tenth-highest num-ber of votes.... When called upon to announce its results, which must be done clearly and distinctly in English or in French, the spokesper-son of each Participating Broadcaster shall first state the name of the country on behalf of which he is speaking and then announce the points allocated to each song in ascending order." Best of all, the win-ning country gets to host the contest the following year.

On paper, this looks straightforward enough, but aesthetics and scoring frequently collide, creating a supernova of international in-trigue and conspiracy theories, all of which are kept fresh by ever evolving geopolitics and constantly updated contest rules. Factoids, gossip, and reports from far-flung juries are analyzed by fans as ob-sessively as many men watch SportsCenter; think of it as Monday morning quarterbacking for women and gays, the contest's most de-voted constituency.

Much has been said about the fact that the contest has actually spawned few stars. It's true that if you're speaking about worldwide fame, only Céline Dion (winner in 1988 on behalf of Switzerland) and Abba would qualify. But actually plenty of Eurovision acts were doing well enough in their respective countries or in Europe as a whole before entering the contest, and others have parlayed their ex-perience into flourishing careers: Sandie Shaw, Cliff Richard, and Olivia Newton-John have sung for the U.K.; Ofra Haza represented Israel in 1983; Julio Iglesias placed fourth on behalf of Spain in

1970. Now many entries come out of reality TV. (Commentating the 2005 contest for France 3, Guy Carlier introduced a pair of competitors by saying, "They're the winners of *Bosnia-Herzegovina Idol*. This sentence gives me vertigo.") But in Kiev, pro or semipro entertainers rubbed elbows with amateurs in the original Olympian sense of the word, like Denmark's Jakob Sveistrup, who teaches in a school for autistic children, and Slovenia's Omar Naber, a dental technician whom I saw sitting outside the arena after the contest, talking forlornly on a cell phone all by his un-starlike self. It's this kind of incongruous sight that made dealing with Ukraine's idiosyncratic sense of organization worthwhile.

Flying to Borispol Airport capped weeks of angst, confusion, and nail-biting frustration. Going to Ukraine was easy enough; going to the ESC in Ukraine turned out to be a trial in which the weak of will and the light of wallet didn't stand a chance. Securing a hotel room, a press pass, and two tickets for the final consumed weeks of my time in the winter and spring of 2005. It required calling and emailing France, Ukraine, England, and Switzerland, and eventually pleading for help from the diplomatic corps. It quickly became obvious that Kiev and the Ukrainian government took the contest as an opportunity to show the rest of Europe they could put on a show, while local businesses took it as an opportunity to make a quick hryvnia. Unlike other major events, getting a press pass didn't guarantee access to the show. In fact, it turned out that nothing save perhaps a suitcase of unmarked Euros guaranteed anything: the ticket sale was delayed for weeks; the website was inaccessible; tickets mysteriously sold out even though nobody was able to buy them; a company that somehow seemed to have gotten hold of the tickets appeared overnight and started reselling them at an inflated price. Finally, some string-pulling and a wad of hryvnias secured two prime seats for the final. By then the trip's bill had climbed to such an alarming high that my

Australian travel companion and fellow Eurovision freak Trevor and I figured we'd have to survive exclusively on bowls of cheap borscht and cut the side trip to hot! hot! hot! Chernobyl.

Many of the Eurogroupies traveling to the show every year lacked our steely determination and gave up in 2005 because Kiev was just too chaotic. A Paris tour operator and experienced Eurovision goer told me he prayed a Scandinavian country would win so the contest would run smoothly in 2006. Hosting the ESC is no easy task in any year, but Kiev's problems were compounded by the fact that thirty-nine countries were slated to participate, making the 2005 edition the biggest one ever.

Thirty-nine? "I didn't realize there were so many countries in the European Union," you may wonder. Well, there aren't. Let's just say it's easier to convince the EBU's Geneva telemongers that you can shake your booty than to convince the EU's Brussels Eurocrats that your balance of payments is healthy and your imams are library-bound pussycats devoted to scholarly research. Turkey, for instance, has been ringing the EU's doorbell for years, but it first participated in the song contest in 1975 and won in 2003. The EBU's ranks are even capacious enough to include North African and Middle Eastern nations such as Morocco (which participated in the ESC once, in 1980) and Israel (a three-time winner, competing regularly since 1973). In addition, the dismemberment of the Soviet Union and of Yugoslavia have created a slew of new nations, all of them dying to put on sequined pantsuits and sing. And so the ESC has grown from seven entries in 1956 to a record thirty-nine in Kiev—Lebanon, which was scheduled to be number forty, belatedly read the rule stipulating that each country must broadcast the concert in its entirety, and it withdrew rather than having to show the Israeli song. I wish the EBU had extended an invitation to Vatican City to fill Lebanon's slot; after all, Vatican City's got some great outfits, puts on fab pageants, and is used to convoluted electoral procedures—it would have been a cinch.

To handle the overflow of contestants, in 2004 the EBU created a semifinal, which takes place a couple of days before the final, in the same city. The top ten finishers in the semi repeat their songs at the grand showdown. They join the so-called "Big Four," i.e., the countries that fork out the most membership dues to the EBU—France, Germany, Spain, and the U.K.—as well as the ten highest-scoring countries from the previous year, including of course the winner and current host. (Starting in 2007, there will be five "pool semifinals" all across Europe in April, bringing the potential number of countries eligible to participate in the elimination process up to a whopping fifty-five; a total of twenty-five will participate in the final in May.) And in Kiev, there was no way we could forget that Ruslana had triumphed in 2004, a feat seemingly as important in Ukraine's cultural history as Mikhail Bulgakov finally completing *The Master and Margarita* around 1940.

The best thing in Kiev: buying Ruslana stamps for my postcards. Actually, buying Ruslana everything, from CDs to key rings to coasters. It's a good thing the singer is easy on the eyes and a charismatic entertainer because she was ubiquitous: Ruslana beamed from billboards; Ruslana starred in TV commercials; Ruslana was sighted on Kreschatyk Street; Ruslana sang at the free outdoors festival; Ruslana was Europartying at the Euroclub; and of course, Ruslana was a guest performer at both the semi and the final, flanked at the latter by dancers who looked like Ming the Merciless's bodyguards. It was as if she had won the Nobel Prize *and* an Olympic medal. Unsurprisingly, it wouldn't be long until the singer switched to politics: in March 2006, she was elected to parliament after running on the Yushchenko list Our Ukraine. (Her bio on that list's official site taught me that Ruslana got her college degree as "symphonic orchestra conductor" and that her husband is "physician-theoretic by profession.") I wouldn't be surprised if she ends up president one day. In the meantime, she is a genuine star and her presence at the semi took a bit of the sour edge off the event.

Not that anything went wrong that evening, technically speaking. Contrary to web gossip suggesting that Kiev's Soviet-style concrete Palats Sportu (sports palace) would not be refurbished on time and the contest would have to be moved to Sweden, the arena was ready. And the Ukrainian presenters' English was perfectly adequate, even if they sounded as if they had learned it by watching 1970s game shows. If only tele-voters had been as alert as Ukrainian contractors and made better choices that fateful night. . . . Holed up in our hotel room (giving up on attending the live semi was one of the purse-tightening measures), Trevor and I almost choked on our lukewarm Rosynka Super Colas when some of our favorites—Iceland's Selma, Lithuania's Laura and the Lovers, and Belarus's Angelica Agurbash—didn't make the cut. Was it because Selma's red pedal-pushers were so hideous that they distracted from her nifty up-tempo number? Did voters eject Angelica (Miss Photo USSR 1991) because if the organization in Kiev was bad, everybody knew the capital of an impoverished police state would be worse? Did Laura fail because her official bio revealed she had once sung backup for the Scorpions? At least the four women in the wonderful Vanilla Ninja made the cut. Who cares if they were Estonian mercenaries representing Switzerland?!

Extraordinarily enough, contestants don't have to be from the country they're representing at the Eurovision contest, a loophole that's long been exploited by small nations—the odds of Andorra and Monaco unearthing a new pop star every year are pretty low. So nobody batted an eye when in 2005 the wily Swiss recruited a quartet of foxy Tallinn girls with a burgeoning career in Germany. And the Ninjas weren't the only traveling Wilburys in Kiev: Belgium's

Nuno Resende was born in Portugal; Finland's Geir Rønning was born in Norway; Andorra's Mariean van de Wal was born in the Netherlands; and Turkey's Gülseren was born in Turkey but has been living in France since she was seven.

Even Britain, which would appear to have access to a deep pool of homegrown talent, has always cast a wide net, recruiting Australian Gina G in 1996, for example, or Kansas-born Katrina Leskanich and her Waves in 1997 (they won). Like a busy Eurocuckoo, Katrina, now Waveless, even tried to find yet another nest and entered the Swedish national selection process, aka Melodifestivalen, in 2005; much to her surprise, she wasn't picked. Still, perhaps this fluidity illustrates a great achievement by the European Union: the free circulation of people within a borderless continent—at least when it comes to singers, not Polish electricians or Kurdish refugees.

And so Vanilla Ninja went on to the final, along with Trevor and me. We were in exotic company: the twenty-four competitors hailed from countries as diverse as Moldova and Israel, Malta and Russia, an impressive range that helps explain why the contest is so entertaining. In comparison, Americano-American brawls come off as hopelessly self-aggrandizing and downright provincial. *American Idol?* Excuse me, but second-guessing intra-Baltic rivalries or post-Yugoslavian alliances is a lot more captivating than watching an Alabaman and a Texan face off while a trio of judges looks on. This is a simple fact of life that NBC obviously didn't grasp when it announced in the spring of 2006 that its own version of Eurovision would include contestants from all fifty U.S. states. Whoop-de-do!

Yet nationalism remains decidedly good-natured at the contest. Waiting to enter the Palats Sportu, I spotted fans with national colors painted on their faces cheer denizens from rival countries. A gang of Swedes wearing matching IKEA T-shirts cordially posed with a man waving a fabulous red-and-black flag that looked as if it had been pulled out of the Tintin book *King Ottokar's Sceptre* but turned out to be from Albania. A man holding a Turkish flag embraced a gaggle of Greeks, seemingly unconcerned by the fact that the two countries have been at each other's throats over the Cyprus issue for more than thirty years. You don't see that kind of effusion at a European soccer match, as anybody who's ever fled from drunken hooligans can testify. At the Palats Sportu, sportsmanship reigned, and the only display of rowdiness came when Belarus was soundly booed for awarding twelve points to Mother Russia. This is what the world would look like if women and gays ran it, I thought, drunk on the excitement of it all.

But what does it all *sound* like? In 2005, Dr. Harry Witchel, a teaching fellow in Bristol University's Department of Physiology, isolated the key elements making up an ESC winner. According to him, they are pace and rhythm; an easily memorable song; a perfect chorus; a key change; a clearly defined finish; a dance routine; and a costume (presumably something sparkly). As vague as that list is, it's still easy to see that it pretty much rules out rock. In fact, the Eurovision contest embodies everything that is *not* rock and, by extension, America.

Like Bollywood, the ESC represents pop culture that happily thrives outside the U.S. Of course, both Bollywood and Eurovision integrate references to American-born idioms, but these idioms aren't considered any better than any number of others such as *schlager* or *variété* (locally rooted popular musical styles from Germany and France, respectively). Both predate rock, and while I can't deny that both carry a certain amount of cheesy baggage, they also can be supremely melodic. Over the years, many Eurovision-spawned songs—Séverine's "Un banc, un arbre, une rue," Lena Philipsson's "It Hurts," Baccara's "Parlez-vous français?," the aforementioned "Waterloo" and "Poupée de cire, poupée de son"—have held a special place in my heart because they are so irresistibly catchy. In fact, only three acts could have remotely been considered to have played rock in Kiev—and what rock! Zdob si Zdub may have been Moldova's answer to the Red Hot Chili Peppers, but they also brought a drum-beating granny on stage; Vanilla Ninja sounded like Electric Light Orchestra covering "Ride of the Valkyries"; Norway's Wig Wam looked like middle-aged glam sausages encased in silver spandex and topped with fright wigs. Americans may take this as yet another sign that Europeans can't rock; I take it as yet another sign that Europeans don't care about rock. Not the same thing at all.

While most of the Kiev songs would be anathema to Smithsonian-addicted world-music purists, enough of them kicked plenty of ass by glorifying melodicism and arrangements descended from Phil Spector's "bigger is better, more is more" school. The Kiev contestants also relished mixing and matching pan-European influences with exotic spices, often producing stunningly lumpy stews. Christof Spörk, from Austria's Global. Kryner, explained that "the concept of our music is Alpine music. . . . It combines Austrian and Slovenian music with Cuban music." In its press bio, Hungarian band Nox stated that "we build a bridge between the ancient Hungarian pentatonic scale with the world of contemporary music."

Indeed the biggest ESC trend over the past few years has been the incorporation of ethnic flavoring in both the music and the ubiquitous dance routines. Ruslana's "Wild Dances" drew from the folk stomping of Carpathia's Hutsul people, and her victory in 2004 led the following year to a veritable epidemic of tribal drumming and traditional outfits customized for maximum garishness. A couple of acts mining the turbo-ethnic vein did stand out in Kiev: Nox benefited from a catchy song and a group of black-clad dancers looking like Riverdancing Darth Vaders; Sistem, the backing band for Romania's singer Luminita Anghel, ended its set by power-sawing the oil drums it had been banging on, Einstürzende Neubauten–style. At least disco—which has been a constant at the contest since the mid-'70s—is likely to remain after the ethnic fad wanes.

No matter the style, however, covers are forbidden. My favorite Eurorule among many, many Eurorules is that songs cannot be longer than three minutes; think of these edicts as pop's answer to the constrained writing favored by the French collective OuLiPo (Ou-vroir de Littérature Potentielle). These restrictions make the songwriters contort themselves in order to stand out within a strict time limit, though whether they write a power ballad or a dance-floor scorcher, they somehow all end up writing in a bridge at around the second minute, following it with a key change, and concluding with a grandiose finish. Brilliant! This is enough to make up for the fact that no more than six performers are allowed onstage for each country, and that the magnificent orchestras of yore have been replaced with backing tracks (all vocals are performed live, though).

The language requirements are a lot more flexible. Contestants have been free since 1999 to sing in whatever language they want; essentially this means they are free to sing in the unique tongue known as English as a Second Language. The lyrics aren't usually completely wrong, but they often feel slightly off and aren't helped by deliciously accented pronunciations. Watching the semi, for instance, I was delighted to hear Vanilla Ninja sing "I can see the danger eyes / In your eyes," though it later turned out they were singing "I can see the danger rise / In your eyes."

Save for pockets of resistance in the Balkans, the biggest exception to the ESL tsunami remain the French. These days, France stands tall (or not so tall, actually, since its candidate, Ortal, was next to last in Kiev) in a depleted Francophone field—especially after neither of

2005's other Francophone entries, Monaco and Belgium, made it to the final. As Bruno Berberes, head of the French delegation, put it, "In France, we want every country to be made to sing in its native language. It makes it more interesting. [In 2004] we had twenty-four countries in a row singing in English, and so songs in French have no chance."

Bruno, please! I can guarantee you that the Palats Sportu's semi-catatonic state during Ortal's performance had nothing to do with her singing in French and everything to do with her singing a bummer of a tune that mysteriously lacked anything resembling a chorus. When I went to buy ice cream and dumplings from the concession stands during the endless point-attribution segment, I overheard a French delegation member hiss to another, "It was the dress! That dress was terrible!" But perhaps Ortal's dress wasn't terrible enough. Perhaps we would have a chance if the *exception français* could just stop trying to be so classy, give up on the thoughtful lyrics and the meaningful choreography, and just go for the sequins, the Hi-NRG, or, if all else fails, the pentatonic-tribal combo. But no: following its pattern of inventing institutions only to grow bored with them (RIP countless constitutions including the European one), France has been dragging its Eurovision heels for the past fifteen years or so. Perhaps we should submit an entry in Volapük or Esperanto. At least there would be an element of surprise, because surprisingly for a contest where stunts are common, nobody's ever performed an entire song in either language. But then some contestants' English is so . . . *unique*, it might as well be Esperanto.

Much mirth has derived from the inane lyrics of Eurovision contest songs. The Kiev rulebook stipulated that "the lyrics and/or performance of the songs must not bring the Eurovision Song Contest into disrepute." Ahem. Over the years, many countries have played it safe by finding refuge in onomatopoeia or filling verses and choruses with an abundance of *la-la-las*. Most eschew intentional irony; only a few have dabbled in anything that could be construed as postmodern (when you're from Moldova or Belarus, two of continental Europe's poorest countries, you'd very much like being modern before you can even consider being post); even fewer have had political lyrics.

Politics are officially unwelcome at the ESC. In the past, some countries have withdrawn to make a point; in 1969 Austria, showing the kind of spine it lacked in 1938, refused to go to Franco's Spain. On the other hand, messages in songs have tended to be couched in hazy rhetoric. In 1977, for instance. Austria's Schmetterlinge attacked the music business in its entry "Boom Boom Boomerang," which opened with "Music is love for you and me / Music is money for the record company." Of course it then went on to a biting Eurochorus of "Boom boom boomerang, snadderydang / Kangaroo, boogaloo, didgeridoo / Ding dong, sing the song, hear the guitar twang / Kojak, hijack, me and you."

There wasn't anything remotely that poetic in Kiev. Ukraine's Greenjolly had to change the lyrics to its entry, "Razom nas bagato"—a popular chant during the Orange Revolution a few months earlier—after the EBU's Song Contest Supervisor, a Swede named Svante Stockselius, expressed his disapproval. Greenjolly obligingly tweaked some lines, though its Midnight Oil–style anthem still kicked off with the line "We won't stand this—No! Revolution is on!" and its singer wore a Che T-shirt. Meanwhile Russia's "Nobody Hurt No One" started with "Hello sweet America, where did your dream disappear? / Look at little Erica, all she learns today is the fear / You deny the truth, you just having fun / Till your child will shoot your gun."

Of course, being political very often has nothing to do with lyrics. Echoing Bollywood's signature style, the ESC represents music as a vessel for liberation and identity through over-the-top performances, larger-than-life singers, and the idea that every number should be a friggin' *show*. Is it any wonder, then, that the contsest is so popular with the gay community?

While same-sex love songs haven't been entered, at least officially, the ESC is more gay-friendly than most international competitions. The turning point came in 1998 when Israeli transsexual Dana International won with "Diva." Israel's Orthodox crew didn't appreciate being represented by a statuesque tranny, but millions of Euroqueens rejoiced. In 2002, Slovenia picked three men dressed as female flight attendants to go to the contest in Tallinn. The following year, the two surly mock-bians of t.A.T.u briefly held hands onstage while singing for Russia, and in 2004 Bosnia and Herzegovina's Deen lispily performed the unofficial anthem of the crystal generation ("I'm lying, I'm late, I'm losing my weight / Because I want to dance all night / Because I want to stay all night / In the disco, in the disco") in what may well have been one of the gayest performances of all time.

In their book *The Complete Eurovision Song Contest Companion*, Paul Gambaccini, Jonathan Rice, Tony Brown, and Tim Rice muse that "MTV, the cultural glue of the younger generation of European music followers, has nothing to do with Eurovision: the culture gap seems to be not between Estonian and French but between those over thirty and under thirty." I would actually argue that the gap is between those for whom pop is a way of looking at the world and those who dismiss it as pap.

In contrast with rock's constant search for "authentic" roots and worthy *artistes* to bring them forth, pop and disco celebrate artifice and masquerade. Just look at Eurovision 1982, when twelve of the eighteen contestants had one-word names that reeked of time-shares in Bratislava: Nicole, Stella, Svetlana, Bardo, Chips, Mess, Lucia,

Doce, Aska, Neço, Brixx, and Kojo. If you find this list appallingly dumb, there's no way you could ever enjoy the ESC; if it makes you laugh in delight, you're also the kind of person who knows that Nicole remains Germany's one and only winner.

And instead of being defensive, fans fight back. Before and even during my trip, I prepped by reading several Eurovision websites—some, like *esctoday.com* or *eurovisionfr.net*, for their straightforward news; others, like the Schlagerboys' entries at *popjustice.com*, for their cheeky humor. Many of the writers on these sites dismantle rockist pretension with humor and verve. They know perfectly well how surreal it is to be mocked by guardians of musical purity who then go on to worship acts as jejune as the Arcade Fire or Arctic Monkeys.

Many countries don't mind being represented by, say, a campy dude wearing a gold lamé cowboy costume (Germany, 2000).They care even less if they used to be communist. In a 2005 *New Statesman* article, Tim Luscombe wrote: "In recent years, Estonia, Latvia, Turkey, and Ukraine have taken Eurovision extremely seriously. Estonia and Latvia realized that membership in the EU lay beyond the gates of Eurovision triumph. These countries saw winning Eurovision (which would make them the contest's hosts in following years) as a chance to showcase their European credentials and hasten EU membership. And they were right." Or, as Marcel Proust once put it, "That bad music is played, is sung more often and more passionately than good, is why it has also gradually become more infused with men's dreams and tears. Treat it therefore with respect. Its place, insignificant in the history of art, is immense in the sentimental history of social groups."

The contest is a huge deal for postcommunist, poorer nations. The Ukrainian authorities and the Kiev municipality went to great lengths to show their capital city could host a major event. The streets were spotless, even during [street] fairs at which beer cost about seventy-five cents a liter; kiosks manned with English-speaking students were set up at popular spots to help lost tourists; we could not have asked for a nicer frisk from the Palats Sportu's impassive, high-cheekboned security force. And once we reached our seats in the arena, we could glimpse President Yushchenko, who handed out the trophy at the end. In a brochure distributed to journalists in Kiev, Belarusian Minister of Culture Leonid Guliako asserted that his country's participation in the contest "is certain to be a worthy contribution to the process of Belarus's integration into the European cultural space." (Although while the power of disco could integrate pretty much anybody into the European cultural space, a move into the European *political* space would be greatly facilitated if President Aleksandr Lukashenko weren't so keen on keeping his country under a dictatorship.)

Because the stakes are so high for so many, outlandish behavior isn't limited to the stage: the machinations start with the national selection processes, which are administered by the companies broadcasting the Eurovision contest in their respective countries. Typically, the road to Kiev was littered with histrionics as exquisitely colorful as what took place at the Palats Sportu. During its selection process, for instance, Russia's Channel One was said to have manipulated the SMS results so that its favored candidate, reality-show contestant Natalia Podolskaya, would be picked. In Bulgaria, runner-up Slavi Trifonov accused winning band Kaffe of rigging the SMS votes; then Kaffe's song "Lorraine" (and its immortal line "I can still remember Lorraine in the rain") was accused of plagiarizing a 2001 song written by . . . Trifonov's company. Things got a lot more serious in 2006, when the Serb and Montenegrin factions of Serbia and Montenegro clashed during their national selection process, leading to a nasty feud that almost eclipsed the concurrent death of Slobodan Milošević and led the country to withdraw from Eurovision altogether when it couldn't agree on a candidate.

But in truth, most of the conflicts swirling about the contest don't arise from the songs or from the singers' sexualities but from the voting—or more precisely from the way the voting is interpreted. Indeed for many ESC aficionados, the allocation of the points by the participating countries is just as fun as the performances.

In a 2005 paper titled "How Does Europe Make Its Mind Up? Connections, Cliques, and Compatibility Between Countries in the Eurovision Song Contest," four Oxford scholars noted that "Irrespective of whether it contributes anything to the advancement of music per se, the Eurovision Song Contest does provide a remarkable and unique example of an annual exchange of 'goods' and opinions between countries. Going further, it is arguably the only international forum in which a given country can express its opinion about another, free of any economic or governmental bias." Which doesn't mean it's free of controversy, as every single year, accusations of bloc voting surface. Frankly, they are getting a bit tiresome, and I for one just don't believe they explain either poor showings or victories anymore, if in fact they ever did. Yes, countries often end up voting for their neighbors or for nations with which they have a cultural affinity. Yes, Cyprus will give twelve points to Greece, which is likely to return the favor. Yes, nobody will blink if the Scandinavian countries award each other a fair number of points. But Malta, to name but one, doesn't have many obvious allies and still made it to No. 2 in 2005, while Sweden was so mediocre that even its Scandi neighbors deserted it and let it sink to an ignominious No. 19.

While phone voting is seen as more democratic and less riggable than the previous system of local juries (two words: *ice skating*), it's also led to intense lobbying as many participants make promo appearances all across Europe in the weeks leading up to the contest in the hope that tele-voters will be familiar with them come final time. Many continued to try to gain visibility in Kiev. There were meet-and-greet parties almost every night at the Euroclub, and contestants tirelessly worked the streets. Everywhere Trevor and I went, for instance, we ran into Spain's Son de Sol, aka the triplets from Seville, filming spots and chatting up vendors at local markets. The effort didn't pay off for them, but lobbying for weeks definitely is the wave of the future. In a refreshing change from the usual sour grapes and mud-slinging, Swedish TV producer Anders G. Carlsson admitted, "We're impressed with how the Eastern Europeans have approached the competition. Down here we almost feel like country bumpkins. We should try to adopt their methods."

The former Soviet-controlled countries tend to do the most pre-contest legwork because the Eurovision contest means a lot more to them than to the jaded French or Brits. Belarus was rumored to have spent one million Euros on a months-long campaign during which its candidate, Angelica Agurbash, visited several countries. Accredited journalists were deluged with promotional material aimed at helping us fully grasp the subtleties in Angelica's song: "It has been a longstanding tradition of the Belarusian pop scene that composers collaborate with the best contemporary poets." One can only assume it's the latter who, in an act reeking of pure Soviet realness, translated what Angelica sang ("I've got no hesitation / It's my infatuation / Your touch is an obsession / I'm addicted now," etc.) into what appeared in the official transcript of her song in the Kiev press handbook: "She was standing near a window, / And her beauty was like a trap, / She was shot by sunny beams, / And gave herself up with an open heart, / With all her essence: / All that she took / Was working and boiled, / And only an adult dream / To feel the woman in / Was realised when / They've decided to be tied up by Hymen." (Laugh, hipster, laugh! After all, it's easier than admitting that these lyrics are no more ridiculous than "I make trips to the bathroom / Yeah my friends all have true grit / I am speckled like a leopard / I'm a specialist in hope and I'm registered to vote / Why don't you come into my barrio / We'll see if you can float." Perhaps Interpol should consider calling Minsk's best contemporary poets.)

Unfortunately, despite two costume changes and the gayest dancers in the entire contest, Agurbash failed to make it to the final; the chink in Belarus's diabolical plan was that its singer turned out to have a grating, metallic voice. She was last seen right after the semifinal debacle, leaving the Palats Sportu in both a huff and a van with black-tinted windows. At least Belarus made up for this failure when its representative, the terrifying moppet Ksenia Sitnik, won the Eurovision Junior Contest later that same year. Yes, despite having reached middle age, the ESC spawned a love child in 2003: the Eurovision Junior Contest, which is open to kids aged eight to fifteen. I was particularly taken by Spain's Maria Isabel Lopez Rodriguez, who won in 2004 with "Antes Muerta que Sencilla." That title translates as "Better Dead Than Banal," which might as well be Eurovision's unofficial motto.

While losing countries complain of bloc voting, they should look closer not only at the realities of modern promotion but also at the fact that England, France, or Sweden won't always define the parameters of European popular music, and the burgeoning idea that these old-school powers won't always define the parameters of European politics. The pendulum swung westward once; it can very well swing the other way: in his *New Statesman* article, Luscombe pointed out that "the political topography of Europe (and the ESC) has changed. The center has moved east. And some people are scared of that."

It was not all that surprising, then, that Greece triumphed in Kiev, bringing the trophy back to the cradle of civilization. Even less surprising, Helena Paparizou stormed to the top with a classic formula in which a turbo-ethnic vibe was laid onto a strong dance foundation; the news that Paparizou was raised and lives in Sweden came as no big shock, either. Call me utopian, but to me this is precisely why there may be hope for Europe after all.

DAVE SIMPSON

EXCUSE ME, WEREN'T YOU IN THE FALL?

The following correction was printed in the *Guardian*'s corrections and clarifications column, Wednesday, January 11, 2006:

> Kay Carroll, the former backing singer in Mark E. Smith's band, the Fall, has asked us to point out that it was she who abandoned the band in America in 1983, rather than vice versa as was stated in the article below.

It's a Tuesday morning in December, and I'm ringing people called Brown in Rotherham. "Hello," I begin again. "I'm trying to trace Jonnie Brown, who used to play in the Fall. He came from Rotherham and I wondered if you might be a relative." "The Who?" asks the latest Mr. Brown. "No. The Fall—the band from Salford. He played bass for three weeks in 1978." "Is this some kind of joke?"

This has been my life for weeks. I've become an internet stalker and a telephone pest, all because of an obsessive drive to track down everyone who has ever played in the Fall. That's 40-odd people, including drummers abandoned at motorway services, guitarists left in foreign hotels, and various wives and girlfriends of the band's provocateur-ringmaster, Mark E. Smith.

The Fall lend themselves to obsession. In John Peel's Record Box—which contained the late DJ's favourite records—Fall records had an entire section to themselves. Peel called them the Mighty Fall: "the band against which all others are judged." More than 25 years after the band first formed, their audiences still include fans who don't follow other bands. Smith's inspired, social sci-fi songs are revered by everyone from comedians Frank Skinner and Stewart Lee to the designer Calvin Klein, artist Grayson Perry and authors Irvine Welsh and Philip K. Dick. Musicians and music critics love them, too: David Bowie, Bo Diddley, Thom Yorke and Alex Kapranos all claim to be fans, and the band's latest album (their 26th), *Fall Heads Roll*, won a five-star review in the *Guardian* for its "paint-stripping riffs, hail of one-liners, withering put-downs and bewildering images."

My own obsession with the band has been a long time in gestation. I first saw them play at Leeds' Riley Smith Hall in 1981: the fact that the singer was called Smith and the guitarist (Marc) Riley seemed to give this some weird significance. As the band approached their 30th year, I began to wonder if the Fall's continued relevance could be attributed not only to Smith's genius way with splenetic observations, but to the trail of havoc left by the revolving line-up. At the very least, I wondered where all these people were. As Peel had said, noting that most former Fallers simply disappear: "I don't know if he's killing them or what." So I resolved to track them down, not realising that this would involve afternoons writing letters to defunct addresses in Doncaster and eight-hour sessions searching for a single person.

I started with Smith, who sank pints of lager in a Manchester hotel as he explained his policy of successively "freshening up" the band. "It's a bit like a football team," he said. "Every so often you have to get rid of the centre-forward." Smith has based his career on looking forward, so he was unlikely to give me numbers for clarinet players who left in 1981. The numerous record companies the Fall have had over the years had only ever dealt with Smith. The Musicians Union claimed to have "no information relating to anybody who was ever in the Fall."

I did have another lead, however. Sixteen years ago I interviewed a man called Grant Showbiz, and remembered that he sometimes produced the Fall. He gave me some numbers, though sadly, most of them were dead—the numbers, not the ex-members. But I did reach former guitarist/sleeves man Tommy Crooks, now an artist in East Lothian. He'd been a part of the Fall's most notorious implosion, when the band (bar Smith) had disintegrated following a punch-up on stage in New York in 1998.

Over a crackling phone line, Crooks recounted what was to become a familiar theme. He describes being in the Fall as "the pinnacle of creativity" but with "a lot of madness." His first day in the band was spent rehearsing in a room where the lights kept going out; Smith would "unplug my amplifier and hold the microphone up to the strings, just to freak me out." The New York punch-up kicked off, Crooks recalls, after Smith had arrived in a particularly bad mood, having just been held at gunpoint by a taxi driver. Things were said on stage and "everything just went apeshit." Crooks saw Smith being bundled into a police car, and hasn't heard from him since. "I remember the band's bus driver asking, 'So what are this lot like, then?' The soundman said, 'This is as weird as it gets.'"

After a few days of trying to track down 43 former members of the Fall, things were getting pretty weird for me, too. Searching on the internet for "Mike Leigh," the band's 1980 jazz-cabaret drummer, was a nightmare: Google offered me 4,500,000 entries relating to the film director. I sent an email to Manchester University asking: "Are you the Ruth Daniel who used to play in the Fall?" and discovered a keyboard player who lasted a day in 2002. She revealed that Smith liked to warm up for gigs by "barking like a dog."

The more people I found, the more punch-ups I heard about. Marc Riley—now a DJ but a Fall guitarist from 1978–82—says he was sacked for hitting Smith back after the singer punished the band for an "average" gig by slapping each musician in turn.

"Smith doesn't do average," says bassist Steve Hanley, who met me in a Manchester pub. "He'd rather do 10 great gigs and 10 rubbish gigs than anything in the middle." Hanley's fearsome bass defined the Fall from 1979 until he, too, exited following the New York rumpus. After taking "two years to calm down," he became a school caretaker. He remembers post-gig inquests that would go on for hours as Smith—seeking a reaction—accused his bandmates of: "'Playing like a fookin' pub band.' Chairs would fly. It was like guerrilla warfare."

Some of this was tongue-in-cheek. Smith confessed to me that he used to fine drummers £5 each time they hit the tom-tom, and that on tour in Europe he would employ the "European phrasebook," sending guitarists to say things like "I am a flower" in German. Hanley's brother Paul, a drummer, remembers how one of Smith's favorite jokes was to "take new members abroad just so he could send them home." Another was to dismantle the band's equipment in the middle of a gig. "When you're playing five or six nights a week the group get slick," Smith said in his defence. For him, routine is "the enemy of music."

For all that he can be surreally funny, Smith's intent is deadly serious. As a man called Eric the Ferret—the band's bassist in 1978, and one of the people at whom Smith threw a chair—comments, sagely: "The Fall don't cruise." Among Smith's tactics for instilling the required creative tension, the trump card is threatening the sack.

I was curious to discover how long the Fall had been in Smith's control, so met Tony Friel, who founded the band with Smith, Martin Bramah, Una Baines and a drummer usually called "Dave," whose surname no one can remember and who was sacked for being a Tory. Now living in a terraced house in Buxton, Friel, about three years ago, played in the Woodbank Street Band; it was thanks to their website that I tracked him down.

Friel had been "best mates" with Smith and even coined the band's name (from the novel by Camus), but hadn't lasted long, quitting over Smith's decision to bring in then-girlfriend Kay Carroll on management and backing vocals. "I thought she muscled in," he says, "although Mark asked me to stay."

I found Carroll, too, in Portland, Oregon. After emailing to ask if I was "a stalker," she mailed me an hour of taped Mancunian vitriol. "I knew that Mark got me in to fuck off Friel, and it worked," she says. She believes Smith is a natural manipulator who knows when people have outlived their usefulness. Carroll—who masterminded the early Fall's hardline approach to the music industry—was herself abandoned in a U.S. bar in 1983.

The more people I found, the more I'd hear how they were recruited from the road crew (Riley, Hanley) or from support bands. Smith told me how once, when the rhythm section were late for a gig, he brought on players from the support band and was delighted when the errant pair walked in to see their replacements. In 2001 he drafted in the whole of Trigger Happy to be the Fall, giving them only eight hours' notice before they had to play a gig.

Brix Smith joined the Fall—and became the first Mrs. Smith—after she met Smith in America. Remarried, and with the name Smith-Start, she now runs Start fashion boutique in London. She tells how, the night they met, she played Smith a demo of her band. "He just said, 'I like your songs. Can we use them? Can you play on them?' He's so fucking smart I can't tell you," she sighs. "He wasn't educated, but he was extremely well-read. The way he looked at the world was so different. Because he wouldn't see things the same way, he wouldn't speak the same way."

A bizarre number of Fall members seem to have come from the same 500 square yards in Prestwich/Salford, or Smith's local, the George, before it was knocked down. Guitarist Adrian Flanagan recalls how, when he was 15, he would "put notes through Mark's door saying: 'You're my hero. Everyone else is rubbish. Maybe when I'm of legal drinking age, we could go for a drink?'" He soon ended up in the band—"He'd always give local kids a break."

One of the strangest entrances is that of Nick Dewey, who attended the 1999 Reading festival as the manager of the Chemical Brothers and ended up on stage with the Fall. "This drunk man [guitarist Neville Wilding] came backstage asking if anyone played drums," he says. "The band had had a fight and left the drummer at motorway services." Dewey hadn't played for 10 years, but once a Chemical Brother put his name forward, Wilding refused to take no for an answer. Dewey was led to a darkened tour bus to meet Smith, "passed out with his shirt off. The guitarist had to punch him in the face to wake him up. Then they began fighting over whether or not they should teach me the songs. Mark said no!" With a blood-covered Smith offering occasional prompts, Dewey pulled it off.

I tried to ask Wilding about this incident but his neighbor said he was "in Guadalajara." The neighbour is Adam Helal, who also appeared in the Fall, playing bass from 1998 to 2001. Perhaps Smith really can take any member of the public and "mould them."

"I was a terrible guitarist when I joined aged 17," agrees Ben Pritchard, who has survived in the guitar hot seat for the past five years. "Maybe that's why Mark wanted me in the group. The challenge is to take someone wrong for the group and make them right." He compares the Fall frame of mind to that at "Boot Camp." He has been abandoned at airports to make his own way to gigs; the band's last tour was so stressful that, at 22, he is losing his hair. Why do it?

"The Fall are making history," he says. "I have nightmares, but it's never boring. It's not Coldplay."

As the search continued, ex-Fallers started suggesting there should be "some sort of support group," while others asked to be put back in touch with people dumped in foreign climes, making me wonder if I should set up a Fall Reunited website. Equally, I was worried by the fates of the disappeared. In particular, Karl Burns—who was hired and fired nine times between 1977 and 1998—seemed to have vanished after punching Smith onstage in the New York meltdown. Several former members worried that he was dead. Some suggested he had "moved to the hills" in Rossendale, Lancashire, but appeals to the area's local papers produced nothing. Riley suggested I "try the prisons," which led me to Ed Blaney, who indeed left the Fall because he was sent to prison ("Dangerous driving," he says). He hadn't seen Burns either.

When I caught up with former Fall/Elastica keyboard player Dave Bush (now studying web design in Wiltshire), he told how Burns once turned up for a U.S. tour armed only with sticks and a hat, was fired, and spent two months riding around on a motorcycle before taking the same flight home as the band. Bush cleared up one of the Fall's biggest mysteries, the fate of founding drummer "Dave." Bush knew him on the Manchester party circuit as Steve, and says he became schizophrenic before throwing himself under a train.

Original keyboard player Una Baines had a lead for Burns—"My friend Barbara says she thinks she saw him a year ago. I'll ask around"—and her own moving story. Over herbal tea in a Chorlton cafe, she recalled how her time in the Fall ended in two drug-induced nervous breakdowns and hospitalisation as a result of "wanting to break down every barrier. Musical. Personal. Mental. But contrary to what Mark says, he never sacked me. I was just too ill." She recovered to make a classic album in Blue Orchids' *The Greatest Hit* (with former husband and ex-Faller Martin Bramah) and is now a singer with the Procrastinators.

There were just two names left. Guitarist Craig Scanlon—Fall fans' favourite—hadn't given an interview since being sacked in 1995 and was rumoured to work in the dole office. Contacting him involved negotiations with a mysterious go-between called "Moey" before an email claiming Scanlon is in "top secret government work" arrived from the Department for Work and Pensions.

"Steve [Hanley] rang and said Mark had sacked the whole band," Scanlon says. "Then it was just me." According to Scanlon, Smith—who revealed in a 2001 interview that firing the veteran guitarist was his "biggest mistake"—later invited him to a gig, something of an olive branch, but "after three hours in the pub with him I realised I was better out of it." Tantalizingly, Scanlon had actually seen Burns, a "while back," when he'd been "scruffy, big beard . . . I thought he was a tramp."

It reminded me of something Hanley said a month before: "Mark's had all these talented people in the band, but not many have done anything without him. He must have something . . . "

WILL HERMES (AS ROBERT BARBARA)

#32—JUST BECAUSE IT'S A SONG DOESN'T MEAN IT'S TRUE

"FIRST NIGHT"—THE HOLD STEADY

So I saw the waitress again. You know, the one from Minneapolis. Those who don't know, please refer back to posts #6 and #22. I apologize this blog does not have an internal search engine.

It was last week. She was without her laptop, and scribbling in a small notebook in the balcony of Irving Plaza at the TV on the Radio show. She was on the VIP side, on the right; I was with the people, directly across from her on the left. The show was extra-terrestrial. Great clouds of weed smoke rose up from the crowd beneath us, and the band churned out waves of soul-drone energy so massive it was all you could do to hold onto the boogie board of your consciousness and ride it until a lull. It's appropriate they're on 4AD, because they totally have that swoon-rock thing down, like Cocteau Twins and Lush, but more gnarly and boyish and groovy and urban and dissonant and hippie-ish and hairy. Dave Sitek, the white dude, had these little windchimes attached to the peghead of his guitar, which he kept wacking against the microphone, and that seemed like an apt metaphor—taking delicate, beautiful things, like Kyp's falsetto and Tunde's soulman tenor and the overall droning ambiance, and smashing them around.

As I believe I've noted before, there's something mannish in this woman's appearance, substantial in that Midwestern Nordic way; broad shoulders, horsey teeth, and strong legs. She wore one of those little half-sweaters, black, affixed beneath her bosom over a leotard, with small green crystal earrings and a wooden cross, which looked half-goth, half-Christian, like it coulda gone either way.

And so it did, as I found out when we spoke after the show. Like many Minnesotan progressives, straight and gay, she apparently couldn't quite shake the Christianity, despite her obvious distaste for the way it's been hijacked by nutjobs and bigots and homophobes and hawks and powermongers and psychotic TV preachers and faux-pious rappers and craven political spin-meisters and clueless Germanic popes. So she made it a fashion accessory and a social networking tool. We talked about first communion and confirmation and *Jesus Christ Superstar*, which was my very first album and hers too. In fact—and this is the first weird thing, but not the most weird thing—she had the words JESUS CHRIST SUPERSTAR tattooed in the shape of a tiny cross on the front of her right shoulder, just below the collarbone. She pulled down her top an inch or so to show it to me.

She explained it was the first album she ever owned as well, and thus the first tattoo. She also said she was embarrassed to have the name of an Andrew Lloyd Weber creation inked into her flesh, but that it only goes to prove that, and I quote here, "you should not get a tattoo when you are young and foolish, just the same way you shouldn't discuss marriage with someone while on ecstasy."

We talked about the show by Merzbow, the Japanese noise artist, which was the last time I saw her. I told her about the mass retching at the show, which she had not seen, but had read something about in *Pop Matters*. It turns out she left early because she'd felt queasy. I told her my theory that he was an activist vegetarian sonically attacking carnivores. Sure enough, she'd eaten hanger steak that night.

It turns out she lives in New York full-time now. She's a copywriter at Ogilvy & Mather, but also writes on music—for *Rolling Stone*, *Blender*, *Spin*, *No Depression*, *Bust*, and *Arthur*. We talked about writing, though I didn't mention this blog. And we talked about tattoos. The Jesus Christ Superstar one she did herself, using a mirror, which I found remarkable.

And that's when the most weird thing happened, the recognition of which was precipitated by my hearing a line from a song in my head, which goes:

> *"Tiny little text etched into her neck*
> *it said Jesus lived and died for all your sins."'*

And then another line that went:

> *"Damn right I'll rise again."*

And yes—I found out her name was Holly. It's a name I like a lot. It's the name of the transvestite in the first verse of Lou Reed's "Walk on the Wild Side," the one who "shaved her legs / then the he was a she," and who is based on the real life Holly Woodlawn. And that's kind of appropriate, given this Holly's boyish demeanor.

But this Holly, as some of you now must realize, has been specifically immortalized not in the songs of Lou Reed, but in those of the Hold Steady, and it's been going on for two albums now. Not accurately immortalized, I now know, but immortalized nonetheless.

"Fucking shitbag liar," Holly says in an Irish bar on 3rd Avenue that we wind up in. There is no Jesus tattoo on her neck, as the song

"Yr Little Hoodrat Friend" suggests, just the one on her shoulder. (She says "Little Hoodrat Friend" is about her too, even though it doesn't use her name.) As for the tattoo on her lower back—the one that Craig Finn snarls about reading as "Damn right I'll rise again"—is actually a knockoff of a Maori moko design like the kind Ben Harper has on his back and has been showing off over the years. No words at all. It's right on her sacrum, in fact. She excused herself, went to the bathroom, unsnapped her Danskin snaps, and came back out to show me. She rolled down the top of her Lee's, and I reached my hand out to steady myself against a pillar. As mokos go, I thought it was a pretty good knockoff.

"It's pagan, not Christian," she said, sitting down in the booth. "That's key. He made me out to be some junkie trainwreck Jesus freak. I'm more pagan than Christian, really."

She shook her head. "Fucking liar," she said.

"Wow," I said.

"And I did go to Hazelden," she said. "But just to chill, really. And my parents didn't name me Hallelujah. It's just Holly. That came from a joke—Craig would say 'Holly-lujah!' whenever he was drunk, which of course was constantly.

"Asshole," she said.

After that she fell quiet. And then she had to leave, because she had work the next day.

"First Night" is the only song explicitly about Holly on the Hold Steady's excellent new record, *Boys and Girls in America*. It's my favorite: it made me teary-eyed before I met her, and it still does. So does the line in "Same Kooks" about "making love to the girls with wrapped up wrists." "First Night" mentions something about Holly, the character, being in a hospital. I didn't ask her about that. But I did look at her wrists, which seemed unmarked under her string bracelets.

Holly doesn't have a blog. She doesn't believe in them. "I don't write for free," she said. "Fuck that. Writing is too hard. I'd rather just keep my thoughts inside my head until I need 'em." She grinned a toothy Midwestern grin.

I also didn't ask her whether she moved to New York for Craig, although I assume she did. And I didn't ask for her phone number, because I didn't want her to think I was hitting on her, because at the time I wasn't sure I wanted to. I just said, "I'll see you around." Stupid. Stupid. Stupid.

But I am certain I will see her around. The movements of music writers, after all, are very predictable.

posted by Robert Barbara @ 9:45 PM

INDUSTRIAL PSYCHOLOGY

The snarl was familiar before I ever put my head on the platinum-buttoned ocelot fur couch. "Get money. Fuck bitches." Eyes closed, I know that my diamond-grilled therapist isn't taking notes and I wonder how much he's even listening, while he hypnotically repeats the mantra—Get money. Fuck bitches. Get money. Fuck bitches— each syllable gurgling like a telltale heart gone hood. I don't remember if I asked him about the major general of the Queen's Navy chasing me up the mountain or when I diffused a bomb while slathered in white paint or why, in my waking hours, I would actually break up with perfectly scrumptious, wifey-material because she once wore a silly hat. I really don't think it'd matter. Dr. Weezy F. Baby (please say the motherfuckin' . . . Ph.D.) has one lesson: Get money. Fuck bitches. And that's why I'm on his decadent couch and he's not taking notes.

"I need something, anything, other than those four words, damn it!" I scream. My outburst shocks me, but it has a point and I intend to pursue it. "What about the dreams and the sweats? What about the deer-skin lamps with the fangs?"

Dr. Weezy F. Baby stays silent.

In reality, Lil' Wayne (aka Weezy F. Baby) isn't licensed to call me crazy, at least not yet. He is studying psychology (or maybe political science?) at the University of Houston and, according to his last report card, he's "on the fuckin' honor roll." Wayne has his own distorted, nonsensical dreams too, and one is to be a celebrity psychologist "'cause they pay." Get Money. Fuck Bitches.

If we look only at the music released from December 6, 2005, to November 21, 2006, then the boasts of this self-proclaimed "best rapper alive" are dead-on. The former date marks the release of his fifth solo album, *Tha Carter II*, and the latter is (fittingly) when his hero, Jay-Z, officially ends his retirement—but for exactly 350 days, it's not even a question. No one rapped better than Lil' Wayne over this period. *Carter II* was immediately lauded as Wayne's magnum opus, the potential of contemporary hip-hop's most unique voice finally realized on record. Born Dwayne Michael Carter in New Orleans's famed and maimed 17th Ward, the newly named president of Cash Money Records followed Jay-Z's blueprint, mining a mixture of string-heavy soul samples and frantic club hits for quotable quips and an inexhaustible collection of danger-soaked—and artistically risky—street tales. *Dedication 2*, his Gangsta Grillz mixtape with DJ Drama released this summer, was even better. Tackling the most monstrous beats of the year ("Hustlin'," "What You Know") and some jaw-dropping originals ("Cannon"), Wayne tears through rap with an incalculable fervor, and by the time it's all over, *Dedication 2* is easily the hip-hop album of the year. Even with just a slim case.

"Don't let that bird shit," Wayne says. "He got a weak stomach." When Dr. Baby talks, he speaks in riddle and I lose track of who's the patient between us. This is his response to another of my nightmares, and sometimes I prefer the 47-foot-tall birds pecking at the webbing of my feet, at least to this nonsense.

"What kind of grown man is petrified of birds?" I ask. "I need a real answer. I'm sick. I don't spit, I vomit. Got it? One egg short of the omelet."

He clears his throat and I sit up to hear his words of wisdom. "Fuck bitches. Get money." I lie back down and maybe lose my grip again.

The truth is, Wayne raps with the swagger of a man on a mission. Much is made of a swagger; it made Rakim's microphone science devastating and not devastatingly boring, it made Big Daddy Kane's dance moves not only OK, but hard as hell, it makes Lil' Wayne's near-nursery rhymes ("Dear Mr. Toilet / I'm the shit") into scathing daggers. Gravelly and hoarse or high-pitched and otherworldly, he makes the simplest words sound alien. He can reflect an apocalyptic air of relaxation, practically making his lungs-open, leaned-back posture in the booth audible on record. Just as easily, he'll push a manic urgency through walls of anger and unrelenting will, not like the anxiety-inducing stress of Ghostface, but with a calm and calculated manner that is even scarier. He exhales repose and inhales exigency. "*I eat rappers and go in my yard and bury their bones.*" His voice is anchored by an intimidating nasality and a mordacious N'awlins drawl that combine to form something like Death's sinewy snarl—but only if Death had "Fear God" tattooed on his eyelids. Weezy does. The effect of his voice, the tattoos on his eyelids, it's all maligned and menacing, and yet the man wouldn't stand six feet tall standing on 16 phone books.

"Let me get 'em / I hope his kids not with him."

What happens if his kids are with him? Does that mean that the job has to wait or that the job just gets uglier? Don't let the laconic lines fool you—he's a lyricist. His punch lines are rarely tired, instead doused in an energized cleverness—"Broke dudes only make jokes funny / I make more than I can fit in this quote, money"—that makes heads shake or just as easily provides narration for fight music.

"I say that after every song, I be like, 'I murdered that shit,'" says the Weezy of this dimension, though it's hard to tell. The question was about a moment of clarity, of understanding and appreciating one man's own creation. For Wayne, the act of creating is spontaneous (he freestyles every line, never writing a word before stepping into the booth), but his response to questions is measured. He leans forward, wary of speaking the braggadocio of his raps in a beat-less conversation. "But you know, I ain't on myself like that, to be like, 'Yeah I'm a beast.' I just do it in my raps."

We're sitting in his tour bus now, at a foldout table possessing a tidiness that suggests a center-of-command for business. Teenie-bopper singing sensation and backflipping extraordinaire Chris Brown sits to my right. BET is filming the back of my head. Nearly a dozen others look on and anticipate the minute tasks that make Wayne's life easier—rolling blunts, timing journalists—and I take note that I should tell my shrink about this, too. Everyone is in Los Angeles as part of Brown's *Up Close and Personal Tour* (supported by Ne-Yo, Juelz Santana, Dem Franchise Boys and Wayne) and, more specifically, everyone is in Hollywood for Young Money/Cash Money artist Currency's debut video shoot. I'm only there to debunk a statement Wayne makes toward the end of *Carter II*, and the longer I stay the more I find myself praying there's something to debunk at all.

On "Feel Me," a sensuous studio journalist asks about Wayne's motivation and he is vehement that it can't be anything but money. "*Is that really a question? Do you really have that written down in your note book? You should be ashamed of yourself. You smell me, I smell like money.*"

Church music cues the very next second and Weezy leaves his heart on a strained track about the kind of devastation that's slightly more tangible than that of his lyrical prowess. "I got to bring the hood back after Katrina / Weezy F. Baby / Now the F is for FEMA / Sick nigga bitch / I spit that leukemia."

"Surely, it is not just about money," I insist.

"If I wasn't getting paid, I wouldn't do it. I represent the new generation of hip-hop," he says. "Back then, you had a generation that was like, 'We don't need no money, we'll do it for nothing.' You know why? Because they wasn't getting money. They don't know how money feel, how it taste. I'm a millionaire!"

I still don't want to believe him. How dare he shatter that romanticized, Kafkaesque image of the starving artist? His thoughtless dismissal deflates everything that an artist is supposed to embody. Where would he be, after all, if he hadn't made his voice heard so many years ago? "I'm a smart man. I'd be in school, probably be scamming, making cons in some kind of way, probably have like 10 black cards," he says. An eerily diabolic grin quietly dominated the conversation, ". . . all in your name."

It's easy to forget that Wayne is just 24; he carries a weight in his shoulders that expresses a world beyond his 288 months. Maybe he just works out a lot. "In reality, I am [an old soul]. I got a seven-year-old daughter, I'm married and divorced, I done been shot twice, I went through three different [record] deals . . . I am old." As vulnerable as he sometimes allows himself to be on record ("I know people who died in those pools / I know people who died in those schools"), he rarely lifts the iron façade of seriousness.

Today's video shoot is one of those rare moments at this point in his ascension, and a lapse in his armor shows as he gropes a green-screened silhouette of Remy Martin (eyeing the director's monitor to ensure his gesture's hilarity), leads a Red Hot Chili Peppers sing-a-long, and loudly fantasizes about slapping the Pussycat Dolls in their foreheads with a stack of $100 bills if they come to his birthday party. Suddenly, someone sneezes and Wayne is the first to say, "Bless you." During every break, everyone's jokes get punctuated with a loud, "Baaaaawll-in!" With every shout of the day's catchphrase—coined by Jim Jones on "We Fly High"—Wayne leans back and looks to the sky, the maze of tattoos on his tattered arms almost reaching the cotton-candy punk belt that hardly holds up his pants. The Cash Money Records publicist is thrilled that I get to see "Wayne's playful side."

"I have fun every day because it could be my last one," he says in a familiar refrain. "Get money! That's the funnest thing—past, present, future—it's the most funnest shit ever! You ever tried it?"

I have, and now I'm back on the couch, looking to the sky—sans pink belt—at Dr. Weezy F. Baby's mosaic ceiling. It's an artistic rendering of legal-tender $100 bills. I ask Dr. Baby about the strive for artistic contentment, about the stress of creating something only because it needs to be created. Is it really an egotistical extension of my search for acceptance? Can that deep-seeded yearning just be self-destruction in order to get people to like me? Which Weezy am I talking to, the wise-beyond-his-years pseudo-Freud, or a developmentally stunted, real-life mogul who happens to be the king of his game? How is it possible to find meaning in a finite world, given all the time I spend quoting Lil' Wayne?

"Fuck bitches. Get money."

SARAH GODFREY

MULTIPLE PERSONALITY DISORDER

Rapper Multiple Man owes a certain lady friend for at least some of his rise to local notoriety. She has blond wavy hair, a luscious red mouth, and stands about 3 feet tall. And she blows up in the back.

The doll that has become an integral part of Multiple Man's stage show was bought at a D.C. adult store in 2000. "I was looking for porn one day, and I found her," he says. "It was a professional purchase. I've never used her for personal use, despite what some might say."

Multiple Man, aka 30-something Kasimir Bovell, revealed his plastic woman to the public during a gig at the Spot in 2000. At the time, he remembers being frustrated with the repetitive acts that crowded the stage. "I was listening to everybody, and the first nigga came out: 'I'm the hardest nigga in my hood—good night!'" says the Petworth rapper. "Then the next nigga comes out: 'I'm harder than him. I'm the hardest nigga in my hood, and I'll shoot you in the face—good night!'"

Multiple Man came out dragging the doll in one hand, a traffic cone in the other. "I got up there," he says, "and [people in the audience] were like, 'What the fuck is this?'" Launching into his performance, Multiple Man held the cone to his crotch, like a big orange dick. Then he used it to simulate sex with the inflatable doll. Multiple Man now sees this moment as a watershed in his career.

"There are two kinds of D.C. rappers," he explains. "Eighty percent are wife-beater-wearin' niggas talking about 'I-ma shoot you, I-ma kill you.'" And then there are rappers like Multiple Man, who "come with some creativity." Having invented the doll bit, Multiple Man went on to incorporate it into most of his future acts. The use of crazyass props beyond the usual liquor bottles and weed paraphernalia became his signature, his way of showing a different side of D.C. rap.

Of course, sex toys alone cannot carry a career—Multiple Man also has crafted an extensive arsenal of songs. His two albums, 2002's *The Multiverse* and 2004's *The Multiplexxx*, are filled with delightful Son of Blowfly–style filth smacked with enough eccentricity to separate the songwriter from his peers. "Celebrity Fuck Match," a track on *The Multiplexxx*, would be blandly freaky if it discussed boning Beyoncé, but instead it sexualizes Oprah. "2 Heads," from his upcoming *Multitudes*, is a Big Love song dedicated to a very special lady . . . and her best friend. Multiple Man believes strongly in good lyrics: "I gotta show you that I got wordplay and I'm a crazy muthafucka," he says, "not just that I'm a crazy muthafucka."

Multiple Man has actually been a ward of St. Elizabeths mental hospital. But he thinks his brain works fine—better than average, in fact—it's just that "sometimes," he says, "the person I am, and the way the world is, don't match."

At a recent performance at the Velvet Lounge, audience members seemed to be in on the joke, eagerly eyeing the doll that sat slumped over in a corner.

Multiple Man made them wait for it, though. He opened with "Metro Line," a description of life on the train that has "two raggedy dykes kissin' / And dirty bums pissin'," and "The Nation's Capitol," in which he proclaims "D.C." stands for "dirty and cruddy" and "dope and crack." But when he switches from local boosterism to raunchier fare, like the sequel to audience fave "Bang That Ass"—a crowd-pleaser called "Still Wanna Bang Dat Ass"—the doll comes into play. He makes her straddle him, eats her out, smacks her on her ass, then gets his autoerotic asphyxiation on and chokes her a little bit. Finally, he pretends to cum on her back and collapses onto the poor thing in a spent heap.

"I think I actually got a nut," he says.

Multiple Man was introduced to hip-hop at the age of 11, in Tulsa, Okla., where he spent eight years of his childhood. "Around that time, everybody was breakin'," he says. "I'd pull a windmill here, a backspin there." But in 1988, Multiple Man left behind the favorable reputation he'd built with his childhood group, the T-Town Breakers, and moved to the District. "Rappin' was just starting to get cool there," he says, "and then I had to come up here."

What he found was a city less than enthralled by hip-hop. "Not too many people were fuckin' with rap," he says. "People were smackin' congas—rap was some bama shit." Multiple Man, who takes his name from the X-Men comic book character, says that while D.C. residents began listening to rap in the late '80s, they weren't interested in creating the music until around 2000. "I hung with a circle of rap friends," he says, "but if you rapped, it was like you were a traitor to the city."

In 1999, Multiple Man attempted to take himself out. He was hospitalized in St. Elizabeths briefly for evaluation. "I tried to knock myself off—took 60-some Tylenol, which can cause hepatotoxicity and brain damage," he says. "That's the most punkass shit I've ever done in my life." But the experience wasn't all bad: Multiple Man was pleased to discover that "they feed your ass good" in the psych ward. And he walked away with the perfect cover art for *The Multiverse*: a photograph of him, with his hands gripping the sides of his head, sitting in front of St. E's front gates.

Multiple Man thinks that because D.C. rappers are late to the party, there's a lot of mediocre product in the city. The old complaint goes that many D.C. rappers are just less-interesting knockoffs of Scarface and Tupac. *The Multiverse* was his attempt to cloud conventional wisdom about D.C.'s gangster rap scene. Tracks included the first incarnation of "Bang That Ass," the jerk-off theme song "Choke My Chicken," and the thick-chick anthem "Phat Young Girl," which was used by plus-sized porn star Lady Nanaja in a girl-on-girl scene in *Fat Young Girls*.

Andrew Elwell, better known as poet, MC, and frequent hip-hop show host Captain Caveman, says that what separates Multiple Man from the pack is that he never follows the crowd. "He has energy on stage, he's coming with a message, and he can rap his ass off."

The Multiverse also featured a fair bit of science-speak, reflecting Multiple Man's decision in 2002 to enroll at Howard University for a Doctor of Pharmacy degree, following in his father's footsteps. "On [*The Multiverse*], I was talking about alimentary canals and nimbostratus clouds," he says.

"He'll be talking about everyday things and then just throws it in there," says Porche' 9–11, a longtime Multiple Man friend and collaborator. "It's like, Wow, I don't even know what that is, but it sounds good."

Yet for his second release, Multiple Man cut out most references to human anatomy and weather systems. "I can admit, between *The Multiverse* and *Multiplexxx* of dumbing it down. . . . The literacy rate in D.C. is 20 percent." Multiple Man thinks D.C. isn't ready yet for weird, dense rappers. Put an MF Doom or Kool Keith record on the stereo at Northeast's Azeeze Bates apartments, where his girlfriend stays, and "niggas'll use it for target practice," he says.

Last year, Multiple Man felt comfortable enough with his place in the rap world—and his ability to make such critical pronouncements—to start reviewing local, independent hip-hop groups. *The Multiple Report*, which he e-mails to a select group every month or so, features his own special rating system. Five skulls, the top score, is accompanied by the explainer: "BIDALOOOOO!!! That's Classic Shit Right Here, Joe!!" "Bid-a-looooo" is Multiple Man's trademark battle cry, which he calls an "optic blast," and the highest form of praise. At the lower end of the spectrum there is one-and-a-half skulls ("Young!!! . . . What the Fuck Was U Thinkin', Young!!??"); one skull ("This is Some Real Bama Ass Shit, Slim!!!"); and the dreaded half-skull ("U Should Be Smacked 4 This Bama Ass Shit!!!").

The language is harsh, but Multiple Man insists that people need strong, honest critiques from someone inside the scene if the city is ever to capture the attention of listeners outside of the region. "Folks are already sleepin' on us—we gotta give them a reason to wake up," he says. "Idaho might come first and rap about potatoes . . . doing things with French fries."

Multiple Man sometimes pisses people off—but never because of a rating itself. A recipient of one of the lowest ratings the *Report* ever handed out called the critic to yell at him because the album critique contained what he felt was a low blow. "I kinda went overboard," Multiple Man concedes.

"I said, 'I can't see his own mother coming to see him perform.' He called me and said his mother was killed by the government. He didn't mind the review, but it was that I mentioned his mother. I knew he was divorced, so I even put that I could see why his wife left him—he didn't mind that, just mentioning his mom.

"So I apologized," Multiple Man says. "But the review still stands."

The upcoming *Multitudes*, which Multiple Man hopes to drop sometime next year, hasn't been reviewed yet, but the rapper imagines the *Multiple Report* will mark it with no less than four, and likely five skulls, just as his other releases have been scored. He's already recorded several tracks for the release but, as he's struggled with toning down cerebral lyrics in the past, he's now toying with another idea.

"I was thinking about cleaning my shit up," he says. "I got stepkids now."

The thought is still simmering on the back burner, though. Multiple Man has too many projects planned that require him to work blue. He intends to release a Christmas album where he'll take traditional holiday songs and "smear dirt on 'em," as well as an all-sex project titled *Multiple Orgasms*.

Besides, going G-rated would mean he'd have to abandon the latest addition to his stage show—a booty-shaking little person. "I found the midget on MySpace," he says. "We got to kickin' it. . . . I said, 'I'll punish your little midget ass'—like that." Multiple Man says the woman was intrigued by one of his promo pics—she thought a shot of him in a hockey mask, holding a big knife over a big plate of ground beef, was "sexy"—and agreed to dance at one of his shows.

"I was like, cool," he says. "Muthafuckas already know I bring out a doll, but I brought out a dancing midget."

MAN IN LOVE

Barbra Streisand, Barry Gibb, and
the Autobiographical Criticism of
Doug Belknap

Some of you I would hope have read Dianne Hart's monograph *Enough Is Enough: Prodigality Celebrated and Condemned in the Carter-Era Recordings of Barbra Streisand*. Although Dr. Hart's study is limited in scope, her thinking is expansive. My own forthcoming book on Streisand's middle period is indebted to her penetrating analyses. I must also thank Hart for exposing me to the criticism of Doug Belknap. A footnote in *Enough Is Enough* led me to the man's review of *Guilty*, Streisand's 1980 collaboration with Barry Gibb, and I have since become an admirer of Belknap's idiosyncratic and loudly autobiographical work.

The review of *Guilty* appeared that year in the September issue of *Spunk* magazine, a formerly influential rock monthly by then considered debased by the relevant tastemakers. *Spunk* at the time was mostly devoted to rock of a decidedly masculine cast. One imagines that *Spunk* readers were united in enmity or at least apathy toward Streisand and Gibb, and would have considered an endorsement of

Guilty distasteful and a pan gratuitous. It's odd, then, that the magazine gave the album any coverage at all, odder still that they ran Belknap's long, discursive review.

What I've since managed to learn about Belknap is that he lived in Minneapolis, briefly attended the University of Minnesota, and worked, moonlighting presumably, as a freelance writer, most provably during 1979 and '80. I found one piece published in the University's *Minnesota Daily* in May of 1972, a recommendation of Weather Report's *I Sing the Body Electric* notable for employing two food metaphors. In the first paragraph Belknap calls the album a "spicy gumbo of New Thing jazz, acid rock, hot-buttered soul, classical gas, and Latin passion"; in the closing paragraph he likens it to a "steaming bouillabaisse."

Belknap may have written as well for community newspapers throughout the '70s, but his byline doesn't return to an officially archived publication until late '79. Again it's attached to a review of a Weather Report album—the concert recording *8:30*—penned for the short-lived *Rhythm-A-Ning* magazine. A warm appraisal of the music quickly gives way to a digression about a record reviewer, apparently a gastronome and fusion buff, who constructs a model suspension bridge from clippings of the 147 reviews he has written for a jazz newsletter. Each review contains at least one food metaphor, a feat of stylistic persistence that apparently went unnoticed by the newsletter's subscribers or its alcoholic editor. The reviewer then takes a fatal dose of sleeping pills and lies down next to the model bridge, in effect jumping off his own work.

Belknap wrote three relatively restrained reviews for *Spunk* in the summer of '80, followed by the Streisand piece, which is quoted in its entirety below, and which seems to mark the end of his career in music criticism. My efforts to track down Belknap have been unsuccessful. If you know anything about his whereabouts, please contact me. I remain eager to speak with him.

Barbra Streisand
Guilty
CBS Records
Reviewed by Doug Belknap

I see that *Guilty*'s liner notes have Richard Tee playing electric guitar on the "The Love Inside." If you know your session men, you'll raise an eyebrow at the credit, and sure enough, the electric instrument Richard Tee is playing is a piano, not a guitar. One thing Barbra Streisand's latest success is guilty of, then, is shoddy liner-note composition. Otherwise it's pretty much blameless.

Maybe you've already seen the jacket, with Gibb, who wrote or co-wrote all of the album's songs, wrapping his arms around a coquettish Streisand, both dressed in angelic white, à la Johnny Mathis on the cover of *Heavenly*. It would be too much to call this music heavenly, but it is ethereal, so light you have to adjust your tone arm to play the LP version. And yet the album's consommé of pop and Broadway, disco and light R&B isn't wholly insubstantial. I find it moving. Streisand and Gibb haven't lent great stores of genuine emotion to their collaboration, but they've given the listener the tools to do so: the bravura phrasing, a drama in nearly every measure; the voluptuous, occasionally capricious melodies and chord changes; the trademark vocal harmonies, both transcendent and rodential, that Gibb honed with the Bee Gees.

I've liked Barry Gibb ever since I heard "Massachusetts" on the radio of a cream Mercedes 450 SEL belonging to Linda Morgan's mom. We kissed that night, Linda and I, standing in front of the car, and her breasts were large and her sweater was softer than any fabric I had ever felt. I hadn't previously associated with people who could afford cashmere sweaters, or even cashmere socks. Our subsequent outings, however, were washouts.

Let me return to "The Love Inside," which is indeed lovely, and not only on the inside. Expansive, resigned, middle-aged, it's like a

Sondheim ballad minus the erudition. The clever turns of phrase have been replaced with clichés—"I'm just an empty shell" and so forth—but the lachrymal high notes are present, yearning and wheedling. During this song one might pause for a pensive break from preparing something out of *Elegant Dinners for Two*, perhaps absentmindedly taking a sip of economical red wine. I did just that earlier this evening. Also, I cut the recipe in half. "The Love Inside" isn't free of the breathless histrionics Streisand brings to nearly every performance, but it is sung with the proper subtlety, which is to say, neither too much nor too little. Streisand remains a stage singer, of course, a belter for whom amplification is a luxury rather than a necessity. Only a fool would refuse to use such a voice to its full capacity.

A fool or an ascetic, because it must be a pleasure to sing like that. It must be a pleasure to be outstanding at something. Yesterday I was given my United States Tennis Association rating. I've decided to play competitive tennis in a league, to meet new friends, as they say, and because Sharon once said I looked good in white. Before signing up, you must have a coach rate your game on the official scale. There's an official scale that goes from one to seven. One is a paraplegic three-year-old with imperfect vision and a carelessly strung racket. Two is a paraplegic three-year-old with perfect vision and a decent lob. A 6.9 is John McEnroe. I've been judged a 3.2, just below the mean. I'm competent, obviously no beginner, but also not impressive, not the sort of player whose strokes inspire admiration from passers-by in the park. I suspect I'm a 3.2 in general. Once I asked a girl from work how she would rate my looks on a scale of one to ten. She said I was a seven, maybe even an eight. I'm not sure how that translates to a one-to-seven scale, but it beats a 3.2. Of course she would never have called me a six or below to my face. And she wouldn't have given me a suspiciously generous nine or ten. Really, then, she was working on a two-point scale, seven acting as one and eight as two. And she went with one, approaching two on a good day. So that probably is a 3.2.

Sometimes when Sharon would play her Barbra Streisand records, I would make noises of disapproval. One time she responded by hissing, "anti-Semite," jokingly. I laughed enough for the joke to become a ritual. Sharon wasn't routinely funny, but when she was, she was, I thought, quotable. My complaints were good-natured, you see, in contrast to how she and Donald would disparage my Weather Report and Chick Corea albums, once quite harshly when I was allegedly reading in the other room. "Oh, don't take off the Chick Corea album, Sharon," Donald said, coaxing a laugh out of Sharon. "I'd love to hear it again and again!" His sarcasm was strictly of the meat and potatoes variety, never clever.

I doubt it would interest Donald or Sharon to know that Steve Gadd, featured on the Chick Corea album derided that night, also plays on *Guilty*. He plays superbly, with manly assurance. Thanks to his hiccuping fills toward the end of "Promises," even Barbra Streisand can claim to have almost made a funk single. What a sad, strange song that is, Gibb's hooks like icicles, Streisand's singing joyfully desperate. "I am the love, don't let me die away," she sings, with several Barry Gibbs answering "die away" in harmony, appropriately stretching out "die" like a last breath. I wish I could hear this album with Sharon. I could listen to it every night with her, twice. I would gently rub it with a pink felt record-cleaning cloth after each airing, apologizing for the tiny needle pricks.

When we first started dating I perhaps mislead Sharon by saying that I liked Barbra Streisand, too. What I meant is that I found her charming in the mid-60s, especially on the *My Name Is Barbra* TV special, flirting with kettle drummers and singing songs about poverty and against materialism while vamping and hamming, by turns enviously and contemptuously, through Bergdorf Goodman. She was brilliant, funny, and gorgeous. I watched the show with my mom. I guess I was fourteen. My mom grew up in New Jersey, and although she was estranged from her family, she missed the East Coast, missed the Italians and Jews she used to hang out with. Not that there aren't Italians and Jews in Minneapolis, but they're much scarcer. My mom loved Streisand, loved her misfit glamour, her wit, her Jewishness, her abnormal voice. "She has the lungs of a beluga whale," said my dad, passing through the room. "You flatter the beluga whale," said my mom.

I also sheepishly enjoyed *The Way We Were*, which I saw on an inauspicious first date with Lorraine Ibsen. But for the most part though, prior to Sharon, I ignored Streisand. I mainly listened to jazz and rock and fusion and hardly ever tuned in AM radio. Streisand's sometimes maligned attempts to sing contemporary material couldn't bother me because, except for the hit she had with Laura Nyro's "Stoney End," I didn't hear them. I was unaware of her version of John Lennon's "Mother," for instance, until Sharon and I moved in together and Sharon's extensive collection of Streisand records and memorabilia arrived as an unwelcome dowry. "She's singing it like it's called 'Second Cousin Twice Removed,'" I cracked, as Sharon arranged the furniture. It came out more cuttingly than I intended, but Sharon chuckled. Later we made love on a mattress on the floor, and the night proved to be the apex of our predominantly healthy sexual relationship. There are at least two images from that night that I still use, not always happily, as masturbatory aids.

Every morning, except Tuesdays and Sundays when she didn't work at Carson Pirie Scott, Sharon would do her ablutions to Streisand's "I Can Do It." Most evenings she would play a Streisand album or two, and occasionally Donald would come over for a "Babsanalia." Mostly this just meant talking and playing records, but sometimes they'd pantomime and dress up, Donald in half-drag, or they'd reenact scenes from Streisand's movies. The Babsanalia were always spontaneous, usually involved pot or coke, and often lasted into the small hours, at which point the accuracy of the reenactments was suspect. My only contribution to these endeavors was the coinage "Babsanalia." I participated once, on a night when I felt it was important for me to get high. It was hard to be the third wheel. I was insufficiently equipped with knowledge or enthusiasm.

Sharon and Donald were too sophisticated to be truly idolatrous, but not sophisticated enough to blend sincere passion and self-aware irony in the manner of high camp. That was how I saw it anyway. The frivolity of it all chafed me. Nothing important was important to Sharon or Donald. Their Streisand club was purely escapist, of course, a means of pretending not to be of our generation and not from Minnesota, or to be witty and urbane and to have a bona fide witty and urbane gay friend instead of a dim closet case. I was never explicitly excluded from the Babsanalia but it became clear that these evenings were for serious fans only and that I should find other amusement. Usually I'd read in the bedroom. Sometimes I'd go to a bar alone.

Donald also worked at Carson Pirie Scott, in the men's casual-wear department. He was not an ethical man. When a shirt came in that he liked he would hide it in the backroom until it went on final clearance. Then he would sneak it back to the sales floor, as if it had been languishing on the rack the whole time, and he'd get it for even cheaper than his employee discount. Donald was reportedly straight, but I knew this to be untrue, at least not entirely true. Sharon accepted his bluff, though she was attracted to his apparent gayness in the way my mom was attracted to Streisand's Jewishness. Sharon did acknowledge that Donald moved and talked in a way that would lead many if not most to unfairly question his sexuality. Then there was his Streisand fixation, his interest in clothes (though he dressed badly if you ask me), his passion for the theater, his insistence on being called Donald and never Don, the fact that he had once lured me into the bathroom at Deborah Curtis' Christmas party, and that once inside Deborah Curtis' bathroom he had whipped out his cock or at least not strenuously protested when I slowly unzipped his jeans and executed my first and only act of fellatio.

Sharon didn't know this last piece of evidence regarding Donald's homosexuality.

Donald had one good male friend that I knew of, a short, part-time actor with Aryan features and the physique of an amateur weightlifter who was even dumber than Donald, and lazy. He didn't work other than the three or four parts he landed a year, usually one lead in a community-theater embarrassment and a few spear-carrying gigs at the big theater in town. Mostly he cadged from girlfriends and half-heartedly sold drugs. I called him the Slothario, which Sharon, who didn't like him either, thought was clever. Donald and the Slothario would go to nightclubs often, reportedly to pick up women. They even bought notch-less belts from a neighborhood cobbler and leather worker, stole a leather punch from a hardware store, and would actually add notches to their belts in commemoration of successful seductions. Of course anyone can punch a hole in a belt, and no way was Donald getting it up for all those girls. My theory was that Donald and the Slothario were lovers. Donald also had steady girlfriends, including a tiny, laconic brunette named Sara with no "h" who, when she worked as a peep-show model, called herself "Sar-ahh!" Donald and Sara dated for almost a year. My theory was that Sara was also gay, either by birth or as an occupational acquisition. During the year that Donald and Sara were going out I sometimes found myself in situations that led me to wonder how effectively the tinted windows at Paulie's Hot Tomatoes cloaked the peeping customers. I figured I caught a break when Donald and Sara broke up.

It was around that time, though, that Donald and Sharon started spending even more time together, mostly away from our apartment. By then there were a few clubs in Minneapolis where one could disco, and they would do that, sometimes going to a party after the bars closed so that Sharon wouldn't return to our bed until 3:00 a.m. One Easter Sunday I remember she was logy and irritable all day. It didn't occur to me until late in the afternoon that she was hung over. I was so slow on the uptake, such a dolt. She started telling me about a group of East Indian guys who were also going out dancing, how charming they were. One, an aloof, lanky guy named Divyanga who was said to have fallen out of favor with his Brahmin parents, came to a party that Sharon insisted we throw. He said, "It's nice to meet you. Sharon's a great dancer," as if I had given her instruction. He wasn't charming.

One night I bought a new edition of Password, the game, and suggested we share a bottle of wine and play a round or two. Sharon and I both liked Password. She however had plans to go out for drinks followed by dancing and then who knows what with Donald, the Slothario, and the East Indians. I was welcome to come, she insisted. But I wasn't. I noted that she took almost forty-five minutes to get ready, roughly twice as long as usual. I also noted that she looked really good. After she left I tried to read but couldn't concentrate and resorted to TV, which, predictably, only aggravated my depression.

That night Sharon came into bed around 3:00 a.m. again, maybe 3:30, and her breath smelled like vodka and orange juice and cigarettes and she tried to arouse me but I rolled over and feigned sleep. The moment was not unlike those described in "You Don't Bring Me Flowers." Later, I suspected that she had gotten horny dancing with the East Indians and had hoped to seduce me in order to pretend I was someone else. Once during lovemaking she had asked me to portray Hubbell Gardiner, the Robert Redford character from *The Way We Were*, but that was different. I didn't mind. After Divyanga moved into our apartment and I moved in temporarily with Gary the building manager, I also began to doubt the plurality of the East Indians, a ruse no doubt, designed to make de facto dates seem like non-threatening group socializing. Only Divyanga, whom Gary the building manager seemed to know well, had come to our party, and when I asked Sharon, a poor ad-libber, what the others were named, she pretended not to hear and then when asked again came up with "Ravi" and, after yet another pause, "Big Ravi."

Two days after my Password proposal was rejected, Sharon told me that she did love me, but she was no longer in love with me. I had no use for the distinction. I fell from the couch sobbing, not a long fall, but dramatic. I held on to the coffee table; my legs were folded up like a little boy's. Sharon was faced with the situation in which you want to comfort the person whom you have just discomforted. She sat there quietly until I stopped blubbering. Stupidly, we slept in the same bed that night. In the morning I stared apocalyptically at her unblanketed body. She was wearing only underwear, which I took for effrontery. In fairness it had been a warm spring night.

I've been crying with decreasing regularity, though still frequently, during the six months since. Actually, my crying has increased over the past few weeks, since I was assigned to review *Guilty*, in six hundred words. *Guilty* is a sad record, a record about being made foolish by love, about desperation and deceit. Gary the building manager is an AC/DC fan and will be glad when my assignment has been dispatched. Gary's a good guy. Divyanga is cheesed with me for extending my temporary stay at Gary the building manager's, and seems to think I'm not allowed to do my stair-climbing and hall-walking exercises throughout our apartment building, as if I had access to some other building. But I guess Divyanga isn't the boss of me. I notice that Donald never comes around anymore. Divyanga has barred him, no doubt. The guy is paranoid, though he's right about Don.

Guilty ends with a song of romantic betrayal called "Make It Like a Memory." But that's silly because what's worse than a painful memory? Barry Gibb has not read his Proust, at least not carefully, though his melodies sometimes approximate Proustian delicacy.

My current favorite is "Never Give Up," quasi-Arabic funk to my ears, potentially a showstopper, but comparatively pared down, the string and horn players sent home for the night, the bass creeping or maybe skulking. Streisand is self-important where she used to be self-deprecating, but she's jive talking on the verses and it's funny, deliberately funny. The lyric has her suffering from a dry throat. She's non-metaphorically lovesick. "I will never give up," she sings, stretching out "I will" for a full measure, eliding the "r" in "never," making the word an even more emphatic "neva!" The point is reiterated on its way to the chorus' staccato conclusion and the album's summary question: "I will never give up, never give up, never give up. I will follow you home. How can you turn me away?"

JESSICA SHAW

PEOPLE, PEOPLE WHO LOVE BARBRA

Christmas Eve. Lauderdale Lakes, Fla. 1976. Lorraine Lipman is going to see *A Star Is Born* with seven friends and asks her 14-year-old daughter, Robin, if she'd like to come. "What else does a Jewish kid do on Christmas Eve?" Robin now recalls, flashing a smile that dimples her cheeks and squints up her eyes. "As soon as I saw Barbra Streisand's face on the screen, I was blown away." Her expression turns deadly serious. "My whole life changed that night."

Lipman went to see the movie again. And again. And again. 163 times, in fact. As soon as school ended for the day, she would hop on the bus and head to the theater. Every weekend, she'd catch screenings from morning until night. She wore out and replaced the soundtrack album three times, weeping through each listen, leaving tearstains all over the record covers. "That was when I decided I'm going to save every penny for the rest of my life for a Barbra Fund," she says. "I saved every birthday present, every Hanukkah present. I sold all my jewelry. I got extra jobs. I'm so glad I had the foresight to start that back when I was 14."

249

Today, 30 years later, Lipman is holding court on a pillowy beige couch in the Boca Raton, Fla., home of fellow fan John MacEachron, where around 50 devout Barbraphiles have gathered at a brunch celebrating the Florida stops on Streisand's 16-city tour. While two acolytes belt out the *Yentl* soundtrack ("Why is it that every time I close my eyes he's there?") on a portable karaoke machine in the bedroom, a bunch are admiring MacEachron's vast videotape collection, and even more are packed in a small den debating the finer notes of Streisand's early-'70s TV guest appearances. As four amazed guests look on, Lipman flips page by page through her "Six Degrees of Barbra Streisand" scrapbook: a 250-plus-page photo album bulging with pictures of people and places somehow connected to her idol. Chris O'Donnell? "Almost was Bernard," the caption reads, a reference to the Prince of Tides role that ultimately went to Streisand's son, Jason Gould. Starbucks? "Where Barbra gets her coffee in Malibu." Bill Clinton? "F.O.B."

"She's like a stalker," dismissively whispers one onlooker, who then goes on to describe her own extensive collection of Streisand's garbage. (Yes, bags of trash, including a torn-up 1983 letter in which Streisand fires an employee.) Others, like Joanna Gilsenan, a peppy 24-year-old newlywed who flew in from Manchester, England, with her husband, Martin (not a fan, he stagnates in the kitchen), are in awe. "I don't have the infinite knowledge some of these people have," she says. "I just know that before the show last night, this wave of panic hit me. I was going to see Barbra. I felt ill."

For these ardent admirers, loving Streisand is a singularly sublime experience. They are, as they see it, the luckiest people in the world, happy not just to shell out $750 for a concert ticket, but to construct their entire lives around her career. In the realm of Madonna maniacs and Phish fanatics, Streisand's faithful seem to hold a uniquely obsessive spot. "A lot of people have been fans since the '60s and '70s," says Allison J. Waldman, author of the 2001 collection *The*

Barbra Streisand Scrapbook, who is making a documentary, *Let Go and Let Barbra*, with fellow bruncher Angelo Guglielmo Jr. about the most loyal of followers. "Other singers have come and gone, but Barbra, she's a survivor. A lot of Barbra fans feel like they've stuck with her through thick and thin, and they're not stopping now."

Just look at Rosie O'Donnell, who can't remember a time when she didn't worship Streisand . . . and says the sole reason she went into show business was to become friends with her. "It's not as though this is an entertainer that people like, and so they put a poster up of her," says O'Donnell, who is making a fan documentary of her own (*Stalking Streisand*). "She has a gift that has been bestowed on few individuals. I think she's got a direct connection with the Light, or whatever you want to call it—the Source, or God. She's definitely channeling something. She's a huge satellite dish."

As the sun sets a few hours before Streisand's Oct. 30 Fort Lauderdale concert, the plaza in front of the sold-out Bank-Atlantic Center has the spirited vibe of a Grateful Dead show. Occasional loners pace with one finger raised in the air, hoping for a miracle ticket, while a group of fans discuss their dream set lists. But instead of dreadlocked crusties, these early arrivers are seven senior canasta buddies who've carpooled over from the Cascades, a gated adult community in Boynton Beach, Fla. Nearby, Barbara Jaramillo, 57, who recently underwent heart surgery, tries to bond with an excited elderly couple. She sits on a bench, stroking a palm tree necklace around her neck, and starts to get *verklemmt*. "I've been waiting 40 years to see her in person," she says, clutching a white handkerchief she brought along for when the tears really start to flow. "When I found out she was doing another tour, I said, 'I don't care what I have to do. I'm going to be there.' And now I'm jumping out of my skin."

Finally it's showtime, and Streisand appears on a round platform raised from below, lifted into a flood of flattering light. During the two-and-a-half-hour show, she expertly works all sides of the rose-filled stage. The crowd loves it, tittering appreciatively when she jokes about a "senior moment" and letting out a whoosh of *ahhhs* when Streisand starts humming the first few notes of "The Way We Were."

One of the Boca brunchers, Todd Sussman (who had impressed his fellow noshers with an extensive knowledge of past tour merchandise), now sits in the fifth row, taking copious notes about each song for a column ("Todd's Corner") he writes in a Streisand fan newsletter called *All About Barbra*. He springs up at the end of each song as if someone had just sprinkled tacks on his chair, and he is stunned speechless when a woman behind him admits she came to see guest artists Il Divo, not Barbra.

At one point, Streisand introduces Linda Richman—Mike Myers' ex-mother-in-law, who inspired his classic "Coffee Talk" *Saturday Night Live* sketches—from the stage, and heads crane to catch a glimpse. (In other cities, actual celebrities have shown up, including Bill and Hillary Clinton, Robert De Niro, and Oprah.) "It's sick how much I love her," Richman gushes during the intermission. "I play her in the car. I play her at home. The voice keeps getting better. The body keeps getting more voluptuous." Her only complaint? "In '94 I got tickets for free. Ever since my daughter divorced [Myers], the perks really have dried up."

Later, after the lights dim and Streisand strolls out for the second set, this lovefest briefly comes to a screeching halt, courtesy of a now-famous incident featuring a plastic cup filled with ice and maybe some liquid. Streisand brings George Bush impersonator Steve Bridges on stage for a presidential mock session, and a heckler throws said offending item at the singer. "*Treyf,*" Streisand snips, using the Yiddish word for unkosher food, as she throws the cup off stage. From across the theater, another man repeatedly yells, "You're a bitch, Barbra!" and "Four more years!" until three burly security guards drag the squirming, screaming disrupter out. "Just buy my records," Streisand yells back. "Don't see me live!"

Barbra would later claim the ice incident was not politically motivated, but rather the result of a guy having a fight with his girlfriend. Whether or not you buy this, some audience members clearly were put off by the sketch. "It's wrong to bash our president under any circumstances," says Dr. Paula Stewart, a dentist responsible for whitening the teeth of Il Divo, speaking a few days later. "I prefer her as an entertainer, as opposed to being held hostage to hear her political views. Nobody wants to hear that crap." But many others couldn't agree less. "It's the artist's job to provoke," says Rosie O'Donnell. "She's real. She's up there. And she's pissed."

On the day before Streisand's Nov. 2 show at Atlanta's Philips Arena, Edmund La Fosse, 53, woke up at 5 a.m., consumed by the knowledge that Barbra could be here, on his home turf, right now. He flipped on the news, expecting a lead story about where the star was staying or what she was doing. "I thought the anchor would say, 'Streisand hits Atlanta!'" he says the following morning in his cozy condo. "That's where my head is at right now."

His arms covered in tattoos of skulls, one punctured by a blood-dripping blade, La Fosse doesn't look like a typical Streisand disciple. In his bedroom are framed pictures from his time as a principal dancer in Eliot Feld's ballet company and a silk-screen signed "To Edmund, Happy Birthday, Andy Warhol." "From my Studio 54 days," La Fosse says affably, referring to life before the past 18 sober years.

With the concert nine hours away, La Fosse is hanging out with Robin Lipman, who flew up last night to crash at his pad. Lipman and La Fosse have been friends since they met at a Streisand convention more than 20 years ago. Today, the two explore his living room like a couple of archaeologists unearthing holy ruins. There are life-size cutouts of the star from store window displays, the red chandelier earrings and blond hairpiece from the 1966 TV special *Color Me Barbra*, and *Yentl* stickers that Lipman boasts she bought for 39 cents at a drugstore back in 1983. Lipman doesn't even blink at the collection's oddest piece: a pinecone from the grounds of the singer's estate that sits alongside its "Streisand Center Certificate of Authenticity." Maybe it's because at home she displays a piece of Streisand's house that fell off during an earthquake and a bottle of water from the pool of Streisand's former Malibu mansion.

La Fosse looks up at the electronic billboard he's programmed to continuously flash his seat assignment for tonight's show (he has just spent nearly $800 on a front-row ticket, which means he'll have to sell the merely decent one he bought months ago). "I'll see any movie she's in," he says. "I'll buy anything she does. She can't go wrong. I've never felt this way about any other performer. And I've met Liza. I've met Baryshnikov. I've met Madonna."

Before the concert, the two cruise around Atlanta, driving past the Ritz-Carlton hoping for a Streisand sighting (no luck) and stopping by a favorite chicken-and-waffle joint in case their girl grabs some preshow eats (nope). Though La Fosse can't afford the airfare and hotel costs to attend more shows, Lipman will have a couple other chances for a run-in when she flies to the Las Vegas and Los Angeles concerts. Her Barbra Fund is "down to pennies" after she purchased tickets and airfare for 10 of the 20 stops on this tour. But while she's been to 23 concerts over the years, she's never managed to meet her idol. "I don't even know what I would do if I met her," Lipman says. "I'd have to tell her what she's meant to my life. She gives me the most pleasure of anything I've ever known."

That night, the audience is intoxicated by Streisand, especially when she tells a heartwarming story about being pregnant the last time she performed in Atlanta, in 1966. They cheer supportively when she stumbles after part of the set she's leaning on breaks. During a second encore, she dedicates the song "Smile" to her white poodle, Samantha—or as Streisand describes her, "a person [covered] with hair." La Fosse soaks it all up from the front row, eight seats down from John Travolta and Kelly Preston, gazing upward as if to take Communion. "It was the night of my life—the word I am going to use is GENIUS," La Fosse e-mails a few days later, still coming down from the experience. "My friends," he says, "know not to call me a month before the show or a few weeks after. I need some time alone to process the experience. It takes me a while to absorb it."

The morning after the Atlanta show, Lipman rents a car and drives five hours southeast, hoping to visit the South Carolina locations where Streisand filmed *The Prince of Tides*. It takes an hour of getting lost on various bridges before Lipman finds the spot where she can recite Nick Nolte's "Lowenstein . . . Lowenstein" line. She has someone take her picture in the house that Streisand rented during the shoot and snaps some self-portraits in the car's rearview mirror. These pictures will be added to her already extensive collection of reenacted scenes from Streisand's movies. Except *Yentl*. So far the Barbra Fund hasn't covered trips to the Czech Republic.

Eventually Lipman is back home in Coral Springs, Fla., counting the days until she leaves for Las Vegas. At first, she had worried that her boss at the elementary school where she works in administration might deny her request for 13 vacation days. In the end, he okayed the time off, but if he hadn't, Lipman knows her priorities. "There's always another job," she shrugs. But not always another Barbra concert, unfortunately; this tour ends in Los Angeles on Nov. 20. "I'm going to be so depressed," she says. "I'm going to go crazy without something to live for." Of course, there are rumors brewing of a European tour in 2007. "I've been waiting my whole life to go to Europe," says Lipman, her voice speeding up, giddy at the prospect. "And now, finally, I'll have a reason to get a passport."

Nitsuh Abebe

MAKING PLANS FOR DANIEL

It's the last day of February, half past six, dark already, cold, insufferably windy. Daniel Johnston has two things on his mind: He's out of cigarettes, and he's about to get a ride in a limousine. I'm with Daniel's companions for the night, gathered in the lobby of a Marriott hotel in midtown Manhattan, and I'm guessing the rest of us are thinking more about where that limousine's going to take us—uptown, to the Whitney Museum of American Art. Tonight is the preview reception for "Day for Night," their 2006 biennial, and 14 of Daniel's drawings are up there, somewhere, hanging in two small, neat rows. This is pretty important, as Daniel's aware: "It's a really big-time art museum," he says. But he's still thinking more about the cigarettes and the ride. Whenever a large enough livery car circles the block, he perks up: "Is that really it?" And then I bother him some more with questions about his art.

Art is complicated, but if there's anything we can learn from "Behind the Music," it's that the art itself is only the beginning. Make art with any value, and you're immediately surrounded by action.

Managing that action can be tough. It's treacherous enough that even savvy, stable artists wind up ruined—by trusting the wrong people, or making the wrong decisions. The art is one problem; the business is another one entirely.

Daniel Johnston isn't surrounded by a pop star's buzzing machine; he's not actually "famous." But his art is valuable. His much-loved songs, recorded largely at home, have gotten him as far as a weird, ill-fated contract with Atlantic Records; his notebook-sized Magic Marker drawings sometimes sell for thousands of dollars each. The action that stems from that is even more complicated than usual, because Daniel just isn't capable of attending to business. The reasons why are familiar to his fans and—following a recent cover story in *The New York Times* Arts section—any number of readers. He's 44 years old and has spent most of his life struggling with bipolar disorder. He's been hospitalized, repeatedly; he's had breakdowns and episodes and scares; at his worst, he's come very close to being responsible for people's deaths. He relies on the care of his family for everyday living—never mind making a career in the arts. His work is valuable, but it's less like a business and more like a natural resource: He makes it, and probably always will, and a whole lot of action goes into figuring out what happens after that.

Which means that Daniel's surrounded by the same machinery as any star—only on a weird miniature scale, and with all the actors curiously replaced. Instead of slick managers and unctuous handlers, Daniel has his family: mostly his father, Bill, and his older brother, Dick. Instead of shady groupies and coattail riders, Daniel has art dealers, some of whom the Johnstons claim have taken personal advantage of both Daniel and his work. On some level, the routine down here in the Marriott lobby feels like some sketched-in version of meeting a pop star—right down to the part where the entourage is finished gathering and Dick runs upstairs to fetch Daniel from his room.

Strange, too, when the man of the hour steps off the elevator looking the way we now know him: paunchy, older than his years, faintly cherubic. He's wearing the usual drawstring sweatpants and track jacket; his gray hair is mussed and his eyebrows shoot everywhere. His medication gives him noticeable tremors in both arms, something you'd never guess from looking at his drawings. If you saw him on the street, you might assume he was homeless, a conclusion several people will leap to later tonight. It's not so far off: If not for Daniel's family, there's every chance he'd be going through the same cycles of institutionalization and homelessness as some other mentally ill people.

There's a lot going on with Daniel right now, so tonight's entourage is not exactly small. When I showed up, Dick Johnston—whom Daniel titles "my assistant manager with my dad"—was chatting with the publicist for *The Devil and Daniel Johnston*, a documentary that's set to premier at the end of March. Nearby sat Jordy Trachtenberg, of the digital distributor Orchard Music, along with his girlfriend; Jordy's involved with a compilation of Daniel's songs that'll be released in April, with the title *Welcome to My World*. Cruising toward us in that limo are Elizabeth Burke, Abby Messitte, and others from the Clementine Gallery in Chelsea, which will host a show of Daniel's drawings in two weeks. And once we reach the Whitney, Daniel will meet with a stream of other parties: curators, patrons, museum donors, owners of his work, fans, the reporter who wrote that *Times* cover story, half of Sonic Youth—even some guy who, strangely enough, really wants Daniel to come check out some show having something to do with the Brian Jonestown Massacre. It is, according to the *Times*, "Daniel Johnston Month" up here.

No one thought Daniel would make it to New York for any of this. Just after Thanksgiving of last year, he ran into a serious health problem—a kidney infection that reduced him to a coma-like state.

It's possible that the medication he takes to control his bipolar disorder had been taking its toll on his body in other ways. He and his family both told the *Times* he wouldn't be here. But here he is, in a good, mellow mood, his conversation jumping back and forth about some of his interests: smoking, making music, the Beatles, and cola, like the strange one he got at lunch. "It was a real heavy glass, it weighed like a ton. It was really weird. They brought me a hamburger and a Coca-Cola that was like a weightlifting Coca-Cola."

And then the limo arrives, and we're ready to go.

A week later, I head to a screening of *The Devil and Daniel Johnston*, a documentary by Jeff Feuerzeig. The film won Feuerzeig a Director's Award at the Sundance Film Festival, along with a nomination for a Grand Jury Prize. Stephen Holden of the *Times*, on the other hand, wrote the film off as "fawning," amid some talk of "fans who confuse brilliance with madness" and "a tendency in the United States to equate weirdness with artistic brilliance."

Turns out the film is fawning—but mostly by omission. Everyone interviewed, apart from Daniel's own family, has a story to tell about first hearing Johnston's home-recorded cassette albums. But the story is always the same: "I was blown away." A work of genius, they say; the typical line is that Daniel's songs are just as special as the Beatles and Bob Dylan songs they draw on, just less professional in their performance and recording. There are countless ways in which this is true: The best of his songs can be just as musically limber and lyrically well spoken as any. But claiming to have spotted that stuff straight off means skipping over the countless things about Daniel that just aren't like Dylan or the Beatles—the strange yelping voice, the cruddy tape-recorder studio, the sometimes harrowing performances, or the unguarded bluntness of the words. It means skipping over what a lot of people are surely getting out of those records, and it means skipping over a lot of what those records give us: the sound of a young man with a chord organ in his brother's garage, singing strange songs into a tape recorder.

It's a funny omission. Several people here make reference to the "myth" of Johnston; they just never stop to wonder why that myth connects with people. What Feuerzeig offers is mostly a timeline of the myth itself, as mapped out by a shocking number of recorded documents. It's astounding how much of Daniel's life has been recorded, whether by himself or by others, and it certainly benefits this film.

The first stop is Daniel's West Virginia childhood, where we see a kid's total immersion in art: He draws pictures, reads comics, plays the piano, listens to records, makes Super-8 films with his brother. In fact, he won't do anything else—won't do his chores, won't get a job, always only the art. Some here look to mythologize that immersion, but I'm not so sure; I keep thinking of one of my favorite novels, *Edwin Mullhouse*, which speaks beautifully to the solemn importance of child-art to the child. When Daniel's Christian parents yell back about his indolence—his mother calling him "unproductive," asking why he wastes all his time on "Satanic" drawings that "pollute the minds of young people"—it all seems even more normal. Everyone wants him to get off his ass and do something worthwhile; he just wants to stay immersed in his world of notebook doodling, comic books, writing little songs, and dreaming of being a famous artist. How many kids are having that argument even as you read this?

The difference between those kids and Daniel, though, turns out to be the illness, which starts creeping up in his late teenage years. He goes off to college to study art, but he can't take care of himself— he misses his classes, seems dazed, and eventually gets sent home. At another school, he falls madly in love with a girl who turns out to be engaged—he doesn't look like he'll ever graduate, and gets brought home again. His parents send him to Texas to live with his brother and look for work—he takes a tape recorder into the garage and records an album. He gets moved over to his sister's house, but he buys a moped and runs off to sell corn dogs with a traveling carnival. And eventually he lands in Austin, Texas, working at McDonald's and trying to get everyone to listen to his tapes.

It's not hard to guess what this mythology offers: For everyone who put away the doodles and got a job, Daniel is a dream of the opposite. Live vicariously through him, and you get to believe in the great artist who runs away on a speeding motorcycle; you get to look at it all as destiny, not as a giant risk you're too psychologically healthy to take. Jordy Trachtenberg, in the Whitney, puts it a different way: "I think we all have some kind of calling in life, but the harsh reality wins out. Daniel wins by default, because what other choice does he have? It pours out of him every which way, a song or a drawing." And when I ask Daniel if there's any job, any other job, he's ever thought would be interesting to have: "I've worked jobs before, but I don't want to. I worked at McDonald's. I don't want to work jobs no more. I'm an artist." When did he decide that? "All my life. I didn't want to work, I expected to be an artist. I finally made it."

And what does it mean for us to assign Daniel that myth? What does it mean for Daniel to embrace it? It's easy to look at Daniel's art as pure, something natural and unmediated, and in ways that's true—but in ways it isn't. Daniel picked up the myth of the exceptional artist from the world, not the other way around. What effect does that have? Louis Black, editor of the *Austin Chronicle*, talks in the film about the moment when he and others first decided to have Daniel institutionalized, fretting about being the sort of person who would put van Gogh in a mental hospital. What we don't see is much wondering about whether it'd have been better for van Gogh, if not art history, to get treatment. Thirty minutes later, Black is explaining how Daniel began to deliberately go off his medication a few weeks before performances, knowing the edge it would bring to the show. He did this before a 1990 appearance at the South by Southwest festival, and we see footage of the show here: It's riveting. Then again, so are the photos of Bill Johnston's wrecked airplane, which Daniel brought down. On the way home to West Virginia, he killed the engine mid-flight and threw the key out the window.

The main thing you get out of the documentary, if you're anything like me, is just plain depressed. It's tough to watch a person be ill, especially when you met him a week ago and saw him happy. It's just as tough to see how that's affected everyone around him: As much as the art has thrilled many, the real Daniel has required a lot of sacrifice and put people through a lot of difficult things. Feuerzeig seems to understand this, and instead of leaving us with a feel-good conclusion—Daniel, happy now in Texas, living peacefully with his parents—he throws in something extra: The realization that Bill and Mabel Johnston are spending the last years of their lives still taking care of their child. I doubt they'd have it any other way, but it's a sacrifice nonetheless.

Daniel, I'm told, had a hard time sitting through the documentary. When I ask him about it, he laughs pleasantly, covers his face, and tells me it was just plain embarrassing; he doesn't even remember a lot of the stuff in it. He tells me he's seen it twice, but Dick only counts one of those viewings—Daniel couldn't make it through the other one. "He was squirming at some parts," Dick says. "And I try to say it's okay, Dan, that was a long time ago, it's all gone. But they have the camera on him when he's totally out of his head. Can we go on to another scene now? No, the camera's gonna stay on him while he's acting like a lunatic. So I grieve for him in that regard. It's an uncomfortable thing for him to watch."

Daniel mentions one part in particular, a song he sings about Mountain Dew: "I don't remember doing that at all." It turns out that the recording in question comes from a period when he was institutionalized. It's a jingle for Mountain Dew—how all the patients drink it, how it'll save them from sin. It is, without question, funny.

Cut to Daniel's former manager, Jeff Tartakov, who hits the punch line, saying he sent it to the Pepsi Corporation and never heard back. Funny and wonderful, yes, but it's also a symptom of a very serious illness, which raises a whole lot of hard-to-answer questions about exactly how interesting you want to find it.

Daniel is much, much better these days. He lives in a limited world, and there are plenty of ways in which he's a lot less functional than the rest of us. But he's mentally ill, not mentally challenged: At his most communicative, he's sharp, witty, friendly, and fun. Once he's in that limousine, headed toward the Whitney, drinking Mountain Dew from the bar, he's practically a comedian, goofing around with Jordy's girlfriend: "Here I am with Carly Simon—she keeps telling me I'm vain. I mean, with a limo like this, and all these people, and the Mountain Dew, how can I be vain? And this is rich people's Mountain Dew—when I buy Mountain Dew it's from an old broken-down gas station."

His tone is exactly the sort that most artists have to remind themselves to fake: It's as if he has a good sense of his cult renown, but remains unaffected by it. He lives, after all, in a small Texan town, next door to his parents, interacting mostly with his family. How much difference does "fame" make there? "He can get it out of his system and make fun of himself in that way," says Dick. "Or he just realizes that in the scheme of things, you're fooling yourself if you go on too much about it. You might as well laugh and be done with it."

Dick's a big part of that, too. Whenever people seem to be turning Daniel into any kind of mythic figure, or walking on eggshells over his condition, Dick turns into a standard-issue big brother and deflates the whole thing. When someone in the limo reminds Daniel again that this is "a big night," Dick brushes it aside: "A big night for him means we get to order pizza." It seems at first like he's cutting his brother down to size, but after a while it begins to feel like he's doing something much nicer—reasserting the comforting everyday order of Daniel's home life. "He's not come up to speed in his mind," says Dick. "As much as I try to describe to him what's transpired and what's getting ready to happen, the next minute it's 'Oh, can we stop and get a smoke?' It's of passing interest to him, because that's not what his world is made up of."

As with a lot of people in this situation, you can tell how close someone is to Daniel by how willing they are to tease him about his behavior. Jordy Trachtenberg, who's accompanied Daniel on foreign tours, is the same way, happily telling stories and prompting Daniel to fill in the funny parts. "Remember when we were in that Applebee's in Virginia, and you stood up and asked a waitress who just happened to be across the room for a Coke?" (Daniel does a mock sheepish look: "Yeah, well, I don't get out much.") "Remember when we went record shopping? And what did you do? You bought the same Beatles bootleg from five different stores, didn't you?"

The folks at the Whitney, of course, are as gentle, accommodating, and professional as you'd expect, from the interns working at the artists' entrance to the string of curatorial types who emerge to say hello—all of them terrifically pleased that Daniel's made it here. Daniel, for his part, is just as professional, happily shaking hands, saying his thanks, introducing everyone to his brother. Daniel, in fact, seems less affected by the atmosphere we've stepped into than I am—"big night" though I knew this was, I hadn't anticipated that it would be arty, wealthy, and exclusive enough to leave me feeling like a bit of a yokel.

The biennial crowd turns out to be a lot like Los Angeles in general—the sort of thing that throws you off balance by conforming to every stereotype you've ever come across on bad TV. A lot of attendees look ready to report to Central Casting: Older Upper East Side women with expensive faces. Men dressed like tycoons who seem to be appraising the art and the people both. Adults who look like Tim

Burton characters. Gaggles of fabulous young folks. Even a man wearing a pince-nez and resting in a motorized wheelchair so futuristic it seems like it should be manufacturing cars; I almost hope it's an affectation. Some skater kids slouch by, being young turks; one of them shuffles along clutching his side like a junkie, then stops when he realizes no one's paying attention. There's plenty of star power from just outside the art world, as well—David Byrne, DJ Spooky, Kim Gordon and Thurston Moore, Taylor Meade, Momus. The last two are actually part of the show.

Daniel meets Phillipe Vergne, one of the show's curators. He has his picture taken with a major donor. He's reintroduced to Randy Kennedy, who wrote last week's *Times* article, but he's a little confused on the timeline: "Didn't you come down to Texas to see me, a couple years ago?" The folks from Daniel's gallery have social and professional obligations around here, and set off to work the room; Dick, Jordy, and Daniel move quickly along to the drawings, which are somewhere on the second floor.

Daniel's colorful drawings are executed in Magic Marker on regular-sized notebook paper, with speech bubbles and title text floating around the central figures. They're cartoonish, both in the drawing style and in their content—many of them feel like individual panels from a larger story. Johnston defines them as "amateur art," despite his formal training. When he says "amateur art," he's just describing what he likes: "Doodles, nervous drawings, things like that."

What separates Daniel's drawings from just plain "doodles," though, is the consistency of their themes and concerns. In all of Daniel's art, sketched or recorded, there is an ongoing battle between good and evil. Many of his drawings feature a Daniel-like character called Joe the Boxer, who's missing the top quarter of his head—he's often found boxing a many-eyed, tentacled creature called Vile Corrupt. Heroes are a recurring theme, including Captain America, one of Daniel's long-time fixations. Hell appears and reappears. So do gunboats, swastikas, military men, and other signs of war. As Daniel told *Pitchfork* a few years ago, "Good triumphs over evil . . . World War II, for instance, who won that war? America!"

One of the drawings at the Whitney depicts a uniformed man, draped in American flags, giving what looks like a Nazi salute. The text above his head reads "God Bless America"; the text below his feet reads "Fear Yourself." Another shows three skeletal figures writhing in fire; the title text reads, "In hell there are no friends." Daniel talks about that one tonight: "That's probably not true," he says. "That may be a little drastic."

In just as many drawings, though, there's peace—they're filled with jokes, bright-yellow ducks, visions of love, and whimsical compositions. They're lively and friendly. The art is defiantly not the work of a tormented mind—it's the work of a guy who believes strongly in good, believes strongly in pain, and believes strongly in fun.

The Whitney's press release classes Daniel Johnston among artists who offer "an archaeology of the present in which irony and critical distance convey a disgruntled relationship with the tired models dominating our media-driven environment." Fair enough, for a quick press release brush-over, but tonight it seems completely wrong. The "irony and critical distance" might be down to an author-is-dead approach, but the last bit is backward. Daniel's inspirations feel older and more media-dominated than anyone's: He's in love with Captain America, the Beatles, and Casper the Friendly Ghost. And when it comes to disseminating art, his relationship with the media is a whole lot more curious than that. When an MTV crew came to Austin in the mid-80s, Johnston went out of his way to bluff his way into their presence—he wanted to be on television, because that meant making it. Apart from stuff like that, it's as if he's blissfully indifferent to the whole idea of mediated art: He wants the amateur stuff, the doodles, the teenage world where a person just makes stuff and hands it to someone else directly.

Jordy Trachtenberg, the music distributor, is big and buzzcut, with a booming presence and an immediate earnestness; two minutes into talking with him, you already get the feeling he'd back you up in a fight. That vibe—loyal, protective—is surely a lot of why the Johnston family trusts him with Daniel's affairs. Just as important is the way he's willing to let them call the shots. "They're not music-industry people," he says. "So sometimes the decisions they make will seem strange. But I have to trust what they think is best." The protectiveness comes out, too: He's happy he'll be in Austin for the South by Southwest festival when Daniel's gallery show opens, because he'd rather not find himself in the same room as certain collectors.

Jordy's lived in New York for a couple of decades. Dick Johnston, of course, has not. He looks about a decade younger than his 51 years, and has the close-trimmed goatee, gray blazer, and crossed-arm conversational stance of the red-state professionals I grew up around. The red/blue cultural divide is, to be sure, a phony one, and here in New York, in the center of this glitzy crowd, Dick seems entirely comfortable, if occasionally amused. When Rufus Wainwright creates a stir a few feet away, Dick just remarks that "those are some pants he's wearing."

At the same time, though, Dick seems keen on reminding me where he and Daniel are coming from, especially when the subject is religion. When I say that he and his brother were raised "very Christian," he's taken aback by the modifier: "Very Christian? Christian," he corrects. I'd read allegations of art dealers sneaking in to see Daniel when his parents are off at church, but when I ask Daniel if he ever goes to church with them, Dick laughs: "That one always takes the moderns by surprise." The last time I heard the word used that way was in the Julie Andrews version of *Thoroughly Modern Millie*.

Religious themes—and that good-versus-evil stuff—are all over Daniel's art. Dick takes them very seriously, and Daniel certainly does, too. "Jeff Feuerzeig once said, 'I think Satan is a metaphor to Daniel, of his illness,'" says Dick. "And I said, well, Daniel really believes in Satan, and so do I. Lots of people suppress the fact that there's a battle going on in you. He never tries to pretend that there isn't. And that's uncomfortable for some people. But the day we start saying we don't have a battle is the day we've lost to the dark side."

He tells me I should probably ask Daniel about his own religion, but he has stories, too. "When Dan was coming in and out of consciousness in the hospital, when he was first waking up, he'd say, 'I need God's help.' And I'd say, 'You're getting it.' You have to see the art to understand his view of reality. I know the public world, the popular world, is very comfortable in their unspiritualized view of living. And that's a shame. They have a misunderstanding about the word 'spirit.' I agree with Dan's perspective, and I think he's stayed true to that perspective."

Daniel's take on it is short and understated: "Yeah, we believe in God. We went to church all our lives—we still do." At the absolute depths of his mental problems, that religion provided the cues for Daniel's delusions: He sensed demons everywhere and obsessed over the devil. Religion was the raw matter—the deep beliefs—the madness had to work with.

There's comfort in being a part of Daniel's crew tonight—this guy, after all, is supposed to be somewhat removed from the big-city art world, so you can be, too. He's good company; it's especially fun to watch him take note of other people's art, which happens mostly with the various video installments. For a while, Daniel ducks into the room where they're showing Francesco Vezzoli's star-packed movie-trailer take on Caligula. Dick follows, but leaves when he sees a woman on screen fellating a strap-on. Daniel watches for two or three minutes, then exits abruptly. A *New York Times* art critic will soon agree with his reaction, pointing out that the piece is a "one-note gag."

Daniel notices music. Our conversation, post-"Caligula," is mostly about Michelle Phillips' appearance in the film. "I love the Mamas and the Papas," he says. "But they always were like a G-rated group, so it's kind of shocking to see that." Later on, across the room, he seems to grow agitated and withdrawn, staring down at his shockingly white sneakers, mumbling and frowning. I try to catch his attention by pointing out the version of "Subterranean Homesick Blues" coming from a nearby room: "You like Bob Dylan, right?" He doesn't seem to hear me, so I step back and let him think, wondering if all the commotion is starting to get to him. A few minutes later, though, he turns to me: "Is this a real Bob Dylan bootleg? It's like he's working on that song." Here I am asking him about it while he's busy listening.

When a Whitney employee asks him who his favorite artists of the night were, he says, "Sonic Youth were here." Which they were— or at least Kim and Thurston. Daniel's worked with them before, so I flagged down Kim; after telling them both how much he loved *A Thousand Leaves*, Daniel says he'd love to work with Sonic Youth again. "Or even just you and me," says Thurston. A week later, in Feuerzeig's documentary, I'll see footage of what happened the last time Daniel and Sonic Youth hooked up—members of the band driving around New Jersey, searching for a lost and unbalanced Johnston so they could put him on a bus and get him back home to his family.

Daniel definitely wants to work on music again. These days, he plays with some kids from his town in Texas, in an act called Danny and the Nightmares. In the limo on the way over, he was thinking grand again, talking about a collaboration he'd done with the band Sparklehorse: "They asked me right away, they said we can record another album. I said that's great, yeah, so I started writing songs, and it's been like two years now, and I have it ready to do, and I'd like to record another album with Sparklehorse."

"You never know," said Jordy. "Anything can happen."

Drawing pictures, though, seems like a better life for an aging Johnston. It's something he can do at home, at his own pace; he just hands the results over to his father and brother, who number and catalog them for exhibit or sale. Compare that process to the one involved in making music: dealing with collaborators, dealing with studios and labels, and—toughest of all—being asked to perform and tour, something that takes a significant toll even on young, healthy people.

But the art comes with issues, too. Even Daniel's "lesser" drawings can fetch prices running up over one thousand dollars, and his inclusion in the Whitney biennial will undoubtedly push that value up even more. The Johnston family sees that as an opportunity for Daniel to support himself and pay for his care. In the world at large, though, the art is inevitably a commodity—and the Johnstons have had problems with at least two collectors, both of whom they claim have tried to acquire Daniel's art behind their backs.

One of them is Tartakov, who appears at length in *The Devil and Daniel Johnston*. Tartakov has been essential to a lot of the things Daniel's accomplished. His label released many of Daniel's early recordings, he organized some of the showings that originally brought Daniel's artwork to people's attention, and he was very nearly the one who landed Daniel a major-label record deal. Just as that deal was looking like a possibility, though, Daniel dropped Tartakov as his manager, something that seems to have hurt Tartakov badly. The picture we get in Feuerzeig's documentary, in fact, is that of a person who made a bad business decision—investing time and energy into an artist who just couldn't be counted on to stay productive, loyal, or even reasonable—and has spent years trying to salvage whatever he can from it. On one message board devoted to Daniel's art and music, he seems exactly that resigned—calmly and politely engaging with fans even as many of them treat him as the villain of the story.

With both Tartakov and Jeff Brivic, owner of the biggest collection of Daniel's art, the Johnston family's main concern seems fairly simple: They want all business dealings to run through them. Dick says that Daniel, like anyone, just wants to be liked—he's friendly and generous, and he knows that his drawings are one of the few valuable things he can give people. He's this way with his family, as well. Dick tells a story about stopping by Daniel's house to drop off groceries and clean up, and having a slightly guilty-looking Daniel offer him some drawings in return: He just wants to feel like he's contributing something. The problem is that while Daniel knows his drawings have value, his exact notions of value can be a little confused. "If you ask him which he would rather have, a hundred dollars or a Coke," says Dick, "well, it depends on whether or not he's thirsty."

After a couple hours at the Whitney, Daniel's tired—and hungry, and thirsty, and craving a cigarette. The entourage moves to a restaurant further uptown, where Daniel has his third hamburger of the day. Once we're done eating, he heads outside for a cigarette, and I tag along. A woman comes down Madison Avenue walking a puppy, looking skeptically at Daniel as we pet it. But with his stomach full and the night's action behind him, Daniel is in the best shape of the entire evening—happy, talkative, and totally lucid, fake-boxing with Jordy and telling me all about the amateurism he wants in his art. The Magic Markers, he says, go all the way back to his youth: His parents would give him a set every Christmas, and he'd draw them dry. As for the albums: "No matter what people might say, my records are pretty amateurish. Who would have ever thought of anything as ridiculous as an album recorded on a chord organ?"

"That was a great night," he says. "You can tell people appreciate it—they're whole hog with the limo, and all the pretty girls at the party. There was that one girl who looked like someone from *Saturday Night Live*." This has been one of the evening's running themes: Daniel says Abby Messitte, from the gallery, looks like someone from SNL, and despite all the night's guessing (Julia Louis-Dreyfuss? Molly Shannon?), it'll take me a few days to figure out that he must mean Mary Gross. "What day is it?" he asks. "Is today Saturday?"

It's Tuesday, I say.

"Feels like a Saturday," he says, "with all this partying going on."

And he's right again, kind of—it's Mardi Gras.

JESSICA HOPPER

SWF, 45

Mecca Normal's new album, *The Observer*, is hard to listen to. Not for the usual reasons—I don't mean it sucks. What makes it tough going is the same thing that makes it great: subtitled "A Portrait of the Artist Online Dating," it's so mercilessly honest and personal it's hard to believe it can exist in the pop-music marketplace. A concept album about Jean Smith's romantic life as a single woman of 45, it develops a grim, intimate picture of the solitary struggle for connection that doesn't go easy on anyone—not Smith, not the men she dates, and certainly not the audience.

The pop canon is full of songs about romantic longings and failures, so that we've been conditioned to expect certain story arcs, delivered in each genre's codified language—blues and its back-door men, hip-hop and its baby mamas, rock and its lonely motel rooms. There's pleasure in having our sufferings and hopes reaffirmed, however approximately, by such archetypes. But Mecca Normal, the Vancouver duo of Smith and guitarist David Lester, have spent two decades hammering away at the musical and social conventions that mainstream culture goads us toward as listeners and as people. They're overtly political artists—anarchist-feminists both, they've developed a traveling workshop called "How Art and Music Can Change the World"—and their loose, abrasive, drumless songs don't rest easily in any genre. And even coming from them *The Observer* is startling.

When we listen to music it's natural to try to relate to the singer's experience or inhabit it as our own, but getting invited along on Smith's blind dates and hookups is discomforting to say the least—as a storyteller, she skips the niceties and just plunks everything down on the table. "He tries to put the condom on / He curses / I try to see what he is doing," she sings in her low, acidic croon. "But I'm pinned beneath him / I hear him stretching the condom like he's making a balloon animal."

All but a couple of the album's 12 songs are connected to its basic theme of relationships between the sexes, and half are diaristic synopses of actual dates Smith went on with men she met at Lavalife.com. She's a keen, literate lyricist, prosy rather than melodic—right now she's at work on her fourth novel—and her attention to detail and detached, acerbic tone make *The Observer* a particularly apt title. Though each diary song is a separate scene, with each man allowed his own particulars, they're unified by Smith's blunt portrayal of herself—we learn about her as a date, not just an artist, and she makes a messy, inconsistent impression, veering from cynical and judgmental to petulant and needy.

On the album's centerpiece, the 12-minute "Fallen Skier," she skips between snippets of dinner conversation and an internal monologue about her date, a 47-year-old student and recovering addict who describes himself as a "fallen waiter/ski bum/party guy." From the moment she says "guy," drawing it out and accenting the word, you can tell she's mocking him. She repeats his story without sympathy, sounding frustrated, almost disgusted: "I feel I'm with a boy, a very young boy / He's only been away from home for 27 years / Only

27 summers, 27 winters / Partying and skiing / I guess that's why he hasn't gotten anything together yet / I don't think he realizes it, but his life has gotten away from him." When he seems concerned that her band might play hardcore punk, she makes a half-indignant aside that lightens the mood: "I stand, a middle-aged woman in a fantastically subtle silk jacket / Hush Puppies / Curly hair blowing in the wind / And this guy's fretting over the possibility / That I'm actually Henry Rollins." But almost immediately her complaints begin to boomerang, telling us as much about her as they do about him. "He never asked the name of my band," she says, "never tried to touch me." Suddenly she sounds vulnerable, even wounded—though her date's clearly wrong for her, she can't keep herself from wanting to be interesting and desirable to him. When she hugs him good-bye at the end of their chemistry-free evening, it's unclear which one of them she's trying to console.

The Observer is a harsh toke, but it's compelling on all fronts— Smith's lyrics force you to think about loneliness, need, and bad dates, but the songs are as engrossing as they are exhausting. Her voice flits and dips like a plastic bag in the wind, moving from a moany sort of sing-speech to a deep, silky quaver to a thick shrill trilling, and she often drawls her words like she's trying to fill the room with distended consonant sounds. The self-explanatory album opener, "I'm Not into Being the Woman You're with While You're Looking for the Woman You Want," is a glowing example of the interplay between her vocals and Lester's guitar, which is equally distinctive and powerful. On "To Avoid Pain" the duo toys with early-60s pop country as Smith hee-haws like a half-drunk Brenda Lee, trying to talk herself down on the way to a first-time hookup: "Take a city bus / To a downtown hotel / I don't feel weird / I don't feel weird / Ask me / Ask me / Ask me if I do." Then, as a dark, discordant synth tone rises out of the music, she eagerly proclaims a dubious victory over her own unease: "Soon enough it's true-ooo!"

On "I'll Call You" Lester's buzz-saw guitar gallops around Smith as she reads a fake personal ad—her version of what a truthful guy would say—that sounds like it was placed by a member of the Duke lacrosse team. "Attraction Is Ephemeral," which provides the most complete picture of Smith and what she's about—the way she begins to doubt her own doubts, wondering if she'd be able to spot genuineness in a man even if it were there—is also the most musically moving track on the album. It's the most romantic too—or rather, it's most explicitly about romance, or at least the yearning for it—though in typical Mecca Normal fashion, it opens up from there, addressing gender and class inequality, patriarchy, and how they can really ruin a date.

In press releases and online materials, Smith provides links to photos she's used in her dating profile, including shots where she's posing in her underwear and others where she's wearing nothing but the ribbon in her hair. But given how unpleasant *The Observer* makes her dating life out to be, it's hard to argue that the pictures are just Liz Phair-style exhibitionism—if you're gonna use sex to sell records, you don't usually linger on the vulnerability that intimacy requires.

In the band bio Smith notes her reluctance to make an album about dating—as evidenced by the fallout late last year over the book *Are Men Necessary?* by *New York Times* columnist Maureen Dowd, romance is a loaded topic among the feminist cognoscenti, perhaps because it's considered unseemly or irresponsible for a feminist to openly admit to wanting or needing something from men (or caring enough to be disappointed with them). Dowd claims that successful men don't want competition from their partners, and thus tend to date or marry down, choosing women who are younger, less educated, and less accomplished. Though she makes her argument largely with generalizations, as opposed to Smith's nuanced particulars, both writers are suggesting the same thing—that independent women wind up alone.

Smith is forthcoming about the concessions she makes for intimacy—while she holds to her standards with men who aren't good enough, she swallows her pride and sells herself out to others who don't have much idea who she is or much interest in finding out. But her artistic integrity never wavers, and throughout it's clear she knows herself and understands the choices she's making. It's a brave act for her to admit that she quietly shushes the "difficult" parts of herself in order to connect with men: she is airing a common secret of women's lives.

GIMME BACK MY BONE

PONDERING THE INEFFABLE SOUND OF
"CLASSIC ROCK THAT ROCKS"

When pressed to define obscenity, Supreme Court Justice Potter Stewart famously opined, "I know it when I see it." For me, a more honest answer would go something like "I know it when I masturbate to it."

Rock music, like smut, offers an equally simple metric for discerning authenticity: if listening to a band inevitably leads to a stoned argument about the fighting prowess of Bruce Lee, then it is probably real rock. I've debated so many Bruce Lee combat hypotheticals while listening to Black Sabbath—Bruce Lee versus genius hammerhead shark, Bruce Lee versus Loma Prieta earthquake, one-armed Bruce Lee versus Willy Wonka—that I never question their place as the supreme suicide-inducing, vengeance-advocating rock band.

The biggest Bay Area radio station that claims to rock is 107.7 the Bone. The Bone consciously sells itself as "classic rock that rocks." When I moved to San Francisco in 2001, it was the only station that reliably got the Led out. It played a ton of Judas Priest, Led

Zeppelin, and Black Sabbath—all the bands that scared me as a small boy because I knew in my heart they possessed evil powers and could, with their music, summon from the soil of the Amazon rainforest an army of cloned Adolf Hitlers. The Bone always comforted me, because it—along with Madalyn Murray O'Hare, pony kegs, bringing M-80s to school, and backward masking—inhabited the same demon-haunted rock-metal world I lived in as a frightened but fascinated child.

FLIRTING WITH DISASTER AND LADY REEBOK

So I'll never forget where I was the first time I heard the Verve's "Bittersweet Symphony" on the Bone. It was 2 a.m. earlier this year, and I was driving west on Fell Street at 60 mph, my 1986 convertible LeBaron catching the timed lights one second after they turned green (Fell's timed lights work at 30, 60, even 120 mph). I wanted rock and prayed for the Bone to twist me up a threefer of Ronnie James Dio. Instead, I found myself thrust into a Lady Reebok ad: vaguely self-infatuated and optimistic about everything but nothing in particular. I defensively smashed my car into a parked Cooper Mini, did a hundred push-ups and sit-ups next to the twisted wreckage, and ran off into the night. As with all time-bifurcating events—9/11, the Kennedy assassination, being told my seventh-grade "sweats" were actually parachute pants—it's often hard to remember what life was like before.

Joe Rock, the Bone's most metal-friendly DJ and assistant program director, told me recently that the station tweaked its format following a 2004 listener-driven "Classic Rock A–Z Weekend" that saw requests for bands like Pearl Jam and Temple of the Dog supplant classic-rock lifers like Derek and the Dominoes and Bad Company. The switch from "metal-oriented classic rock," the station's previous Arbitron-monitored format, to "heritage rock," a mix of old metal, new guitar-based grunge and post-grunge, and both old-school and contemporary Reebok rock, elicited a mild-to-moderate shitstorm from old-school Boneheads.

Why change the formula? I think the economics of commercial radio came into play. Few listeners in the 18-to-34-year-old demographic really care about Deep Purple deep tracks anymore, so the Bone started dropping in Staind and Godsmack amid Jimi Hendrix and Ozzy Osbourne. If you're an old-school Bonehead, the change means that now you only hear KISS once in a while, unless you count all the time you and Strutter, your albino python, lock yourselves in your room and listen to every single KISS song on tape, vinyl, CD, CD box set, digitally remastered CD, and digitally remastered CD box set. If, however, you believe Stone Temple Pilots and Buckcherry are where Ted Nugent would have ended up if he didn't OD on elk jerky and NRA propaganda, then you feel much like John Hinckley probably did after his psychologist let him watch *Taxi Driver* on DVD: deeply appreciative but still wondering what all the fuss is about.

THE SONG NOT THE SAME?

The mythology of classic rock holds that everything used to be one big fantasy sequence from *The Song Remains the Same*: coked-up druids, trashed Hilton suites, and roadies deep into black magic. The reality is that the vast majority of classic rock is nerdy or nonthreatening. You're more likely to hear Supertramp, Fleetwood Mac, Yes, Journey, and Jethro Tull on an Aflac commercial than see them carved into the arm of a berserker teen. The Bone has always needed to appeal to men and women, hawks and doves, parolees and non-parolees. Until the change in format, ubiquitous classic rock loser ballads like The Who's "Behind Blue Eyes" and Pink Floyd's "Mother" represented the shadow self of the average Aleister Crowley–worshiping Bonehead. After the tweak the Bone forced its aging listeners to ask themselves a fundamental and humbling question: "Am I getting too old for this I-Roc?" Bone listeners older than 40—who weren't impressionable suckers when music, fashion, advertising, and public relations merged with movies, television, and politics in the late '80s—had to swallow a bitter pill: it's really all the same now, just younger.

The old Bone—despite its marketing and popularity with grown men who paint their faces silver and black and dress up as Norse war gods for their children's Pop Warner football games—always played an embarrassing amount of lame music. For every "Dirty Deeds (Done Dirt Cheap)" or "Kashmir," there were two pieces of shit like "Gimme Three Steps" and "China Grove." The new Bone basically employs the same formula: Rainbow, Metallica, and Alice in Chains but now with acoustic Nickelback and blink-182 thrown in for the women and the younger sensitive guys.

This, objectively, is no wimpier than the old wimpy stuff, just more corporate and more easily marketable. The new Bone plays songs that strippers born after 1984 can lap dance to and still seem credible to their under-30 clientele. A lot of the new Bone stuff—by so-called active rock bands such as Audioslave and Velvet Revolver—easily out-rocks anything by Don Henley and anything he ever touched.

Sometimes it's better to just sound good than appear consistent. What rocks for me doesn't necessarily rock for my next-door neighbor, unless Alice Cooper is now living in a pupuseria on 24th Street and Harrison. As for the ultimate judge, Bruce Lee's legacy, I say the Bone still facilitates a Bay Area dialogue, even if it's only seen *Enter the Dragon* and the first 10 minutes of *Game of Death*.

DAVID BYRNE

HEAVY THEATER

Saw Sunn0))), the minimal metal band, last night. Last Sunday there was a huge article about them in *The New York Times* which I suspect might dash my hopes for them joining the lineup for one of the nights at Carnegie Hall I'm curating next February. But who knows? I expected a sell out last night as a result of that article, but I guess the *Times* demographic and the audience for extremely loud minimal metal has a small overlap. I can see the Venn diagram in my mind.

The opening act, Boris, was similar to Sunn0))), though much less rigorous in their minimalism and visual presentation. Some prefer their less extreme approach.

Well, it's not the sort of music you go home humming to yourself. It's a sensory assault—intense and strangely pleasurable (I wore earplugs). Most of all, it's theater, well conceived and beautifully executed—and in perfect context (this club venue was a former church). It is also deeply ritualistic.

The stage is cleared before the band enters. There is no drum set or anything else on stage, just a semicircular wall of massive amps across the entire stage, with one amp swiveled slightly to allow the players to enter—this "door" would later be shut behind them.

A bit of dry ice smoke wafted across the bare stage and what looked like six Sith Lords entered carrying guitars (one guy went to a little Moog set up on the side). Without an introduction the "show" began: a deep throb and rumble that grew in volume and, at given signals, there were added tones and changes in the harmonics around the central deep tone.

As there were no drums, the rhythm was present, but more a felt slow pulse than a groove. Heavy is putting it mildly. It could easily tip over into camp or parody, but it never does. Like standing next to a jet engine, it's no joke.

I thought of Tony Conrad, La Monte Young and other extreme minimal modernist composers from decades ago. Young attempted to insert a bit of theater into his presentations, but never came close to the power of this. I thought of global warming (again), the melting icecaps, the earthquake in Java, the Mayan ruins in Yucatan, computer viruses, government surveillance eating itself from the inside out, Donald Rumsfeld's mind, ant colonies, big science, Jesus' dick, Mary's cunt, and the McDonald's meal a suicide bomber ate, minutes before detonation.

This is contemporary theater.

IMPERFECT SOUND FOREVER

This article started life as a Soulseeking column about my new head-phones, a rather delicious-sounding pair of Grado SR60s. The original opening line was meant to be as follows:

> "You'd think I'd know *Spirit of Eden* pretty well by now. I've
> listened to it often enough. But maybe I haven't listened to
> it *well enough?*"

And I was going to go on to detail how much, well, detail my wonderful new cans had wrung out of this fantastic record, about how I'd noticed the sound of rain against the window of the building they recorded in during a few seconds of what I had previously con-sidered to be near-silence at the start of "The Rainbow." I was going to witter on about the timbre of instruments, about how when I lis-tened to Mark Hollis' eponymous solo album from 1998 I could hear the creak of the stool he was sitting on during recording. I was going to talk about how those little details, the accidents, the colourations of sound that remind you that people made this music, are almost as important as the music itself. But I got distracted. I got distracted because it suddenly dawned on me that an awful lot of recent music, much of which I adore, sounds horrible.

So, this new article starts like this:

IMPERFECT SOUND FOREVER

The new Flaming Lips CD is the kind of cod-metaphysical psyche-delia (there's a reason actual philosophers don't take acid—it stops them from thinking properly) that's bound to garner glowing reviews from broadsheet critics to whom all music blends into a homogenous morass and to whom cosmic platitudes equal great spiritual insight. It's pretty good; you could argue that they're running out of ideas and melodies and are compensating by being weird for the sake of it, and that Coyne's voice, never strong, is now so shot that you fear for his ability to even talk, but it's not a bad record. It is, however, an incredibly LOUD record. So it might as well be bad because I simply cannot stand to hear it.

I don't mean that it's lashed with savage, Angus Young-esque guitar riffs or grindcore percussion, because it's not (it's the kind of luscious, unpredictable-yet-lucid-dream futurist collage that *Yoshimi* . . . predicated, occasionally punctured with some rowdiness and energy); I simply mean that the CD itself when played back bashes out of your speakers at a massive, wearing volume. It's not alone in its pummeling attack, either. In fact it's far from alone.

Don't get me wrong; music sounds better loud. It's more dynamic, more exciting, you can hear more detail, you get a better sense of space as instruments and sounds surround you and involve you (like a Taoist says, the space between the spokes is the most important part of the wheel—as it is with music), and the physical pleasure of feeling a ripple of bass run through your body simply can't be beaten.

But loudness and dynamics aren't the same thing. Loudness is relative. *Surfer Rosa* by The Pixies is an old CD that seems daintily quiet next to *At War with the Mystics*, but if you nudge the volume dial up and then up a little more and maybe up a little further, it gets better and better, louder and louder, the juxtapositional leap from whispered, undulating verse to hammer-attack chorus getting more and more exciting and visceral, guitars and bass and drums and Black Francis' yowling curses all clear and vibrant and dangerously realistic. It could maybe do with a little more bass now that we're more able to reproduce low frequencies than we were in 1988, but that's a very minor gripe. *At War with the Mystics*, on the other hand, just gets painful and messy and starts "clipping" when you turn it up.

I'm pretty anal about sound, and I'm prepared to admit it. I'm not a super-duper audiophile (I can't afford to be), but I have spent thousands of pounds over the years on stereos, headphones, hi-fi separates, portable audio systems, and even (in my more gullible moments) biwired speaker cables and limestone slabs to position my speaker stands on, all in pursuit of the "perfect" sound: slightly more sparkle and physical *ping* in the treble (hearing the stick hit the hihat, perhaps, rather than a vague *splash*); a more rounded and tighter bass sound that doesn't bloom like ugly bathwater and overwhelm the song; more realistic vocals that put the singer right in front of you, spittle-filled lips and all. You know the kind of thing . . . It's like when serious wine buffs talk about being able to smell diesel or orange peel in a bottle of Shiraz: it seems like nonsense until you immerse yourself in the sensations of the discipline and find that you too are scrabbling for ridiculous metaphors to describe how something tastes or sounds or smells when you suddenly realise there are more nuances than you ever imagined.

It started when I was about sixteen and listened to "I Am the Resurrection" through shitty headphones out of a shitty boombox while trying to write an essay for school, straining to hear all these sounds buried in the song that I could faintly perceive but had never heard before when wheeling around my bedroom air-guitaring like a delirious fool. That moment planted a seed in me, made me want to hear everything possible, every detail in every song, soak it in and lose myself in it. For the last eleven years I've been trying to find that sound, and the equipment that will make it for me.

I'm not about to claim that you can't "properly" enjoy music unless you're running it through some multi-thousand-pound Naim system with enormous £900 Epos floorstanding speakers, because we all know that you can get a kick out of a great tune running off a crappy C90 cassette in a bog-standard car stereo. Or by playing the new Flaming Lips album through your iBook speakers, or through the earbuds that came with your MP3 player. But that's not the only way to listen to music, and certainly not the best way to listen properly, and I doubt anyone would disagree for long if you confronted them with even a modest hi-fi set-up that can *really* play.

I think music journalists have a responsibility to listen to records on at least half-decent equipment—film critics wouldn't (I hope) review a film based on viewing it on an iPod Video during a train journey, and film studios would be aghast if they did. Certainly you could ascertain the plot from that, but film is about more than just story in the same way that music is about more than just song. Sadly very few music journalists appear to be concerned with the nuts and bolts of actual sound quality though—possibly because it "gets in the way of the music, *maaaan*," but more likely because they're scared that they'd look as if they didn't know what they were talking about if they tried. I know more than a few people who've reviewed albums based solely on MP3s—I've done it myself in the past, to my shame. An art critic wouldn't evaluate a painting based on a black & white Xerox, and while some people will be up in arms saying it's not the same thing with music, I disagree—MP3s lose colour, space, and depth, all of which can affect your relationship with a song.

So what's the actual problem here? The reason *At War with the Mystics* is so punishingly loud is because of how it's recorded, mixed and mastered, how the components and levels of the music are arranged and set in the processes before it gets put onto CD.

A quick lesson from someone who doesn't fully understand (and I am very much a novice learning this stuff on-the-job as I research this article)—in basic, layman's terms "producing" gets the music out of the musicians; "recording" and "engineering" get it onto tape; "mixing" arranges the elements of the music on that tape; and "mastering" polishes the songs up to a cohesive shine and sets the final levels for the finished whole—it makes a bunch of "songs" into an "album," if you like.

Record companies these days (and I don't just mean nasty behemoths like EMI or Sony—your favourite indie are probably just as bad) are eager to make CDs as loud as possible because they think, with some justification, that this is what people want. In order to get CDs to be consistently loud, they get compressed—essentially this means that the quieter moments are made louder in relation to the, um, louder moments, to make the entire CD a consistent, and high, level of volume. During the compression process, the tops of signals can be cut off, or "clipped." Compress a record too much, and it sounds bad. Make it "clip" even slightly, and it sounds worse.

There are two ways to measure "loudness"—peak levels and average levels. The former refers to the loudest part of a piece of music or sound; a crescendo or climax. The difference between the highest and lowest points makes for the average level. Sadly, the science of psychoacoustics suggests our ears generally respond to the average level rather than the peak level of volume—hence we would perceive a consistently loud piece of rock music as being "louder" than a piece of classical that reaches the same or even a higher volume level during a crescendo, simply because the rock song is "loud" all the way through. "Loud" records grab our attention (obviously—being louder they are harder to ignore on first impression) and in order to grab attention quicker and more effectively in a crowded marketplace, record companies and artists have been striving to make their records as loud as possible from the second the first note is played, whatever the cost.

This isn't a recent thing. The "Loudness War" has been going on almost as long as pop music has existed, and probably longer—nobody has ever wanted their record to be the quietest on the jukebox or the radio. The Beatles lobbied Parlophone to get their records pressed on thicker vinyl so they could achieve a bigger bass sound more than 40 years ago. The MC5 apparently mixed their second album, *Back in the USA*, at such extreme volume in the studio that they failed to notice how tinny and thin it sounded—there's practically no bottom-end to it at all. Then there's Phil Spector's legendary "wall of sound" production style, mixed and mastered to sound good on tiny, tinny transistor radios, squeezing as big a sound as possible into as small a space. Three or four decades ago record companies would send out compilations of singles to radio stations on a single vinyl record—if a band or producer heard their song on one of these and it was quieter than the competitions' song, they would call the mastering engineer and get him to up the levels until it was the loudest, even if that meant corrupting the sound quality.

The advent of CD technology in the early 80s changed the game, albeit not initially for the worse. CDs allowed for a greater dynamic range than vinyl or tape (live music spans approximately 120 dB; vinyl covers approx. 75 dB; CD ranges across approx. 90 dB)—meaning that they could be encoded with a much larger differential in volume between the quiet moments and the loud moments of a piece of music. The 90 dB range of CDs encouraged mastering engineers to exploit the potential of the new format for a while, which made for a few awesome-sounding (but relatively quiet) albums mastered for the early days of CD, even though much of the industry hadn't yet cottoned-on to how to best exploit the new format. Of course the music itself wasn't always great however well-mastered, but for every Dire Straits there was a Blue Nile (almost). The early 90s are considered by many to have been a golden age of mastering and sound engineering, when the industry had become familiar with CDs, technology had yet to be overtaken by commercial concerns, and albums were being mastered to exploit the medium rather than the market.

Levels have crept up over the last decade though, and alarmingly so. *Nevermind* is 6–8 dB quieter than, say, *Hopes & Fears* by Keane—to contextualise this, those 6–8 dB will make *Nevermind* sound approximately half as loud. On most modern CDs the music is squashed into the top 5 dB of a medium that has over 90 dB of range. It's like the oft-quoted myth that humans use only 10% of their brain, only real—imagine what we could do if we realised potential. Think of the classic, exciting Pixies formula again—it doesn't exist anymore, because those dynamic leaps have been ironed out. Keane should NOT be twice as loud as Nirvana.

In fact you don't need to imagine—just go back to *Laughing Stock* or *Giant Steps* or *Selected Ambient Works 85–92* or *Siamese Dream* or *Hex* or *Music for the Jilted Generation* and listen for yourself. Play "Hey Ladies" from *Paul's Boutique* again, a song that's almost 20 years old, and feel just how head-snappingly phantasmagorical it is when the soundstage suddenly flips into widescreen during the intro. Is there anything remotely approaching that on the headachingly dense and loud *St. Elsewhere* by Gnarls Barkley? Not even slightly. Friends of mine (and fellow music writers) often cite *Paul's Boutique* as a record they'd like to hear remastered, but it sounds absolutely wonderful to my ears—it just needs turning up a touch on your own amplifier if you think it's not loud enough!

Music with an incredibly loud signal is referred to in the industry as "hot." One way to make music "hot" is by compressing it—essentially this means lowering the peaks so they're almost level with the troughs, and then increasing all of the signal to make it as loud as you can before it starts "clipping." Only a lot of people seemingly don't know when to stop. Compression can be added at almost any stage of the recording process, in large or small doses. Small increments added at recording, mixing and mastering are more effective in preserving sound quality than huge leaps taken at the final stage, for instance.

One result of this is that modern CDs have much more consistent volume levels than ever before. But when is it desirable for music to be at a consistent volume? When it's not being actively listened to; i.e., when it's intended as background music. Sudden (or even gradual) dynamic changes in ambient volume disturb people from what they are otherwise doing (shopping, eating, working) by making them pay attention to the fluctuating sound rather than the task in hand—I only notice the air conditioning at work when it switches off ten minutes before I go home every day, for instance; for the previous eight hours, my brain tunes the hum out so I can concentrate. So it is with music too—it may grab your attention more effectively at the start, but it's ultimately easier to ignore too. All music becomes background music if it's at one flat level, no matter how loud. And flat, hypnotic background music is a form of social control—I used to work in the catering industry and there was significant research suggesting that diners played ambient music with a low BPM and steady level ate slower and made less mess when eating. Similarly a faster BPM made them eat quicker—the type of establishment you piped music to determined the music used; fast food restaurants wanting multiple table covers play pop, rock, and R&B, while classier, more sedate places play jazz or classical.

Not only are the volume differentials flattened when you compress music, but bass and treble frequencies are pressed into the midrange and the space surrounding instruments is lost, making them less easy to separate when you listen. Bass frequencies drive music, they give us a physical sensation to hold onto and ride through a song. Play "Unfinished Sympathy" on a decent hi-fi and the sub-bass shots that open the song hit you like a punch in the belly and a pillow-whack to the chest. Play Girls Aloud's superficially sonically savage "Wake Me Up," Nine Inch Nails meets Gwen Stefani, on the same set-up, and it sounds flat and lifeless. Treble frequencies by contrast add imaging— a sparkling, accurate treble hit can almost be seen—think Jacko's early 80s work with Quincy, all those pointillist pricks of light over the top; cymbals, shakers and twinkling keys. Try The Killers though and their cymbal work is so muddy and indistinct that it's hard to even identify, let alone hear clearly. Speakers work by moving air molecules. Overly compressed music moves a LOT of molecules, but it doesn't move them very precisely.

Artists want to make their CDs excessively "hot" for the sake of being louder on the radio, but this is fallacious. The sad thing is that radio equalises music anyway, songs are run through a whole other set of compressors during the broadcast process to even-out differences in volume, which means CDs don't actually need to be mastered loudly to sound loud on radio—in the UK even relatively open-sounding channels like Radio 3 and Radio 4 are compressed in order to send the signal as efficiently as possible. They're also very quiet compared to the uber-compressed Radio 1, which is designed for a punchy, consistent sound, the poor quality of which isn't fully apparent when listening on a dodgy mono set in a workshop or in the car, which is what demographic research suggests are the most common listening environments for Radio 1. Television is much the same—watching VH1's *A-Z of Anthems* the other night I was stunned to hear how much the level of vocals and synths in Underworld's "Born Slippy" dropped when the beat came in, presumably because neither the television nor the station could handle the dynamic shift. As for DAB . . . well, the payoff for having a million radio stations is that most of them transmit at 128 kbps or less. I wouldn't listen to an MP3 encoded that badly, so I'm certainly not going to listen to radio at that bitrate.

If there's a jump-the-shark moment as far as CD mastering goes then it's probably Oasis. In 1987 *Appetite for Destruction* averaged about –15 dB RMS volume, and was considered loud. By 1994 the average loudness in RMS power for a rock record was –12 dB. *(What's the Story) Morning Glory* in 1995 hit a phenomenal –8 dB on many tracks. The 1997 remaster of *Raw Power* reaches an extraordinary –4 dB, making it supposedly the loudest rock record ever. In 2005 the average RMS volume is –9 dB. Audiophiles and people who work in audio engineering largely agree that this is too loud, but in the face of massive commercial impetus their say is often ignored. Arguably *(What's the Story) Morning Glory* became so successful in the UK precisely because it was so loud; its excessive volume and lack of dynamics meant it worked incredibly well in noisy environments like cars and crowded pubs, meaning it very easily became a ubiquitous and noticeable record in cultural terms.

Music isn't meant to be at a consistent volume and flat frequency; it's meant to be dynamic, to move, to fall and rise and to take you with it, physically and emotionally. Otherwise it literally is just background noise. Compressed CDs grab your attention in the same way that people who shout grab your attention, and they're just as tiring and annoying in the long run if you're standing too close to them. They sound fine if you're playing them back through some satellites and a subwoofer hooked up to your PC, or through a half-decent pair of headphones and an iPod, or in your car where the compression helps the music rise above engine and road noise; but if you push them through a system designed to reproduce sound as realistically and effectively as possible, they can and do sound pretty poor— forced, lifeless, wearing and flat. Some mastering engineers claim that a huge amount of professionally released CDs since the turn of the decade (and earlier) have been so compressed that they don't even consider them to be "musical." I can't bear to play back some of my favourite records from the last few years through my hi-fi and pay them full attention, and this is upsetting.

Dynamic range compression may be responsible for a multitude of recent record industry sins, but it's a difficult phenomenon to identify if you're not aware of what you're looking for. Aside from making records simply sound louder and flattening the delivered frequencies, it also sucks all the space out of music, but many people simply aren't accustomed to listening to what isn't there.

In the days before digital coaxial and optical recording to minidisc or CDR, home taping enthusiasts would have to set the analogue recording levels so that the peak level, i.e., the loudest moment of the song, was to just below the red on a cassette recorder's level indicator. Pushing it into the red clips and distorts the signal, and blows your speakers if you hammer them too hard. But the key thing is that the levels would vary—low for quiet moments, high for louder. It's stultifyingly obvious. Modern CDs hit the peak level from the off though, and stay there resolutely. When the music gets louder there is literally nowhere else for it to go on the CD because the CD is already "full" (i.e., the music is already at the top of the CD's dynamic range and thus as loud as it can be), and it maxes out, resulting in clipping of the signal.

It used to be said that a valve gear, when pushed to distort, makes the right type of harmonic distortion to make music sound better (valve compressors and desks backing up that claim) and that solid state (i.e., digital) makes a very different type of (un)harmonic distortion. Digital distortion is unacceptable, because unlike analogue where the sound goes through a subtle "furring" as you start to overload signal levels, an overloaded digital signal remains the same until it suddenly goes QUACK through the speakers (similar to a scratched CD skipping). This can and does damage equipment if it's driving music at high levels.

On *At War with the Mystics*, for instance, there is so much clipping during the crescendos (which aren't real crescendos anyway, because they're the same volume) that it almost seems as if it's being used deliberately as another instrument in the mix. It's this flatness, this clipping, this unwavering attack, that wears and tires and means you won't listen to your favourite records, if they're from the last few years, as often as you might want to, because they are intrinsically unmusical and unpleasant. Hence, perhaps, the perpetual merry-go-round of seeking the newest flavor-of-the-month; over-compressed music sounds great for a couple of listens, but there is little desire to replay the music because your brain recognises that there is something fundamentally unmusical about the sound.

Music is about tension and release. With very "hot," un-dynamic music there is no release because the sensory assault simply doesn't let up. By the time you've listened closely (or tried to) to a whole album that's heavily compressed, you end up feeling like Alex at the end of *A Clockwork Orange*—battered, fatigued by and disgusted with the music you love. I think the reason I suffer from a musical malaise for the first couple of months of every year recently is largely because October, November and December are spent frantically listening to a morass of the year's records in an effort to concoct "best-of" lists for end-of-year polls. By Christmas I simply have a massive dose of listening fatigue that takes 8–10 weeks to re-cover from. I very much doubt that this is just me.

Who's guilty then, beyond Wayne Coyne's merry psychedelic troubadours? The simple answer is almost everyone, but some of-fenders are much, much worse than others. *Californication* by Red Hot Chili Peppers is so loud and suffers from so much digital clip-ping that even non-audiophile consumers complained about it. *Hot Fuss* by The Killers is one of the most unpleasantly flat and harsh recordings I have ever heard, so much so that I couldn't bring myself to play it again and recently sold it. Sounds great on the radio though . . . The new Embrace album, as much as I love the songs and arrangements, is like a shock and awe assault designed to prepare for a later land attack. Part of the reason Mogwai's new album fails to truly engage me is that the quiet bits are pretty much as loud as the loud bits—if you too consider that the real thrill of the Scottish postrockers was their dizzying command of dynamics as demon-strated on "Like Herod," then it's no wonder that *Mr. Beast* has ar-rived to such a muted reception. The Liars' *Drum's Not Dead* is meant to be some kind of percussion odyssey, but it has one of the worst, most over-compressed, hollow and unrealistic drum sounds I've ever heard. Try listening to *Songs for the Deaf* by Queens of the Stone Age while thinking about compression and it becomes almost unbearable. But perhaps that's the point? It's sequenced with skits to make it sound like listening to a car radio, after all—a concept album about sounding horrible. Noise artists like Merzbow routinely master CDs so "hot" as to render them almost unlistenable, simply because they want their music to be like that.

Even The White Stripes, those fashionistas of vintage recording and mixing technology, compress their records massively; it's just not as obvious (or wearing) because there are usually less elements being crammed into the mix in the first place. It's similar with a lot of R&B and hip-hop—minimal music without many compositional elements (a bassline, a drum track, a single synth and a vocal, perhaps) can be compressed to seem much louder than a more densely layered piece of music with more elements, because each ingredient can be made to take up that much more space on the CD itself in terms of raw information/signal. To try and apply that EQ and compression to a densely layered or orchestrated piece of music is futile. But people will try it anyway.

Compression loses space and realism and involvement. Why go back to a piece of music that's hard, unnatural and unpleasant? This is not saying "only listen to acoustic guitars" because this affects ALL music—minimal hip-hop and heavily textured electronic music both sound better if you can hear them properly, if they have dynamics that you can ride as you listen, that take you somewhere emotionally rather than just battering you in order to get your attention.

How many times have you been blown away by a band's demo only to find the professionally recorded version of it, mixed and mastered properly, sounds lifeless and dull? One repeated complaint against Arctic Monkeys' debut album is that it lacks the excitement of the early demos that caused such a fuss online. Why? Because the final recording and release is compressed to hell, loses its space, its dynamic, its vitality and its excitement.

Compression in itself isn't bad though; many state of the art rock records and iconic sounds from the last 40 years would not exist without the good old compressor. "Tomorrow Never Knows," John Bonham's drum sound, "Song 2," Lennon's piano sound on *Plastic Ono*, Ride, Public Enemy and countless others, basically anyone with a savage electric guitar or really driving drumbeat, would not sound the way they do, punchy, exciting, intriguing, otherworldly and brilliant, if it weren't for compression. The recent and escalating problems with compression are "user errors"; people falling victim to negative instincts and misguided commercial desires, a kind of penis envy transposed to volume, and sabotaging their own records in the process. The key, as always, is to use the available tools with taste in sympathy/empathy with the actual music you're creating, not just to max them out because you can.

We know why artists, producers and labels want loud CDs, but why do consumers want them if they sound so bad when played through good hi-fi equipment? As with anything, technology and the pace of modern life are probably to blame. Possibly we're just too lazy to reach for the volume knob. If people listen to music in sub-standard conditions where they can't even hear it properly, why bother to make the music that they're listening to worth listening to well in the first place?

Think about how you listen for a moment. I'd wager that a large chunk of your listening is done during a commute, whether that's in a car or on a bus or train or a walk through a city centre. I listen a lot on the train myself, running my iPod (songs encoded as 192 kb AAC files) through a pair of Koss Portapros and trying to sit next to other people who have earphones in so my leaking sound doesn't offend commuters who want to read or whatever. Unsurprisingly I see a lot of other people with MP3 players, most of them using tiny earbuds of various kinds. Often their ears are plugged and their eyes are intently focused on a book or magazine or even a mobile phone screen too, senses shut to the horror of public transport. I get the impression that they're not listening to music so much as avoiding what's outside.

I fidget when I listen to music in public. I tap my feet, nod my head, drum my fingers together. Occasionally, if I'm pretty sure no one's looking, I'll break out into a spectacular air-drum roll, swooshing my invisible sticks across fifty tom-toms, thirty cymbals and heaven-only-knows how many snares and kick-drums. While full-on drum rolls might be rare, the rest is commonplace whether I'm on the train or walking through the woods. Other people I see out and about wearing Walkmans or MP3 players seldom seem to tap, or nod, or hum along at all though; instead their gazes seem fixed with a steely resolve, their bodies tense and their minds seemingly tenser. To me that isn't the body language of someone enjoying music.

The story goes that Brian Eno "invented" ambient music after a car accident, when he was forced to stay in hospital dosed on painkillers, and someone left a radio playing so quietly that he couldn't properly hear the music it emitted no matter how much he strained. The genre that this happenstance spawned has produced some truly wonderful music over the years, music that both floats absently in a room and that can be paid great attention to; like a painting hung on a wall that you see every day but seldom look at. It strikes me that the way many people are listening to music these days—on trains, in offices, on the street—is not a normal listening experience. It is neither conscious engagement nor ambient enhancement. It's a hermetic seal, a blockade to the outside world. It's the opposite of ambient music, in that it doesn't become a part of or complement the environment it is played in, but rather destroys it. How often do people simply sit down and *listen* to a record, rather than putting on some music while they do something else?

The rise of the iPod (or other generic MP3 player of your choice) initially made me hopeful that people would start putting a greater level of thought into mixing new music with headphones in mind, and it looks as if my hope has been borne out—sadly I was thinking more of increased ambient detail and stereo-imaging than outright sonic attack. Mixing for headphones is a very different thing from mixing for iPods—binaural recording already exists, for instance, and is a very different approach to the idea of making music to be listened to via headphones. I've read countless articles about people shunning their iPods because they encouraged them to over-saturate themselves with music (and even written one myself, almost), but there are countless more by people who think that all music, all the time is a great thing, even if they never actually *listen*.

Compression is a way of life. A week's worth of radio broadcasts have become an hour-long podcast. Think of those plastic bags you can get for clothes with a hole to stick a vacuum cleaner nozzle in so you can suck all the air out and pack them tighter. We squash fruit into smoothies, social policy into soundbites, vitamins into pills, entire meals into cans and English into txt spk, all so we can consume things quicker than ever before. But quicker is not the same as better. Meanings, subtleties and understandings are lost because we don't have the time to pick up on them.

People are forgetting how to listen, and who can blame them? Music is ubiquitous—it pervades every shop, every café, every workplace, every restaurant, every television programme and every film. It is pervasive to such an extent that some of us, who would profess to love music, find ourselves trying to actively avoid it during the day so that we can more fully enjoy it when we choose to, when we know we can appreciate it. Increased availability and increased choice do not equal increased quality—we're taught that we can have everything we want, but not taught how to decide *what* we want.

But people are slowly realising that so many modern CDs sound so bad because they're too loud—they may not consciously know the reasons, but subconsciously listeners are shunning overly "hot" music; a swift analysis of album chart sales suggests more people are buying modern easy-listening and AOR types than rock, pop, hip-hop, or dance albums, presumably because people are simply tired of being shouted at. The increase in home cinema and the wonderful dynamics it can bring is making people aware that today's music, by comparison, is flat and dull, even if it's "louder." The recent Kate Bush album was a strike against unnecessary volume, and *Leaders of the Free World* by Elbow contains some startling dynamic shifts. Nashville is beginning to understand how its music is harmed by the pursuit of loudness, and country records are being clawed back from the brink.

Please, just stop a moment and think about how you're listening, about what you're listening to and how it *sounds*. If you want to listen to something loud, there's a simple method—turn it up.

Thanks to MD and ME for opinions, photos and facts, and ER for putting up with me not shutting up about this for the last two months.

Robert Forster

A TRUE HIPSTER

On May 6, on a Saturday afternoon while preparing a housewarming party, Grant McLennan, a friend and working partner of mine for 30 years, died of a heart attack. He was 48 years old. This is a remembrance.

Grant and I started the Brisbane band The Go-Betweens in January 1978. We'd met two years earlier in the drama department at the University of Queensland, where we were both doing Bachelor of Arts degrees centred mainly on English literature. Most of the drama subjects were taught at a small off-campus theatre called the Avalon. It was a jostling atmosphere in which Grant and I felt immediately at home, and our friendship began and blossomed here, amid the costume trunks, the works of Beckett, Genet and Ionesco (perfect for a pop band), and a genial professor, an Englishman by the name of Harry Garlick. It was action, and fun, and good learning, and it's where The Go-Betweens started.

Grant was a whiz-kid when I first met him. His passion was film. He was either going to be a director or the greatest film critic this country had ever seen. At 18, he was writing reviews for a publication called *Cinema Papers*, while working at the Schonell, the campus cinema where he assisted with the programming. At 19, he'd done his BA. It was as if he'd raced so hard, and with such brilliance, that he'd got slightly ahead of himself. His application for the film and television school in Sydney was turned down on the grounds that he was too young. Which is where I came in, to fill a gap that was to be merely a year or two, before further adventures took us elsewhere.

While Grant had been pouring himself into film, I'd been falling into music. My academic record at university was patchy beside his. I never finished the degree. The electric guitar and stirrings overseas sighted in the music press were starting to consume me. Grant knew I had a band with a university friend and a drummer, and this intrigued him. The band, which went under two names, The Mosquitoes (taken from *Gilligan's Island*) and The Godots (from Beckett), only did three shows over two years, of which Grant saw the last two. At the final show, we played the first good song I thought I'd written. It was called "Karen."

The similarities between us were strong. We were both private-school boys who'd done well academically but come out of the system with no idea of a career. We were both looking for something that bohemian-free Brisbane couldn't offer, except in the traditional, safe form of an Arts degree. And we were both uneasy and difficult, having emerged from families who looked on somewhat bewildered at the eldest sons they had produced. When Grant and I met, we didn't know it but we'd found each other. Rough mirror-images. And when the friendship that had begun in classes grew to the point where I visited his house and saw his bedroom stacked with film books, novels and posters, I realised his "thing," film, wasn't just an enthusiasm; it was an obsession. And I knew that was exactly how I felt about music.

We began a slow exchange. He told me about French new wave cinema and film noir. I told him about the greatness of the Velvet Underground. He told me about auteur theory and the genius of Preston Sturges. I told him about Dylan in the mid-'60s. He mentioned Godard and Truffaut. We became Godard and Truffaut. Brisbane didn't know it at the time, but there were two 19-year-olds driving around in a car who thought they were French film directors.

So we started the band when he accepted my offer to teach him bass guitar. But it was more than that. It was the decision to pool our ambitions and resources and go for something greater than ourselves, and in this we were aided by one piece of luck: Grant was musical. He could have remained a film student who played the bass, but instead he quickly became a musician. He had a fantastic singing voice and a perfect melodic knack, unknown when I asked him to start the group. What I did know was that, given his obvious creative tendencies, he would write songs. That it took only six weeks surprised me. But after such a short time, he showed me a bass riff, I wrote a chorus, and it became the first Forster-McLennan composition. It was called "Big Sleeping City," and we played it for a year.

Being in a band and releasing our first single—"Lee Remick / Karen," in September 1978—gave us a certain instant notoriety, which we both enjoyed. For Grant it gave him things at 20 that a film career mightn't have handed him until he was 30: recognition, creative adventure, the instant smell that we were going places. The journey had begun. The first vial of our friendship was put aside and we became The Go-Betweens. And from then on we set off on the crusade, with the band as first priority in our lives. We travelled, recorded, added and lost members, and built up the best body of work we could until we crashed 11 years later. Occasionally, through these years, Grant and I would catch each other's eye—as we flew into New York, or played a big Danish rock festival, or went on a French TV show—and think this is what we did it for, these pop moment milestones that both of us had dreamed of back in Brisbane, at the beginning.

Through all of this we stayed good friends. There was something special about our friendship that we could take deep into our work, making crucial creative decisions along the way and never flaring up or tearing at each other. We operated on two rules: each was to have the same number of songs on every album, and we both had to agree on something before we did it. Our confidence in what we could do was amazing. It was as if being in The Go-Betweens gave us an invisible shield, allowing us to believe that nothing could knock us out. Grant was central to this. Every album was "our best so far," and any time I dipped in confidence he was there to pick me up. He was a great working partner. Not only the songs—"Cattle and Cane," "Bachelor Kisses," "Bye Bye Pride," "Streets of Your Town," "Finding You," "Boundary Rider"—but also as an up-close inspirational artist in my life.

This is what he was like. I'd drive over to his place to play guitar and he'd be lying on a bed reading a book. Grant never felt guilt about this. The world turned and worked; he read. That was the first message. He'd offer to make coffee, and I knew—and here's one of the great luxuries of my life—I knew I could ask him anything, on any artistic frontier, and he'd have an answer. He had an encyclopaedic mind when it came to the arts, and his knowledge always had a personal twist. So, as he worked on the coffee, I could toss in anything I liked—something that had popped up in my life that I needed his angle on. I'd say, "Tell me about Goya," or, "What do you know about Elizabeth Bishop's poetry?" or, "Is the Youth Group CD any good?" And, his head over the kitchen table, he'd arch an eyebrow just to ascertain that I was serious, which I always was. Then he'd start. Erudite, logical, authoritative and never condescending—not one ounce of superiority came with the dispensing of his opinion. God. I'm going to miss that. And of all the holes his departing has left, this for me is the largest: the person you can go to who is so much on your wavelength, stocked with shared experience, whom you don't ask for life advice (Grant would be one of the last people there!) but who, as a fellow artist, you can go toe to toe with and always come away totally inspired by. Well, that's a great thing.

And it wasn't only me. Since his death, his role as inspirer and informer has come out strongly in remembrance. An old friend, Steve Haddon, says, "Meeting Grant in 1976 was like getting an education." Another friend, Andrew Wilson, writes, "Thank you for playing 'Johnny Jewel,' *Blonde on Blonde*, and Jane Birkin to me in a wooden Spring Hill room." Of the 1500 responses that quickly sprung up on the internet, many spoke of a meeting with Grant, in a bar, a café, somewhere in the world, when he told them something of someone—made an inspired artistic connection, a tip that these people carried with them. His place here is as a true hipster, in the 1940s and '50s sense of the word. Someone perched on the streets, in the saloons, on the lower side of life, possessing razor-sharp and deep knowledge of the cultural front—but never lording it in the traditional manner. Half jokingly, I once suggested he return to academia. He laughed the idea off, preferring to be the secret holder of wisdom "on a barstool throne."

The break-up of the band in 1989 was savage and abrupt. Grant and I had had enough. We'd written six lauded albums and the band was broke. In the end, we were doing Sydney pub gigs to pay ourselves wages. It was a nasty treadmill. Grant and I had planned to go off as a duo and do an acoustic album, but this got blown sky-high when his girlfriend left him on the day she was told the band was over. The next weeks were chaos. Grant was destroyed. I stayed, consoling him and trying to make sense of the mess that we had brought on by trying to gain our freedom. Then I had to follow my own heart and return to Germany, where I'd found a new life over the last six months. The duo idea hit the rocks when Grant informed the record company he wanted a solo career. The fact that he told them before me hurt. But he had a girlfriend to try to win back—though, as it turned out, that was unsuccessful.

For the remainder of the decade we had fulfilling solo careers. It was great to work alone and to grow. And every eighteen months or so, an offer would come in from some part of the world, attractive enough for Grant and I to do a one-off acoustic show together, catch up, and then go back to our own lives.

There was one other thing, though: the film script. This was a crazy dream dating back to the late '70s. When Grant and I started working together, The Go-Betweens was to be the calling card, the most visible and instantly attractive thing we did. Behind it, we had a number of other ideas we were going to unleash upon the world once the band was famous, which our twenty-year-old minds figured would be in about three years. It was the Orson Welles theory: get famous at one thing, and then bring on everything else you can do. So there was a film and a book in the wings. The film was a jewel-heist caper set on the Gold Coast and then Sydney, a vehicle aimed at our favourite American actor of the time, James Garner. The book was going to be a microscopic dissection of and ode to our favorite pop-star of all time, Bob Dylan, and it was going to be called *The Death of Modern America: Bob Dylan 1964–66* (which still sounds like a great book title to me).

Neither got beyond rough fragments, though the wish to write a film together stayed. So, in 1995, with both of us back in Brisbane, we spent three months in the bowels of the Dendy cinema in George Street writing a film called *Sydney Creeps*. It was wonderful being in a room together working on something other than music, though the script is not as good as it should be. The wrestling over each line and plot twist robbed it of flow and a strong voice. Still, it was done, and there it was: a thick notebook written in longhand, many lines crossed out and written over, lying in a trunk of Grant's last possessions.

We reconvened the band in 2000. Over the next six years we recorded three albums, toured and took the whole thing, to our great pleasure, up another level. We were on the cusp of something. It's strange to say that about a band that had existed for 17 years, but with Adele and Glenn, our bass player and drummer, by our side, all doors still felt open. We were still up for the championship, and we had a growing audience willing us on to bigger and better things. And we had new songs: Grant had a fantastic batch for an album we were going to do next year. I said to him that all my writing up until the recording would just be catching up to what he had. Album number ten was going to be something special.

Yet he wasn't happy. He was proud of the band's recent success, and his private life, after a long bumpy ride, was settled; in general, he was the most contented and up I'd seen him in a long time. But deep down, there remained a trouble, a missing piece that he was always trying to find and that he never did. Family, a loving girlfriend, a circle of friends: all could count for so much, and it *was* a hell of a lot, but it could never cover over a particular hurt. When Grant was four, his father died. Perhaps it stemmed from this. He was moody, and you always hoped you got him on a good day. Sometimes I'd visit and it would take me an hour to pull him out. Twice in his life I was with him when he was totally shattered. And there were many years I missed when we weren't in the same city.

I can remember being hit by the lyrics he put to his first songs. I was shocked by their melancholy and the struggle for joy. I'd known the happy-go-lucky university student. As soon as he wrote, there it was. Any appreciation or remembrance of Grant has to take this into account. He didn't parade it, but it's all over his work, and it was in his eye.

His refuge was art and a romantic nature that made him very lovable, even if he did take it to ridiculous degrees. Here was a man who, in 2006, didn't drive; who owned no wallet or watch, no credit card, no computer. He would only have to hand in his mobile phone and bankcard to be able to step back into the gas-lit Paris of 1875, his natural home. I admired this side of him a great deal, and it came to be part of the dynamic of our pairing. He called me "the strategist." He was the dreamer. We both realised, and came to relish, the perversity of the fact that this was an exact reversal of the perception people had of us as artists and personalities in the band—that I was the flamboyant man out of time and Grant the sensible rock. In reality, the opposite was true.

The last time I saw him was about two weeks before he died. The circumstances of the visit were the same as they'd been for almost 30 years: to play guitar together and do the catch-up with an old friend. He had a two-story granny flat at the back of the house he lived in, and we played on a small deck there. A railroad track runs behind the house, and occasionally trains passed through the songs. We took breaks from the playing, and talked; we had such fun together. Talking. Always talking and gossiping—silly stuff we'd go round and round on.

After four hours I left. He was standing on the front veranda as I walked down to the front gate. In the mailbox was a wrapped copy of the *New York Review of Books*. I took it out and looked at the cover. I called to him, saying I didn't know he got this. He told me he had a subscription, and if I wanted to I could borrow back-issues. I thanked him, said I would and then said goodbye. As I walked to the car and got in, I wondered how many singer-songwriters or rock stars in the world got the *New York Review of Books* delivered on subscription. Not many, I thought. Maybe just one.

RICHARD HELL

ROCK 'N' ROLL HIGH SCHOOL

CBGB's shuts down this weekend.

There's not too much left to say about the character of the joint. It's the most famous rock 'n' roll club in the world, the most famous that there ever has been, and it's just as famously a horrendous dump. It's the archetypal, the ur, dim and dirty, loud, smelly, and ugly nowhere little rock 'n' roll club. There's one not much different from it in every burg in the country.

Only, like a lot of New York, CBGB's is more so, way more so. And of course, for three or four years in the mid-70s, it housed the most influential cluster of bands ever to grow up—or to implicitly reject the concept of growing up—under one roof.

On practically any weekend from 1974 to '76 you could see one or more of the following groups (here listed in approximate chronological order) in the often half-empty 300-capacity club: Television, the Ramones, Suicide, the Patti Smith Group, Blondie, the Dictators, the Heartbreakers, Talking Heads, Richard Hell and the Voidoids, and the Dead Boys. Not to mention some often equally terrific (or equally pathetic) groups that aren't as well remembered, like the Miamis and the Marbles and the Erasers and the Student Teachers. Nearly all the members of these bands treated the club as a headquarters—as home. It was a private world. We dreamed it up. It flowered out of our imaginations.

How often do you get to do that? That's what you want as a kid, and that's what we were able to do at CBGB's. It makes me think of that Elvis Presley quotation: "When I was a child, ladies and gentlemen, I was a dreamer. I read comic books, and I was the hero of the comic book. I saw movies, and I was the hero in the movie. So every dream I ever dreamed has come true a hundred times." We dreamed CBGB's into existence.

The owner of the club, Hilly Kristal, never said no. That was his genius. Though it's dumb to use the word genius about what happened there. It was all a dream. Many of us were drunk or stoned half our waking hours, after all. The thing is, we were young there. You don't get that back. Even children know that. They don't want their old stuff thrown away. Everything should be kept. I regret everything I've ever thrown away.

CBGB's was like a big playhouse, site of conspiracies, orgies, delirium, refuge, boredom, meanness, jealousy, kindness, but most of all youth. Things felt and done the first time are more vivid. CBGB's is where many things were felt with that vividness. That feeling is the real identity of the club, to me. And it's horrible, or at least seriously sad, to lose it. But then, apparently, we aren't really going to lose it.

CBGB's is going to be dismantled and reconstructed as an exhibit in Las Vegas, like Elvis. I like that. A lot. I really hope it happens as intended.

It's occurred to me that Hilly's genius passivity is something he has in common with Andy Warhol. Another trait of Warhol's was that he fanatically tried to keep or record everything that ever happened in his vicinity, from junk mail in "time capsules" to small talk to newspaper front pages and movie star publicity shots to eight hours of the Empire State Building.

We all know that nothing lasts. But at least we can make a cool and funny exhibit of it.

I'm serious. God likes change and a joke. God loves CBGB's.

John Swenson

THE BANDS PLAYED ON

Music is the food of life in New Orleans, as ubiquitous as the summer sun, Spanish moss and palmetto bugs. As inevitable as death, which is at once welcomed and overcome by the unique New Orleans institution of the jazz funeral. But after Hurricane Katrina ripped through the city and breached levees, leaving most of New Orleans underwater, the city's mystic voice was silenced.

But the music has come back. A year after Katrina, it's the musicians who have struggled to their feet to paint a fragile patina of hope over the battered façade of our own Baghdad on the Mississippi, and the story of the music's return is a tale of individual heroics, people of vision who refused to let lack of basic amenities or a curfew enforced by an occupying military sporting automatic weapons stop them from playing music. It's also the story of a people realizing that music is at the center of their spiritual life, the glue that holds their culture together.

Some will argue what event constituted the "real" return of New Orleans music. Like the 800,000 people who now claim to have witnessed Hank Aaron's 714th home run or the 10 million who were "at" Woodstock, the stories will only grow more colorful and elaborate over time. What matters is that the music did come back and that it is giving every last person who remains tied to New Orleans a good reason to be here.

Two French Quarter institutions, Molly's at the Market and Johnny White's Sports Bar on Bourbon Street, refused to close even as the city turned into a disaster area after August 29. Johnny White's Sports Bar, whose slogan is "Never Closed," doesn't have a lock on the front door and bartender Marcy Kreiter simply stayed on, pouring shots and serving warm beer by candlelight. The jukebox was useless without power, but a reporter from the *Manchester Guardian* wrote about an Alabama man in the immediate aftermath of Katrina playing an acoustic guitar on the street in front of the bar.

As for Molly's, the club hosted a live music event September 27 that many recognize as the first music back in the city when Coco Robicheaux performed.

Robicheaux was one of the many who stayed through the storm. He didn't leave because he had gigs to play, a steady stream of engagements at the Apple Barrel, d.b.a. and elsewhere that had gone uninterrupted by the fiercest of maelstroms for years.

"The house shook," Robicheaux recalls. "The windows blew out. The door blew in."

But what he saw when he went outside challenged Robicheaux's imagination.

"There was death everywhere," he says in a choked whisper. "Dead animals, dead dogs, people . . . water everywhere. I stayed until Thursday evening to see if I could find anybody but after a while I just couldn't stand it. I was on one little dry piece of land and everything else was way under water. It was terrible stuff—explosions and fires, dead people floating around and dead animals, fish, alligators, frogs, people, flies and mosquitoes. And the smell. I couldn't take it after a while. No food. No water. I loaded up all my stuff, guitar and amps and decided I would try and drive out of there. I had a four-wheeler, so I figured I could work my way out. They tried to carjack me. I had my .357 and I had to pull it out a couple of times."

Robicheaux went to Texas, then Georgia, but couldn't stand being away from New Orleans and drove back into town.

"It was worse when I got back. It looked like an H-bomb had gone off. People were going crazy, looting and shooting, and the flies were like in Africa. You might be talking and there would be 20 of them on your face trying to get in your mouth as you speak crawling up your nose [and] in your ears."

Robicheaux walked his beat up and down Frenchmen and Decatur streets and found Jim Monaghan holding court at Molly's, which had become a haven for many remaining New Orleanians.

"I was at Molly's when the lights came on," he says. "I said to Monaghan, 'What does that mean to you?' He said, 'I'm back in business. My beer cooler's on.' I said, 'It means music to me. I got my shit parked right outside.' I set up and I started playing 'Baby You Don't Have to Go.' All these people came in, the girls were dancing on top of the bar, removing clothing. Everybody was partying. I just kept playing, never took a break. I have no idea how long I played, longer than usual and I usually play four or five hours. There was a curfew but we didn't care, Monaghan said, 'The hell with it, man.'"

The show at Molly's was spontaneous, but uptown at the Maple Leaf, Hank Staples was itching to get things going. The Riverbend still lacked power, but Staples obtained a generator and put the word out to musicians. Drummer Kevin O'Day helped put together a band called the MREs after the "meals ready to eat" that locals were living on post-Katrina. At the Maple Leaf, the anagram stood for "Music Ready to Enjoy."

"I got a call from Andy Ambrose telling me that Hank Staples wanted to open up the Maple Leaf and do a show on September 30," says O'Day. "I called Walter ['Wolfman' Washington], I hadn't heard from him for about 11 days. The day before I got the phone call for the gig was the first time I'd heard from him since the storm. He had made it up to Ohio, so it was a big relief that he was still alive. He turned around and came back, drove 17 hours to do the show. We made a few more calls and it grew like that."

Somebody tipped off National Public Radio and its area affiliates, so in addition to the roughly 400 locals at the show, some 150 journalists were on hand to anoint the event as the official return of music to New Orleans.

"We had CNN and NPR and CBS there," O'Day recalls. "Everybody showed up to document it. It really was a crucial moment. I think a lot of people were inspired by what went on that night. We started really early, about 4 o'clock in the afternoon. My wife Julie cooked red beans in a huge pot. There were a lot of mixed emotions but it was incredible from the first note until the end of the concert just to be playing. It was like the music was really serving its purpose. All the practice and the years of playing really meant something to everyone at that time. We did what we were supposed to do, which was uplift the souls of everybody. It was an intensely spiritual moment for me.

"Eventually, the National Guard came in and shut down the music and kicked everybody out. That was about 8 o'clock. That was after curfew; we got an extra hour, I think."

Ad hoc combos like the MREs dominated the local musical landscape in October. Ed Peterson and the Ultimate Test—a one-time only combo with Peterson, Steve Masakowski, Don Vappie and Ricky Sebastian—opened Snug Harbor October 14, three days after Frenchmen Street had power. Similarly, Chris Boone and members of Sol Fiya played with Anders Osborne, Willie Green and Stanton Moore at Le Bon Temps Roule.

Boone began playing in the front room of Le Bon Temps right after it opened in early October.

"I came back in the first week of October and stayed with my friend Pepper Keenan, who owns the Bon Temps," says Boone. "I was there when the club reopened. There were a lot of people there because there weren't many bars open. There wasn't any music going on, so I started playing in the corner of the front bar by myself. I thought everybody needed some music to pick them up because of what had just happened, and people were really happy just to hear some music. Then we started in the back room two weeks later. It was Anders Osborne and myself and a couple of members of Sol Fiya, and it was really packed. I think we made about $900 in tips alone."

While the House of Blues and many higher profile clubs remained closed, smaller and less conventional venues slowly came alive. In October, John Autin and Julie Jules were back at the Carousel Bar. In the Bywater, the wine store Bacchanal started hosting live music with Davis Rogan. The Plowboys reopened the Kingpin on Lyons Street.

"It was absolutely fucking jam-packed; people were so excited to hear music it was unbelievable," says Kingpin owner Steve Watson. "You could have put a can with a string on it with a stick and packed the place out. All people wanted was a hamburger and to listen to some music."

Suddenly there was plenty of work for the musicians who returned. "A lot of neighborhood bars started having new music," says Washboard Chaz. "Frenchmen Street was back in action fairly quickly—the Apple Barrel, Spotted Cat, Snug's, and d.b.a. Angeli's never had music before."

"On October 17, I moved back into town for good," says O'Day, "and I was immediately working again. I started playing the Maple

Leaf with Walter on Saturdays. We began our Wednesday night shows at d.b.a. right off the bat, that was huge. Maria opened up the Banks Street Bar. She had to use candlelight at first, but eventually she got the electricity back."

Though Mid-City remained shrouded in darkness, Maria Guth started hosting music at the Banks Street Bar outside the club. "It was pretty amazing," says guitarist Bill Iuso. "Banks Street ran a gig in the open air, a mixed bunch of people, mostly a sit-in. We played acoustic by candlelight and had coolers for the beer. As soon as Maria got power, we started working there weekly."

O'Day also played the emotional reopening of the Ogden Museum of Southern Arts on October 27 backing trumpeter James Andrews. The Ogden was the first mainstream cultural institution to open its doors to the public after Katrina. Special events director Libra LaGrone, the architect of the Ogden After Hours music program, made Andrews a featured element of the ceremonies. "James was a logical choice being from Treme, considering the devastation that happened to that historic neighborhood, as well as his importance to the city as a musician and member of an accomplished musical family," she says.

As the only member of the museum's management team living in the city at the time, LaGrone had to overcome daunting logistical problems to open.

"The museum staff stayed in touch by e-mail," she says. "We wanted to reopen on October 1 but because Hurricane Rita was on its way during that planning period, we decided to wait until after Rita hit. With the devastation of Rita, we settled on October 27. That was a Thursday and we had music the night we opened. I saw James Andrews one night, went up to him and said, 'We want to reopen the museum and I think you'd be the perfect person to do it.' He was right on it. I had no sound equipment and no engineer but

Michael Blum and Pete Winkler from Motorway were in town and they agreed to lend us equipment to do it.

"We expected around 200 people that night. Prior to the storm, our average audience was about 145. We had close to 400 people by 6:30, minutes after the doors opened, and ended with over 600 people. When James hit his first note, I remember standing outside of the museum. There were hundreds of people everywhere and I was home. There was no looking back. Despite all the things I lost in the storm, I realized how fortunate I was to work for an institution that cares about the city and cares about the musicians and artists in the city.

"The museum became a meeting place to find out where your family and friends were. After 9/11, people posted pictures and signs of all of their friends; well, after Katrina people were coming to the museum to hear the music, have a drink and find out where all of their friends were. It was absolutely beautiful. There were parents with newborns and 2-year-olds, and there were grandmothers and grandfathers. There were some contractors and some military people, but I'd say 80 percent of it was local. Every race, age, you name it—they were here. It was truly a remarkable evening."

Andrews was brimming with emotion as he played traditional New Orleans standards that night. The same songs that served as crowd-pleasing light entertainment before the storm became powerful vehicles of transcendence in its wake.

"It was great to see so many people that I knew from New Orleans come to the show to see me play," says Andrews. "It was great to know that they were still alive and that they made it through Katrina. I guess that gig at the Ogden Museum was more like a homecoming. Everybody was seeing their neighbors and friends for the first time since the hurricane, and it was more like a gathering of New Orleanians for the first time since the storm. That's when I knew that a lot of New Orleans people were coming back to New Orleans. Old school New Orleans people really care about New Orleans. That was the crowd that really cared for New Orleans."

The experience wasn't Andrews' first return to town, though. He played for the TV cameras in Jackson Square just days after the storm in what is most likely the first live musical performance after Katrina.

"We played in Jackson Square a week after the storm," says Andrews. "We came back to do a TV show on MSNBC with Rita Crosby. I was up in Monroe, Louisiana, and my brother Troy was in Houston, but we came back to play this show.

"It was difficult to be positive," says Andrews. "Every time you look around, you see sadness. Everything was destroyed; there were no people in New Orleans at that time. No places open, no food stores, it was sad. Even today, family members are still displaced by the storm. Around here now, you've got a few musicians who've come back but it's kind of tough to even find musicians to put together for a gig."

The numerous clubs and music bars that reopened after the storm have been anxious to give musicians a reason to return to New Orleans by providing them with work.

"If we want musicians to come back to town we have to provide gigs for them," argues Cindy Wood, who owns Vaughan's, "so I need to have music more than one night a week."

For years, Vaughan's has been known for its Thursday night Kermit Ruffins shows, but post-Katrina, the club has Washboard Chaz on Wednesdays, Kermit on Thursdays, and the Treme Brass Band on Sundays.

"We came back October 13," says Wood. "We opened to clean the place the next day, but people started coming in so we were open. I was in contact with Kermit by cell phone. It was really kind of scary for a while that he might not come back because they were really trying to keep him in Houston. They were doing everything they could to keep him; they even gave him a club. But they can't stay away forever, especially Kermit. As soon as he got an apartment, he stopped going back to Houston."

Halloween was the first really big weekend, with many bands returning to play Voodoo. Rebirth Brass Band played three gigs that day including one at Voodoo, one in the French Quarter in the afternoon, then a packed gig that night at Tipitina's.

"A big turning point for me was when we performed Halloween night at One Eyed Jacks," says Josh Cohen of Morning 40 Federation. "The curfew was still on. When the place got packed, I realized that the people will go out and party and not necessarily wallow in their misery or hold their head in their hands. They were there to have fun and celebrate the moment. The high points to me are when everything's perfect between the crowd and the band; you're in New Orleans and somehow this whole combination of stuff creates perfect moments in life. We get a limited amount of those moments."

The Zydepunks played Voodoo in the afternoon and Café Brasil that night.

"The band came back into town to play Voodoo Fest, but I had come back in September, right after Rita," says Christian Kuffner. "It was dead, a total ghost town. It was disturbing. I went to Bourbon Street and some of the clubs had just started opening. They had those guys on the mic doing karaoke and it was all police officers in the audience. There was no music. Nobody was playing in the clubs or on the street."

The Halloween weekend was the opposite of that, and as Kuffner surveyed the raucous Frenchmen Street scene outside his Café Brasil gig, a sobering reality tempered his mood.

"I realized a lot of people were there to say goodbye to New Orleans," he says. "I kept running into people who were coming back just to see everybody one more time before they left the city for good."

That feeling of loss is a harsh reality that all New Orleanians understand, but for those who've stayed, music is a big part of what keeps them here.

"I think the ground itself is too powerful," says Shannon McNally. "It's sacred ground, like Stonehenge or the Grand Canyon, and I don't think that thing that makes New Orleans great has left the city. It's there in all of the musicians who know and love New Orleans. We just have to gather frequently, keep in touch, learn how to continue to laugh. We'll all rise to the occasion. We lost Gatemouth Brown, which really shook me, but we still have Snooks Eaglin and Dr. John and Allen Toussaint, and I'm going to follow their lead."

KELEFA SANNEH

NEW ORLEANS HIP-HOP IS THE HOME OF GANGSTA GUMBO

For thousands of people—we'll probably never know exactly how many—Hurricane Katrina was the end. But for listeners across the country, that not-quite-natural disaster also marked the beginning of a party that hasn't ended yet. Ever since those awful days last year, the country has been celebrating the rich musical heritage of New Orleans.

There was a blitz of benefit concerts, including "From the Big Apple to the Big Easy," a pair of shows held simultaneously at Madison Square Garden and Radio City Music Hall last September. A New Orleans jam session closed the show at the Grammy Awards in February. There have been scads of well-intentioned compilations, including *Our New Orleans: A Benefit Album for the Gulf Coast* (Nonesuch), *Hurricane Relief: Come Together Now* (Concord) and *Higher Ground Hurricane Relief Benefit Concert* (Blue Note), a live album recorded at the Jazz at Lincoln Center Benefit. At the Rock and Roll Hall of Fame induction ceremony last month, a video segment paid tribute to New Orleans music through the years, from

Louis Armstrong to the Neville Brothers; there was also the inevitable New Orleans jam session.

But one thing all these tributes have in common is that they all ignored the thrilling—and wildly popular—sound of New Orleans hip-hop, the music that has been the city's true soundtrack through the last few decades.

Rap music remains by far New Orleans's most popular musical export. Lil' Wayne, Master P, Juvenile, Mannie Fresh, B. G., Mystikal and many other pioneers have sold millions of albums, and they have helped make their city an indispensable part of the hip-hop world. Unlike all the other musicians celebrated at post-Katrina tributes, these ones still show up on the pop charts, often near the top. (Juvenile's most recent album made its debut at No. 1, last month.) Yet when tourists and journalists descend upon the city next weekend, for the New Orleans Jazz and Heritage Festival, they'll find only one local rapper on the schedule: Juvenile, who is to appear on the Congo Square Louisiana Rebirth Stage at 6 p.m. Saturday.

Maybe New Orleans rappers don't mind being left out. No doubt most of them prefer popularity—and its rewards—to respect. But why should they have to choose?

Hip-hop was long considered unfit for polite society. And yet the extraordinary snubbing of New Orleans hip-hop comes at a time when the genre is gaining institutional validation. The Smithsonian Institution's National Museum of American History recently announced plans for a hip-hop exhibit. The Rock and Roll Hall of Fame and Museum exhibited "Roots, Rhyme and Rage: The Hip-Hop Story" in 1999. Colleges and universities around the country are offering conferences and courses devoted to hip-hop history. At the same time that hip-hop is being written out of the history of New Orleans, it's being written into the history of America. Could that possibly be a coincidence?

The story of New Orleans hip-hop begins in earnest with what is known as bounce music: festive beats, exuberant chants, and simple lyrics that ruled local nightclubs and breezeway parties in the late 1980s and early 90s. The future hip-hop star Juvenile got his start in the bounce-music scene. But like many New Orleans musicians before him, Juvenile found out that having a citywide hit wasn't quite the same as having a nationwide hit.

By the mid-90s, Southern hip-hop was starting to explode, and so some New Orleans entrepreneurs figured out ways to go national. Master P, a world-class hustler and less-than-world-class rapper from the city's rough Calliope projects, founded a label called No Limit, and used it to popularize a distinctively New Orleans-ish form of hard-boiled hip-hop. For a time Master P was one of pop music's most successful moguls. (He made the cover of *Fortune*, and he never let anyone forget it.)

Master P's crosstown rivals were the Williams brothers, proprietors of Cash Money Records, which eventually replaced No Limit as the city's dominant brand name. Cash Money signed up the hometown hero Juvenile (who was raised in the Magnolia projects), as well as the city's greatest hip-hop producer, Mannie Fresh. Working with a great group of rappers including Lil' Wayne and B. G., Fresh perfected an exuberant electronic sound; he did as much as anyone to pull the musical legacy of New Orleans into the 21st century. You could hear brass bands in the synthesizers, drum lines in the rattling beats, Mardi Gras Indians in the singsong lyrics. (If you're wondering where to start, try Juvenile's head-spinning 1998 blockbuster, *400 Degreez*, which has sold 4.7 million copies.)

Like most musical stories, this one doesn't really have a happy ending—or any ending at all. Master P's empire dissolved, which explains why you might recently have seen him on *Dancing With the Stars*. Mystikal, one of the city's best and weirdest rappers, split with No Limit in 2000, and he's currently serving a jail sentence for sexual battery and tax evasion. Juvenile, B. G. and Mannie Fresh have all left Cash Money, though Lil' Wayne remains.

Then came Katrina. Not all of the city's stars were living in New Orleans when the storm hit, but all lost houses or cars or—at the very least—a hometown. Lil' Wayne moved his mother to Miami; Mannie Fresh set up shop in Los Angeles; B. G. is living in Detroit.

But the music never stopped. Juvenile's "Reality Check" (UTP/Atlantic), released last month, was the fastest-selling CD of his career; for the defiant first single, "Get Ya Hustle On," he filmed a video in the devastated Lower Ninth Ward. B. G. recently released a strong new album, *The Heart of tha Streetz Vol. 2 (I Am What I Am)* (Koch); it was strong enough, in fact, to earn him a new record contract with Atlantic. In "Move Around," the album's first single, Mannie Fresh sings (sort of) the cheerful refrain: "I'm from the ghetto, homey / I was raised on bread and baloney / You can't come around here, 'cause you're phony."

And then there's Lil' Wayne, who last fall released *Tha Carter 2* (Cash Money/Universal), perhaps the finest album of his career (it has sold about 900,000 copies so far). In his slick lyrics and raspy voice, you can hear a city's swagger and desperation:

> *All I have in this world is a pistol and a promise*
> *A fistful of dollars*
> *A list full of problems*
> *I'll address 'em like P.O. Boxes*
> *Yeah, I'm from New Orleans, the Creole cockpit*
> *We so out of it*
> *Zero tolerance*
> *Gangsta gumbo—I'll serve 'em a pot of it*

All right, so this isn't the stuff that feel-good tributes are made of. Despite the topical video, "Get Ya Hustle On" is a mishmash of political commentary and drug-dealer rhymes. (The song included the well-known couplet, "Everybody tryna get that check from FEMA/

So he can go and score him some co-ca-een-uh.") And much of the music portrays New Orleans as a place full of violence and decadence: expensive teeth, cheap women, "choppers" (machine guns) everywhere. If you're trying to celebrate the old, festive, tourist-friendly New Orleans, maybe these aren't the locals you want.

Furthermore, much of the post-Katrina effort has focused on "saving" and "preserving" the city's musical heritage. Clearly top-selling rappers don't need charity. In fact, many have been quietly helping, through gifts to fellow residents and hip-hop charities like David Banner's Heal the Hood Foundation.

But it's worth remembering that many New Orleans hip-hop pioneers—from DJ Jimi to the influential group U.N.L.V.—aren't exactly millionaires. And for that matter, many rappers aren't nearly as rich as they claim. In any case, glowing recollections aren't the only way to pay tribute to the city. The story of Katrina is in large part a story of poverty and neglect; it's no coincidence that many of the rappers come from the same neighborhoods that still haven't been cleaned up. Surely the lyrics to a Juvenile song aren't nearly as shocking as those images most of us saw on television.

The language of preservationism sometimes conceals its own biases. If all the dying traditions are valuable, does that also mean all the valuable traditions are dying? If a genre doesn't need saving, does that also mean it's not worth saving? If New Orleans rappers seem less lovable than, say, Mardi Gras Indians or veteran soul singers, might it be because they're less needy? Cultural philanthropy is drawn to musical pioneers—especially African-American ones—who are old, poor and humble. What do you do when the pioneers are young, rich and cocky instead?

Believe it or not, that question brings us back to the Smithsonian, which has come to praise hip-hop. Or to bury it. Or both. The genre is over 30 years old by now, and while its early stars now seem unimpeachable (does anyone have a bad word to say about Grandmaster

Flash or Run-DMC?), its current stars seem more impeachable than ever. From 50 Cent to Young Jeezy to, well, Juvenile, hip-hop might be even more controversial now than it was in the 80s; hip-hop culture has been blamed for everything from lousy schools to sexism to the riots in France. In a weird way, that might help account for the new-found respectability of the old school. To an older listener who's aghast at crack rap, the relatively innocent rhymes of Run-DMC don't seem so bad. If the new generation didn't seem so harmful, its predecessors might not seem harmless enough for the national archives.

Maybe the New Orleans hip-hop scene—"gangsta gumbo"—just hasn't been around long enough to make the history books. But that will change, as the rappers start seeming less like harbingers of an ominous future and more like relics of a colorful past. New Orleans hip-hop will endure not just because the music is so thrilling, but also because the rappers vividly evoke a city that is, for worse and (let's not forget) for better, never going to be the same.

After all, long before his name was affixed to an airport, Louis Armstrong, too, seemed manifestly unfit for polite society. Back when he recorded "Muggles," an ode to marijuana, he was a symbol of the so-called "jazz intoxication" that was corrupting an earlier generation the way hip-hop is corrupting this one.

A quarter-century from now, when the social problems that Juvenile and others so discomfitingly rap about have become one more strand of the city's official history, they may find themselves honored in just the kinds of musical tributes and cultural museums that currently shut them out. By then, their careers will probably have cooled off. They'll be less influential, less popular, less controversial; not coincidentally, they'll have a less visceral connection to the youth of New Orleans. And finally, their music—and maybe also their recording studios, their custom jewelry, their promotional posters—will seem to be worth saving. Perhaps, like so many other pop-music traditions, "gangsta gumbo" is a dish best preserved cold.

Douglas Wolk

THE SYNCHER, NOT THE SONG

The Irresistible Rise of the Numa Numa Dance

In 2003, the Moldovan-Romanian boy band O-Zone released *DiscO-Zone*, their second or third album, depending on how you count. Their earlier Eastern European hits like "Despre tine" were the sort of thing you'd play an advanced level of *Dance Dance Revolution* to: fast, formulaic, useful for dancing, nothing special. This time, though, they sang a song that changed the world, "Dragostea din Tei."

O-Zone's Dan Bălan had previously been in the doom metal band Inferialis; sensing that Backstreet Boys clones were where the money was, he formed the first version of O-Zone with Inferialis's singer, then ditched him to form a lineup with two much prettier dudes, Arsenie Todiras and Radu Sârbu. For a while, O-Zone mk. II were major celebrities in Romania—"Dragostea din Tei" wasn't even the first single from *DiscO-Zone* there.

Written by Bălan, it's a brilliant piece of boy-band fluff. There's scarcely a second without some extraordinary hook, starting with the wordless keening at the beginning, flipping back and forth between someone's tenor and falsetto voices: "Ma-ia-*hii*, ma-ia-*huu*, ma-ia-*haa*, ma-ia-*ha*-ha." Then the beat comes in: synthesized disco octave bass and an F-C-G-Am riff that underpins every part of the song in one way or another.

The lyrics of "Dragostea din Tei" are as detailed and nonspecific as the words to "I Want It That Way" or "It's Gonna Be Me." They seem to be one side of a phone conversation; the gist is "Oh, hi there, I'm an outlaw type and I beeped you; I hope you will allow me to make you happy, but actually I don't expect anything. Also, you want to go but you won't take me."

Just when the first verse has meandered almost to the point of getting lost, we are unshackled, de-blindfolded, and shoved out of the van into brilliant sunlight, and realize that the verse was just distracting us until we could be plunged into the chorus. It's as big as an abandoned government building, and in precisely the range that huge legions of drunk people can sing easily. "Vrei sa pleci dar nu ma, nu ma iei / Nu ma, nu ma iei, nu ma, nu ma, nu ma iei," it starts. The title of "Dragostea din Tei" is apparently difficult to translate—it means something like "love among the linden trees" but also alludes to a hipster neighborhood in Bucharest and to first love. The video involves O-Zone romping around on the wing of an airplane.

"Dragostea din Tei" was a hit in Romania in late 2003; the next February, it became the No. 1 record in Italy. But the Italian hit wasn't O-Zone's version; it was a cover by the Romanian/Italian duo Haiducii ("The Outlaws"—as in the song's line "sunt eu, un haiduc"), who performed it as a badly sung boy-and-girl duet. The original recording promptly spread across the rest of Europe like an oil slick. By the summer of 2004, it was inescapable anywhere on the continent; even in the U.K., it peaked at No. 3. The Japanese label Avex picked it up for release, too.

This is where the cat comes in. Japanese internet geeks like to make little illustrations with typed symbols; on a very popular forum called *2channel*, there's a cat a lot of people draw with them. The cat's famous catchphrase is "omae mo na," which means, in essence, "you too!" He's consequently known as Mona.

In Japan, Avex released "Dragostea din Tei" under the title "Koi no Maiahi" ("Passion's Maiahi"—the second word's the transliteration of the yodel at the beginning of the song), and a fan known as Ikari made a Flash animation video for it, starring a cat who looked a lot like Mona. Ikari's video is based on mishearing the Romanian lyrics as English or Japanese lyrics: *salut* is accompanied by an image of a monkey (*saru* in Japanese), *fericirea* ("happiness") is *panchira* ("looking up a skirt"), and best of all, *nu ma nu ma iei* sounds like *noma noma yay*—or "drink! drink! yay!" Avex jumped on the video's popularity and started selling merchandise depicting "Noma neko" ("Noma cat"). Inevitably, there were howls of outrage from Mona buffs—and, reportedly, death threats against the head of Avex.

The Ikari video quickly spread beyond Japan; evidently inspired by it, an Oregonian who calls himself Yansa made a pretty amazing Flash video of his own, based on mishearing the lyrics in American English (*mi-amintesc de ochii tai* became *now mintesque, tha Okie play*, accompanied by images of sprigs of mint and the *Oklahoma!* soundtrack). The "nu ma nu ma" bit features dancing gnomes; "fericirea" is steaming plates of fettuccine. And there the story might have ended—"Dragostea din Tei" might have been a little meme confined to hardcore webophiles over a few weeks, like "All Your Base Are Belong to Us" or the LiveJournal Batgirl-drawing thing.

Allegedly, though, Ikari's animation was also the vector that carried "Dragostea din Tei" to a nineteen-year-old kid named Gary Brolsma in Saddle Brook, New Jersey. He liked the song; he made a video of himself sitting in his chair in front of his computer, dancing to "Dragostea din Tei," and posted it as a Flash video to a site called *Newgrounds* on December 6, 2004. He called it "Numa Numa Dance."

Brolsma's video singlehandedly justifies the existence of webcams. His squarish head and shoulders are in the center of the shot. He's got a short haircut, glasses that are slightly too small for him and reflect his computer's monitor, and cheap headphones; he's sitting in a dismal-looking suburban room. And he is *going for it*: rolling his eyes back in his head, shaking his face, shooting his hands into the air with the beat, saluting along with the word *salut*, gesturing grandly, lip-synching the whole thing with his grand opera of a mouth, flirting with the camera, utterly given over to the music. It's a movie of someone who is having the time of his life, wants to share his joy with everyone, and doesn't care what anyone else thinks. In other words, it's a movie of a total geek. Also, it's only ninety-nine seconds long, which is, coincidentally, the exact length that it's capable of being funny—it cuts off in the middle of a verse.

No matter. Within a few weeks, millions of people had watched "Numa Numa Dance." Brolsma appeared on *Good Morning America*; he sent *Newgrounds* a revised version of the clip, without the cutaway gags he'd inserted (like a quick image of some feta cheese during "fericirea"). But by the time Alan Feuer and Jason George wrote about him in the *New York Times*, at the end of February 2005, he'd grown sick of the attention and refused to talk to them. Heartbreaking graf from *Times* story: "These days, Mr. Brolsma shuttles between the house and his job at Staples, his family said. He is distraught, embarrassed. His grandmother, Margaret Telkes, quoted him as saying, just the other day, 'I want this to end.'"

It was only beginning.

Brolsma's video, Dan Bălan apparently realized, could be the thin end of a wedge to break O-Zone in America. He tried to piggyback onto Numanumamania, using the O-Zone name to record a slicked-up English-language version of the song with a throaty-voiced co-singer named Lucas Prata. The chorus of "Ma Ya Hi," as the ghastly English version was called, goes "When you leave, my colors fade to gray / Oo-aa-oo-aa-ay / Oo-aa-oo-aa-oo-aa-ay / Every word of love I used to say / Now I paint it every day." Being open to interpretation is a healthy thing for a boy-band song; making no sense isn't, and "oo-aa-ay" doesn't have the juicy baby-talk singability of "nu ma nu ma nu ma iei." "Ma Ya Hi" briefly pressed its nose up against the bottom of the American charts, then disappeared. The song had already taken O-Zone as far as they were going to go; shortly thereafter, the band announced that they were breaking up.

But the Numa Numa Dance was better advertising for the universality of "Dragostea din Tei" than anything a record label could have paid for. Musicians all over the world started recording their own versions of the song. The Spanish group Los Morancos rewrote it as "Marica tú," and mangled the Romanian chorus into "fiesta, fiesta, y pluma, pluma gay": a plea to party and come out of the closet. (There's a clip of a South American TV show where they sing it with a horde of disco dancers behind them doing the Numa Numa Dance.) The Brazilian DJ Latino borrowed the melody for "Festa no Apê." The Japanese female impersonator Maeda Ken made a Eurodisco-style recording and video of "Koi no Maiahi Chiwawa," a medley incorporating "Dragostea din Tei." Singapore's Jocie Kok recorded a rewritten version, "Bu Pa Bu Pa," about overcoming fear of cockroaches. The Italian trailer for *Chicken Little* featured C. L. doing something very much like the Numa Numa Dance to "Dragostea din Tei." There are Dutch versions, Hebrew versions, Russian versions.

Most of all, there are homemade versions—not of "Dragostea," as such, but of "Numa Numa." In early 2005, upload-your-own-video sites like Google Video and YouTube started to have a significant public presence, and suddenly the big difference between Brolsma's video and, for instance, the infamous video of a kid practicing his light-saber moves became apparent. Everyone laughed at the Star Wars Kid; everyone wanted to *be* the Numa Numa Guy—to feel that un-self-consciously self-conscious joy he felt in his body, flailing around in his chair and lip-synching a stupid pop song in a language he didn't understand.

Type *numa numa* into Google Video's search box, and you'll get well over 400 hits; in YouTube's, you'll get over 1,500. Virtually all of the results are cut from a single template. A kid, in a bedroom or living room somewhere, sits in front of a computer with a webcam perched on top of it. "Dragostea din Tei" plays in the background, and the kid lip-synchs to it, duplicating every facial expression and motion of Gary Brolsma's Numa Numa Dance, except that the kid keeps breaking into a smile. Everyone knows how it goes—it's the internet's equivalent of the Macarena or the Electric Slide, except that it involves facial gestures, too. (And how many people can say they've invented a dance that everyone can do?)

The youngest Numa Numa performers are about two ("I'm *doing* it, Kayla!" one little girl yells to her big sister as she watches Brolsma on the screen and flings her hands into the air. "Me and the guy are doing it together! Ma ya *heeee* . . . "), the oldest I've seen are a couple who look to be in their fifties, but most look to be between thirteen and eighteen years old. The gender balance is roughly equal. There are a few overt parodies of Brolsma—in one, for instance, his gestures are duplicated by a guy in a Darth Vader suit and mask, breathing like the Sith Lord. Generally, though, the Numa Numa people are simply doing exactly what Brolsma did, marking themselves as being just like him. Sometimes they do the Numa Numa in groups of two or three or six; more often, they do it on their own, carefully setting up the shot to look as much like Brolsma's as possible, except with their own domestic scene in the background. They don't just lip-synch to the O-Zone recording but to whatever version of "Dragostea din Tei" happens to be available. It's like *The Family of Man* with crappy webcams in place of Edward Steichen's camera.

Watching one after another—and Brolsma was right, there's no way to sustain interest in any of them for more than ninety-nine seconds, but it's very easy to watch the opening sequences of dozens in a row—they start to look less like an infectious joke than like a new cultural order. These kids aren't mocking the Numa Numa Guy; they're venerating him. They are geeks honoring the King of the Geeks, and they're beautiful to see, because they're replicating and spreading his happiness. They're following a ritual that's meaningful if not yet venerable: learning the dance, lip-synching the song, documenting their performance just so, making it available for the world to see. And they probably have no idea what the words mean, as if that mattered. "Dragostea din Tei," not even the words but the sound of the recording, is now part of the fabric of the internet. It's bypassed the monolithic American entertainment industry to become a standard; the very few records it's sold in the States are accidental by-products of its actual significance, as a mechanism for amateurs to show their love without a hint of the shame that overcame their hero.

In 2006, O-Zone's Arsenie Todiras, now calling himself Arsenium, was chosen to represent Moldova at the Eurovision Song Contest in Athens in May. He'll be singing a song of his own composition, "Loca." Dan Bălan has left the boy-band sound behind and formed a rock group, called simply Balan; there's footage of them playing a bloodless grunge version of "Dragostea din Tei" in front of a screaming Russian crowd. Today, a pair of fourteen-year-old girls in Japan and a tough-looking Eastern European dude with a little mustache and an American middle-school girl with a bad asymmetrical haircut and a nine-year-old boy in a muscle tee and a male college student in terrible drag with greasepaint eyebrows all filmed themselves performing Brolsma's choreography, and uploaded the results. Someone far away, they knew, would see them in their homes, understand their pride in geekdom, and love them for it.

OTHER NOTABLE ESSAYS OF 2006

Benjamin Anastas, "Three Variations on a Theme by Max Weber" (*Moist Works*, February 15, 2006).

Eric K. Arnold, "Dummed Down"(*Vibe*, July 2006).

Marke B., "Fag Fridays: 10 Years of Faggoty Goodness" (*San Francisco Bay Guardian*, May 5, 2006).

Nick Barat, "Beyoncé, Art School Girls and Warp Speed Bass? On the Floor with Chicago's Juke DJs" (*The Fader*, July/August 2006).

Dan Bilefsky, "Finland Squirms as Its Latest Export Steps into Spotlight" (*New York Times*, April 24, 2006).

Oliver Burkman, "How Many Hits" (*The Guardian*, November 11, 2006).

David Cantwell, "Pennies from Heaven" (*No Depression*, November/December 2006).

Josie Cotton, "Josie Cotton: The Story of 80s New-Wave Hit 'Johnny, Are You Queer?'" (*Magnet*, October/November 2006).

Kandia Crazy Horse, "The Black Atlantic or, 2006—the Year the Music Died" (*Creative Loafing*, December 27, 2006).

Suzanne Cusick, "Music as Torture, Music as Weapon" (*Transcultural Music Review*, No. 10, 2006).

John Darnielle, "Thirty Short Poems About My Favorite Metal Band" (*Last Plane to Jakarta*, November 19, 2006 to January 22, 2007).

Justin Davidson, "Measure for Measure: What Conductors Convey to Musicians" (*The New Yorker*, August 21, 2006).

Francis Davis, "The Singing Epidemic" (*Atlantic Monthly*, January/February 2006).

Matthew Duersten, "The Arkivists" *(LA Weekly*, April 5, 2006).

Daniel Felsenfeld, "Putting the 'I' back in H*story" (*New Music Box*, March 22, 2006).

Mark Fisher, "Memorex for the Krakens: The Fall's Pulp Modernism" (*k-punk* blog, May 8, 2006).

Bill Friskics-Warren, "To Beat the Devil" (*No Depression*, March/April 2006).

Matthew Fritch, "Frontier Days" (*Magnet*, July/August 2006).

Gillian Gaar, "Smells Like Big Bucks" (*Harp*, November 2006).

Nick Green, "Invisible Oranges" (*Decibel*, May 2006).

Michael Joseph Gross, "Paris Hilton" (*Blender*, September 2006).

Keith Harris, "Bitter Without Bite" (*Chicago Reader*, March 17, 2006).

Joel Hartse, "Cheat Sheet" (*Sacramento News*, December 14, 2006).

Wil Haygood, "Frank Jr., the Unsung Sinatra" (*Washington Post*, July 9, 2006).

Geoffrey Himes, "A Change Is Gonna Come" (*OffBeat*, September 2006).

Mark Hogan, "Self Portrait" (*Pitchfork Media*, February 20, 2006).

Hua Hsu, "After the Snow" (*Village Voice*, January 17, 2006).

Elton John and Jake Shears, "When Elton Met Jake" (*The Observer*, November 12, 2006).

Lenny Kaye, "Joe Meek: The Meek Shall Inherit the Stars" (*eMusic*, September 2006).

Monica Kendrick, "Just Three" (*Chicago Reader*, September 29, 2006).

Rob Kenner, "The Real Revolutionary" (*Vibe*, May 2006).

Allya S. King, "Behind Closed Doors" (*Vibe*, August 2006).

Jordan Levin, "Salsa Pioneer Still Hearkens to a Rebel Beat" (*Miami Herald*, July 28, 2006).

Chairman Mao, "Problem" (*XXL*, September 2006).

Evelyn McDonnell, "Hip-Hop Hustler" (*Miami Herald*, May 26, 2006).

Melissa Meinzer, "Juggalos Are Us" (*Pittsburgh City Paper*, November 9, 2006).

Phillip Mlynar, "Lone Star" (*Hip-Hop Connection*, January 2007).

Tracy Moore, "Never in Nashville" (*Nashville Scene*, August 10, 2006).

Chris Neal, "Nothin' but a Good Time" (*Nashville Scene*, July 6, 2006).

Chris Norris, "Hooray for Holly'hood" (*Blender*, December 2006).

David Owen, "The Soundtrack of Your Life" (*The New Yorker*, April 10, 2006).

Eric Pape, "Future Shock" (*Vibe*, March 2006).

Whitney Pastorek, "It's a Pearl Jamily Affair" (*Entertainment Weekly*, May 12, 2006).

Nadia Pflaum, "Horn Dog" (*The Pitch*, February 16, 2006).

Andrew Phillips, "Library Privileges" (*Lost Magazine*, January 2006).

Alex Rawls, "What's Happening Brother" (*No Depression*, Fall 2006).

Simon Reynolds, "Lady Sovereign, *Public Warning*" (*Observer Music Monthly*, December 10, 2006).

Matt Rogers, "From Doo Wop to Funkadelia" (*Wax Poetics*, August/September 2006).

Alex Ross, "Fascinating Rhythm" (*The New Yorker*, November 13, 2006).

Jay Ruttenberg, "Kicking the Jams" (*Time Out NY*, April 13–19, 2006).

Jeff Salamon, "Frank Sinatra's Not-So-Golden Nuggets" (*Austin American-Statesman*, December 7, 2006).

Peter Scholtes, "Can't Go Home" (*City Pages*, April 5, 2006).

Jesse Serwer, "Bomb the Suburbs" (*Wax Poetics*, June/July 2006).

Will Sheff, "Okkervil River Tour Diary" (*Yeti*, Issue 4, 2006).

Philip Sherburne, "This Month in Techno: Picturing Minimalism" (*Pitchfork Media*, November 11, 2006).

Sara Sherr, "Death of a Salesperson I–IV" (*Phawker*, December 11, 2006, to January 2, 2007).

Kirk Silsbee, "Bronzeville Gypsy" (*LA Downtown News.com*, May 22, 2006).

Sylvie Simmons, "Lemmy" (*MOJO*, July 2006).

Floyd Skloot, "Eartha Kitt: The Reigning Queen of Song" (*Oxford American*, Summer 2006).

Christopher Sorrentino, "Michael of Arabia" (*Blender*, July 2006).

Deanne Stillman, "Death Behind the Wall of Sound" (*Spin*, April 2006).

Neil Strauss, "The Men Who Disappeared" (*Rolling Stone,* December 28, 2006–January 11 2007).

Ned Sublette, "P-Funk Politics" (*The Nation* online, June 5, 2006).

John Jeremiah Sullivan, "The Final Comeback of Axl Rose" (*GQ*, September 2006).

Skye Sweetnam, "Profile" (*Myspace.com*, 2006).

Marqeaux Watson, "Flavor Flav: Totally Cuckoo?" (*Entertainment Weekly*, August 11, 2006).

Ben Westhoff, "Private Enemy" (*Village Voice*, November 7, 2006).

Ken Whitehead, "Jazz Is for Lovers" (*eMusic*, June 2006).

Chris Willman, "There's Something About Merry" (*Entertainment Weekly*, December 15, 2006).

MacKenzie Wilson, "Kool Thing: the Making of Sonic Youth's Goo" (*Rockpile*, May/June 2006).

Charles Young, "The Killer Returns" (*Rolling Stone*, October 19, 2006).

Corrections: In the 2006 *Best Music Writing* edition, the *Seattle Weekly* piece "A Day in the Life" was cowritten by Rachel Shimp, and the *Revolver* piece "Age of Quarrel" was written by Dan Epstein.

LIST OF CONTRIBUTORS

Nitsuh Abebe is a writer of fiction and music journalism. He lives in New York City.

Jay Boronski is a writer for the *San Francisco Bay Guardian* and *Night Moves*. He is currently at work on a trilogy based on Vivaldi's *The Four Seasons*, the first installment of which is titled *1.33333333333333333333333 3333333333333333333 Seasons*.

Daphne A. Brooks is an associate professor of English and African-American Studies at Princeton University, where she teaches courses on literary and cultural studies, performance studies, and popular music culture. Brooks has published articles on black women's R&B, black rock and post-Soul satire, and post–Civil Rights rock nostalgia. She is the author of two books: *Bodies in Dissent: Spectacular Performances of Race and Freedom, 1850–1910* (Duke University Press, 2006) and *Jeff Buckley's Grace* (Continuum, 2005).

David Byrne is well known as the musician who cofounded the group Talking Heads (1976–1988) in New York. On record and in concert, the band was acclaimed by critics and audiences alike; more importantly, however, they have proven to be extremely influential. Talking Heads took popular music in new directions, both in terms of sound and lyrics, and also introduced an innovative visual approach to the genre.

Byrne has also been involved with photography and design since his college days and has been publishing and exhibiting his work for the past decade. Like his film and musical projects, his artwork is often described as elevating the mundane or the banal to the level of art, creating icons out of everyday materials to find the sacred in the profane. Byrne's works are about interiors, both physical and emotional, as much as exteriors.

Jane Dark formerly made his living as a music critic for glossies and alts, maxing out at $3/word for *GQ*. The higher the pay, the duller the published piece, as a general rule. Now a teacher, he reviews music for free at *jane dark's sugarhigh!* (janedark.com), focusing on hip-hop and country music, the two most vital indigenous North American musics.

Erik Davis is the author of *The Visionary State: A Journey Through California's Spiritual Landscape*, the media-studies cult classic *TechGnosis*, and the 33 1/3 volume on Led Zeppelin's fourth album. He has contributed articles and essays to scores of books and publications and has taught at a number of universities and institutes. A steel-string fingerpicker in his free time, Davis also edits book reviews for Erowid.org and posts regularly to his own www.techgnosis.com. He lives with his wife in San Francisco.

Andréa Duncan Mao is a senior writer for *XXL*. Her work has appeared in *Vibe*, the *New York Times*, *Modern Bride*, and *Essence*. She has contributed to several hip-hop anthologies, including *Vibe's History of Hip-Hop*. She is currently cowriting rapper Lil' Kim's memoir and working on her first novel.

Arye Dworken is managing editor of *DIW Magazine*, music editor of *Heeb Magazine*, and news editor of *ArtistDirect.com*. He is also a freelance writer whose work has appeared in *Spin*, *Giant*, *New York Magazine*, *FLAUNT*,

Planet, VH1.com, and *Real Simple.* Additionally, Arye is working on his first novel, a sci-fi, conspiratorial thriller involving the four members of the Beatles. For more of his work, please visit his personal irony-free website *Bring Back Sincerity.*

kris ex is a Haitian-born, Brooklyn-bred writer. In the past he's written for God, the children, himself, and any editor willing to pay him. Recently, he's come to the conclusions that there is no God, the children can take care of themselves, and there are few editors willing to pay him his worth—leaving him to write just for himself. He prefers it that way.

Jack Erwin is associate editor at *Complex* magazine. The first concert he attended was Eric B. & Rakim with MC Lyte and Rob Base & DJ EZ Rock. He lives in Brooklyn with his wife, Melissa, and their two cats.

Robert Forster lives in Brisbane, Australia. He is the cofounder of The Go-Betweens and is the music critic for *The Monthly* magazine.

Sasha Frere-Jones was born in New York, and he's lived there his whole life. He'll probably come to die in that town: lived there his whole life.

Sarah Godfrey writes about hip-hop, go-go, R&B, and sometimes pop for the *Washington City Paper* and the *Washington Post.* She lives in Washington, D.C.

Rob Harvilla is the music editor at the *Village Voice.* He's also written for *Spin, Pitchfork Media,* and *Entertainment Weekly.* Previously he did stints at the *East Bay Express* in Oakland and *The Other Paper* in Columbus, Ohio. He lives in Brooklyn with a burgeoning author of vampire romance novels and a cat named Bumf.

Richard Hell is a writer and musician. His career retrospective CD *SPURTS* (Sire/Rhino) was released in 2005, and his most recent book is the novel

GODLIKE. He's at work on an autobiography. A disclaimer: he doesn't actually believe in any God or any religion, despite his fondness for the word "God."

Will Hermes is a regular contributor to the *New York Times* and *National Public Radio*, among other outlets, and is an assistant professor of journalism at the State University of New York–New Paltz. He is coeditor, with Sia Michel, of *SPIN: 20 Years of Alternative Music* (Three Rivers), and author of the mostly fictional MP3 blog *Loose Strife* (http://loosestrife.blogspot.com). He is currently writing a book about New York City's music culture in the mid-1970s.

Dylan Hicks insists on living in Minneapolis. His fiction, criticism, journalism, and back work have appeared in the *Rake*, the *Village Voice*, the *New York Times*, *City Pages*, and elsewhere. In the late twentieth and early twenty-first centuries he led a nonprofit rock band.

Jessica Hopper is a feminist music and culture critic living in Chicago. Her work regularly appears in the *Chicago Reader*, *Plan B*, *Chicago Tribune*, *ANP Quarterly*, and other spots. She is the author of the forthcoming book *Old Timey Time: The Land of the Oldest Time* (Teardrops).

David Kastin is the author of *I Hear America Singing: An Introduction to Popular Music* (Prentice Hall, 2002). His essay "From the New Frontier to the New Millennium" appears in the National Endowment for the Arts online curriculum *Jazz: An American Story*. From 1993 to 2003 he taught a course in American literature and popular music at Stuyvesant High School in New York City.

Jonathan Lethem was born in Manhattan in 1964. His seven novels include *You Don't Love Me Yet*, *The Fortress of Solitude*, and *Motherless Brooklyn*. The winner of the National Book Critics Circle Award for Fiction and a MacArthur Fellowship, he lives in Brooklyn and Maine.

Sean A. Malcolm is the lifestyle editor at *King* magazine, as well as contributing editor at *RIDES* magazine. In the Brooklyn native's five-year career, his work has been seen in *XXL*, *Scratch Magazine*, and *Allhiphop.com*. When Sean is not having fun at his job, he can be spotted having fun behind the wheels of steel, spinning alongside a who's who in the New York club scene.

Michaelangelo Matos is the author of *Sign 'O' the Times* (Continuum, 2004) and lives in Seattle.

Adam Matthews chronicles pop culture and social issues for finer venues such as *RADAR*, *The Globe and Mail*, *Vibe*, *King*, *Complex*, and *XXL*. He holds an MSJ from Northwestern's Medill School of Journalism and is the winner of the Press Club of Long Island's Feature Award. He's spoken at Northwestern University and the University of Wisconsin and is a frequent commentator on BBC radio. He lives in Brooklyn with his fiancé, Jocelyn, and their nonbreed standard Shiba Inu, Dylan. Visit him at www.byadammatthews.com.

Justin Monroe is a senior staff writer at *Complex*. His writing has also appeared in *XXL*, *Vibe*, *Scratch*, *Rides*, *Blender*, *Inked*, and *Mass Appeal*. He grew up in Fort Greene, Brooklyn, and now lives in Washington Heights.

Brandon Perkins is the senior editor for *URB* magazine and only slightly disheartened by the current state of hip-hop. After attending Emerson College in Boston, he spent the first few postcollegiate years dodging student loan payments and creating a hip-hop 'zine, *The Beat Reporter*, which really looked more like a punk rock rag but was all about the indie rap. Now, he contributes to the *Los Angeles Times* and is procrastinating on a novel that really wants to get written.

Ann Powers is the chief pop critic at the *Los Angeles Times*. She is the author of *Weird Like Us: My Bohemian America*; coauthor, with the artist, of *Tori*

Amos: Piece by Piece, and coeditor, with Evelyn McDonnell, of *Rock She Wrote: Women Write About Rock, Pop, and Rap*. She lives in the Northeast L.A. neighborhood of Mt. Washington with her husband Eric Weisbard and their daughter, Rebecca Brooklyn Weisbard.

Jody Rosen is the music critic for *Slate* magazine. He is author of *White Christmas: The Story of an American Song* (Scribner, 2002) and the producer of the CD *Jewface* (Reboot Stereophonic, 2006), an anthology of vaudeville-era Jewish novelty records. He is at work on a book about Benjamin Franklin's musical invention, the glass harmonica. He lives in Brooklyn.

Chris Ryan is from Philadelphia, lives in Brooklyn, and writes about rap and basketball.

Anselm Samuel has been a music/entertainment journalist for over nine years. After a four-year stint as culture editor at *The Source*, the New York native became the founding editor-in-chief of *The Ave*, an independent quarterly publication that combines entertainment, social issues, and politics. Currently serving as music editor at *XXL*, his writing has appeared in *Essence, Blender, Penthouse, Complex, Scratch, King,* and *Rides*. Samuel is also a weekly radio hip-hop correspondent for "Phat Saturdays" on 100JAMZ in the Bahamas.

Kelefa Sanneh writes about music for the *New York Times*. He lives in New York City.

Vanessa Satten is the executive editor of *XXL* magazine. She has been with *XXL* for nine years and has contributed to several other publications including *King, Slam,* and *Scratch*. In addition to *XXL* magazine, Vanessa also works on xxlmag.com. When she's not working, you can find Vanessa chilling in Harlem.

Jessica Shaw, a senior writer at *Entertainment Weekly*, has been covering television, movies, and style for the magazine since 1993. She writes the weekly "Shaw Report" column in which she designates what in pop culture is in, five minutes ago, and out. She's written stories about everyone from Phyllis Diller to Tori Spelling, with plenty of *American Idol* stories thrown in for good measure. Shaw has appeared on the *Today Show*, *Good Morning America*, *The Early Show*, CNN's *American Morning*, *PrimeTime Live*, *20/20*, *Entertainment Tonight*, *Access Hollywood*, and countless VH-1 and E! shows. Shaw graduated with a degree in medieval literature from Barnard College.

Dave Simpson has written in *The Guardian* since 1994. Now one of the paper's primary music writers, he expounds on pop and rock and pounds the motorway from an isolated base in the north of England. A Fall fan since 1979, he is currently writing up the story of his search for members as a book, *The Fallen*, and continuing with the biblical quest of attempting to locate the missing drummer, Karl Burns.

Nick Southall was born in southwest England at the tail end of the 1970s and is the youngest of three brothers. He has a degree in popular culture and philosophy and has written about music for *Stylus Magazine*, *The Guardian*, and *LA Weekly*, amongst others. He likes red wine, expensive headphones, spicy food, and the Hungarian national football team of the 1950s. His favorite record is the last one he listened to.

John Swenson has been writing about music since 1969 for *Crawdaddy!*, *Rolling Stone*, *Circus*, the *Village Voice*, and other publications and worked as a syndicated music columnist for United Press International for 20 years. He has been an editor at the New Orleans publication *Offbeat* since 1999. He has published fifteen books, including biographies of Stevie Wonder, The Who, Bill Haley, and the Eagles as well as *The Rolling Stone Record*

Guide (with Dave Marsh), the *Rolling Stone Jazz Record Guide* and the *Rolling Stone Jazz and Blues Album Guide*.

Elisabeth Vincentelli is the arts and entertainment editor at *Time Out New York*; she also contributes to publications such as the *New York Times*, *Salon*, *Slate*, *The Wire*, and *The Independent*. Her book *Abba Gold*, part of Continuum's 33 1/3 series, came out in 2004. When she has a minute to spare, she writes about the arts at determinddilettante.blogspot.com. Born and raised in France, Elisabeth now resides in Brooklyn, NY.

Carl Wilson lives in Toronto, where he's a writer and editor at *The Globe and Mail* and runs the blog *Zoilus.com*. His work also has been published in the *New York Times*, *Blender*, *The Nation*, *Pitchfork*, *Slate*, and *Said the Gramophone*, among others, and presented at the EMP Pop Conference in Seattle. His essay on Princess Diana and Joey Ramone appeared in *Da Capo Best Music Writing 2002*, and his book about pop culture, bad taste, and Céline Dion, *Let's Talk About Love*, is part of the 33 1/3 series of books on albums (Continuum). In Toronto, he helps out with the show Trampoline Hall, in which people give lectures on subjects they're not experts in, once a month, upstairs at a rock bar. He tries to write with that feeling in mind.

Douglas Wolk is the author of *Reading Comics* and *Live at the Apollo*, runs the tiny record label Dark Beloved Cloud, and writes for magazines including *Rolling Stone*, *Blender*, and *Print*. He lives in Portland, Oregon.

CREDITS

"If Music Is the Answer, What's the Question? Pere Ubu's 'We Have the Technology'" by Carl Wilson. First published on saidthegramophone.com, July 7, 2006. Copyright © 2006 Carl Wilson.

"Critic's Notebook: Latinos Give a New Life to Neil Diamond Anthem" by Ann Powers. Published May 9, 2006. Copyright © 2006, *Los Angeles Times*. Reprinted with permission.

"A Double History of the Supremes' 'Love Child.'" Copyright © 2006 Michaelangelo Matos. Originally published on *Back and Forth* blog (beatresearch2.blogspot.com).

"white bread black beer" by Jane Dark. The author claims no copyright for this material, which is available unrestricted on the blog *jane dark's sugar high!* (janedark.com).

"On Top" by Sasha Frere-Jones. First published in *The New Yorker*, April 2006. Copyright © 2006 Sasha Frere-Jones.

"Suga Mama, Politicized" by Daphne A. Brooks. Reprinted with permission from the November 30, 2006, web edition of *The Nation*. For subscription information call 1-800-333-8536. Portions of each week's *Nation* magazine can be accessed at http://www.thenation.com.

"Yeah I'm Threatening Ya! I Keep Hedge Funds!," "Buy Kingdom Come and Get a Free Fucking Tote Bag!" and "I'ma Fuck Around and Barf!" by Chris Ryan. Published on *Gabe Said, "We're Into Movements"* blog November 16 and December 9, 2006. Copyright © 2006 Chris Ryan.

"Being James Brown" by Jonathan Lethem. Published in *Rolling Stone*, June 29, 2007. Copyright © Rolling Stone LLC 2007. All Rights Reserved. Reprinted by Permission.